AMERICA'S
MONEY
MACHINE

AMERICA'S MONEY MACHINE

The Story of the Federal Reserve

Elgin Groseclose, Ph.D.

*Prepared under the sponsorship of the
Institute for Monetary Research, Inc.,
Washington, D. C.
Ellice McDonald, Jr., Chairman*

*Arlington House Publishers
Westport, Connecticut*

An earlier version of this book was published in
1966 by Books, Inc., under the title *Fifty Years of
Managed Money*
Copyright © 1966 and 1980 by *Elgin Groseclose*

Library of Congress Cataloging in Publication Data

Groseclose, Elgin Earl, 1899–
America's money machine.

Published in 1966 under title: Fifty years of
managed money, by Books, inc.
Bibliography: P.
Includes index.
1. United States. Board of Governors of the
Federal Reserve System–History. I. Title.
HG2563.G73 1980 332.1′1′0973 80–17482
ISBN 0–87000–487–5

Manufactured in the United States of America

P 10 9 8 7 6 5 4 3 2 1

For
My Beloved Louise
with especial appreciation for her editorial assistance
and illuminating insights
that gave substance to this
work

CONTENTS

Preface

O
N SEPTEMBER 30, 1913, at a moment when American attention was focused on the revolutionary monetary reform then under debate in Congress, the *New York Times* astounded and diverted its public by a bitter attack on a former president of the United States. The former president was Theodore Roosevelt who had, the year before, broken away from the Republican Party to run as the Progressive Party (Bull Moose) candidate for president. He had been defeated by Woodrow Wilson, but he had been a powerful candidate who had attracted the greater part of Republican Party votes, and his views on public questions still commanded a large following among the electorate.

What had aroused the mortal apprehensions of the *Times'* editors was an article in the *Century Magazine* in which Roosevelt had outlined his proposals for a reorganization of government and society. The editorial attacked his blueprint as "super-socialism." Without going so far as to charge Roosevelt with being a Marxist—this was before the Russian Revolution, but Marxism was even then anathema on these shores—it declared that he would in effect bring a Marxian redistribution of wealth in a "simpler and easier way."

"He leaves," the editorial went on to say, "the mines, the factories, the railroads, the banks—all the instruments of production and exchange—in the hands of their individual owners, but of the profits of their operations he takes whatever share the people at any given time may choose to appropriate to the common use. The people are going to say, We care not who owns and milks the cow, so long as we get our fill of the milk and cream. Marx left socialism in its infancy, a doctrine that stumbled and sprawled under the weight of its own inconsistencies. Mr. Roosevelt's doctrine is of no such complexity. It has all the simplicity of theft and much of its impudence. The means employed are admirably adapted to the end sought, and if the system can be made to work at all, it will go on forever."

The means by which Roosevelt would achieve these ends, the *Times* explained, drawing from the *Century* article, would be by a monolithic one-party political system, along with an indefinite expansion of government powers and functions. ("It will be necessary," the *Times* quoted Roosevelt as saying, "to invoke the use of governmental power to a degree hitherto unknown in this country, and, in the interest of democracy, to apply principles which the purely individualistic democracy of a century ago would not have recognized as democratic.") Roosevelt would also abolish competition. ("The business world must change from a competitive to a cooperative basis.") He would remove the restraints of an independent judiciary. ("The people themselves should . . . decide for themselves . . . what laws are to be placed upon the statute books, and what construction is to be placed upon the Constitution. . . .") He would confiscate the great fortunes (by a "heavily progressive inheritance tax" and a "heavily graded income tax.")

This was the Roosevelt who had been the idol of the Republican Party, then as now regarded as the citadel of plutocracy and special interest. This was the Roosevelt whose portrait, despite his 1912 defection from orthodoxy, still adorns the walls of the Union League Club and other Republican strongholds. And this is the *New York Times* which became the loyal supporter of Franklin D. Roosevelt, his New Deal, and the successor Fair Deal, New Frontier and Great Society administrations that have out-Roosevelted Roosevelt.

The Theodore Roosevelt article and the *Times'* editorial are significant in disclosing how far the political economy of the country was even then being borne on the currents of authoritarian dogma. What Roosevelt failed to see was that these immense changes which he proposed were even then in course of execution. They were brought about by means far more subtle and invisible than those he proposed, and without the necessity "to invoke the use of government power to a degree hitherto unknown in this country," without abolishing competition, or the independence of the judiciary, without quite confiscating the great fortunes. The succeeding years witnessed the extension of a system whereby government became the senior partner in most businesses, in which it determined what expenses should be incurred; at what prices the product should be sold; how much employees, from the lowest to the highest, should be paid, and how long they should work; how much of the income of the business should be retained and how much distributed; and what share should go to the senior partner. At the same time the government would undertake to create or modify the climate in which business was conducted; it would influence, if not determine, the general level of prices; it would determine the optimum rate of business activity, either to stimulate or retard as in its wisdom appeared most desirable; it would conclude what forms of business activity should be favored and developed, what forms should be discouraged; it would determine the costs of capital to those who would embark in enterprise, according to its judgment; and it would make such capital available or not available, and set the rate of interest to be paid. It would even, for a season, reach down into the household and decide the important questions of household finance: is an electric washing machine a capital investment or a convenience of luxury?

The means by which these ends would be accomplished without the strong arm of the state police were then in process of formation through two legislative enactments of the year in which Roosevelt penned his *Century* article. The first of these was the income tax; the other was the Federal Reserve Act. Our concern here is with the latter, and for that purpose a thumbnail sketch of the monetary system as conceived by the founding fathers and as developed through the first one hundred and twenty years of our history is necessary.

The word money, derived from the Latin *moneta,* and its equivalents in European tongues, have always meant *coinage,* as has the term *specie* in the U. S. The framers of the Constitution, having before them the experience of the Continental paper currency, were of one mind that the only authorized currency should be coinage; a proposal in the Convention for the issuance of paper currency ("to emit bills") was rejected without a record vote, and there was added a further provision that no state might issue paper currency or declare anything to be legal tender except gold and silver coin. Despite these further declarations, an ambivalence has persisted in regard to the standard. Hardly had the Constitution come into effect before Congress, under the influence of Alexander Hamilton and with the tacit approval of President Washington, authorized a national bank to issue notes of limited legal tender (acceptable in payment of federal dues). Despite a famous opinion by Chief Justice Marshall in support of "implied powers" in the Constitution,[1] doubts as to the constitutionality of such issues led to their eventual termination. The Civil War crisis, however, led the Congress to authorize circulating notes issued by the Treasury, together with a national bank system in which banks could issue notes against government obligations: after several wavering opinions the Court finally ceded Congress *carte blanche* to do as it pleased in regard to the monetary system.

Nevertheless, explicit provisions of the Constitution have never been modified, and despite the subsequent withdrawal of all gold and silver intrinsic coin from circulation, and the cessation of mintage, the dollar is still defined by statute in terms of a weight of precious metal.

The Constitution gave Congress the power to coin money and "to regulate the value thereof." Actually, the question is relevant whether, regardless of the Constitution, or any other authoritarian decree, government is able to regulate the value of money. Certainly the early experience with coinage would dispute that view (and the later experience with paper money will be examined in the pages to follow). The first coinage act provided for silver dollars weighing 416 grains, .89243 fine* and they were given a legal tender parity with the current Spanish milled dollar, which then formed the bulk of the circulation. However, as the silver was undervalued at this rate, U. S. dollars began to disappear into the melting pot, and the government was compelled to suspend the coinage of dollars in 1805.

At the same time a corresponding effort to regulate the value of the gold dollar also failed under the realities of the market place. The original coinage act had set the content of the gold dollar at 27 grains, .916 2/3 fine (24.75 grains) but as this undervalued gold in relation to silver, the content was altered in 1834 to 25.8 grains, .900 fine (23.22 grains).

While the impotency of legislative fiat in regard to coinage is well demonstrated by both U. S. and universal history, in the case of paper money the operation of public influence is less obvious. In the case of paper the power of the state to obtain acceptance of its fiat is bolstered by a system of sophistries that deceive the most astute. We shall observe the subtleties of argument in the debates over monetary reform leading to the Federal Reserve System.

Almost from the first, monetary discussion, and with it monetary policy, became clouded by a confusion of terminology among *money, specie,*

---

*89,243/100,000 pure silver, with a fine silver content of 371 1/4 grains. Act of April 2, 1792. Actually, it appears that the first mintings were at a fineness of .900, giving them 374.4 grains of pure metal.

cash, lawful money, legal tender, and in recent times M_1, M_2, etc. Today the word *money* is commonly used to designate any form of purchasing power —an error into which our discussion here may occasionally lapse. *Money,* however, as we have noted, properly refers only to coinage, as do *specie* and *cash.* The terms *lawful money* and *legal tender* arose after the establishment of a mint in 1793. Before then foreign coins were common currency, particularly the Spanish milled dollar, and the first U. S. dollars were struck at the equivalent of the Spanish dollar. After the mint was set up foreign gold and silver coins continued to circulate and were, until 1857, "legal tender" at various rates according to their precious metal content; but they were not "lawful money," and only U. S. coinage was the "money of account" for all public records. Until the Civil War only coinage was legal tender, although from as early as 1812 the Treasury from time to time issued interest-bearing bonds of low denomination that were receivable for government dues (limited legal tender); state bank notes redeemable in "specie" or "cash" were also in general circulation but without legal-tender quality. With the Civil War crisis bank notes were turned in for cash in such quantity that toward the end of 1861 all banks suspended convertibility. In 1862 Congress authorized the issue of Treasury notes ("greenbacks"), which were declared legal tender for all payments public and private except imports, and by a peculiar inconsistency also "lawful money." They were inconvertible into coin but could be exchanged for interest-bearing bonds.

In addition to the greenbacks, as a further means of war finance Congress in 1863 authorized a national bank system by which federally chartered banks could issue circulating notes redeemable in coin against the deposit of U. S. Treasury bonds to the equivalent of 90 per cent of the value of the notes. The notes were declared to "circulate the same as money" but had limited legal tender; i.e., they were not receivable for import dues, nor payable as interest on the public debt nor in redemption of the "national currency" (greenbacks).

The legality of the legal-tender provisions was at first denied by the Supreme Court but later upheld in a series of decisions in which the Court practically abdicated jurisdiction to Congress as a "political" question in which it would not intervene. Thus Congress was established in its right to issue paper currency without limit.

Other factors contributing to monetary confusion and leading to further experiments in state management of money and credit were the convenience, for large transactions, of paper currency over coinage, the divergence in the gold-silver ratio, and the phenomenon noted by Adam

Smith in 1776 that "no cry is more common than that of a shortage of money."

Paper notes that were certificates of deposit for gold held by the Treasury to the account of the note holder were authorized in 1863 and 1882. Silver certificates, issued against standard silver dollars deposited, subsequently entered circulation along with the U. S. notes (greenbacks) of the Civil War. During the war these last named had fallen to a market low of 40 per cent of their gold value, but gradually recovered as the war waned and prosperity returned. A policy of redeeming them by the Treasury was at first commended by Congress, then suspended, and finally forbidden, with a minimum of $300 million to remain in circulation by reissue if necessary.

Since both gold and silver coin were lawful money, the divergence of market values of the two metals had created problems in making payments. The question was resolved in 1873 by ceasing the mintage of silver dollars (except for a "trade dollar" useful in foreign trade) and limiting legal tender of silver to $5. The demonetization of silver coincided with a general demonetization of silver in favor of gold in all the principal countries of Europe, a movement that hastened the market fall of silver and created agitation for government relief.

Although total monetary circulation was steadily growing and the Treasury was able in 1879 to effect convertibility of the greenbacks into gold, public pressure forced the resumption of silver coinage in 1878 and restoration of the bimetallic standard (silver dollars again full legal tender). As a further means to stem the drop in silver prices, the Treasury was directed to purchase and coin a minimum of 2 million silver dollars monthly—a figure increased to 4 1/2 million monthly in 1890.

The action of the British government in 1893, demonetizing silver in India, caused a further drop in silver prices, while the U. S. silver purchases had correspondingly weakened the international value of the dollar and led to gold exports; these developments, combined with a general overexpansion of bank and commercial debt, precipitated a crisis in 1893. The silver purchase acts were repealed, and in 1900 gold was declared the single standard of value.

Left unanswered, however, were the problems of the silver miners and the agricultural interest struggling to find markets for its surpluses, along with the voracious demands for credit for the development of the Great West. For all of these problems, manipulation of the monetary system appealed to the public as the easiest solution.

In the Democratic Party, William Jennings Bryan, a Nebraska lawyer, editor, and subsequently Congressman, became the champion of monetary expansion and a cheaper dollar. He so electrified the 1896 Democratic convention by his advocacy of a return to bimetallism (free coinage of silver at a fixed ratio) in an address known as the "Cross of Gold" speech ("You shall not crucify mankind upon a cross of gold") that he was nominated for president and for the next sixteen years ruled as undisputed leader of his Party.

Within the Republican Party Roosevelt had demonstrated a hostility to Wall Street, and was advocating authoritarian controls over the economy with a vehemence that reached its crescendo in the *Century* article to which the *Times* took editorial exception.

Such was the nature of the tide upon which the monetary reform known as the Federal Reserve System was launched. Our purpose here is to narrate the events and explore the issues that led to its enactment and that subsequently modified it into its present form and structure. We will dwell but briefly upon the techniques by which it operates. Those aspects have already been so exhaustively examined as to leave the essential question buried in a debris of verbiage. In particular the later years that have witnessed the maturing and hardening of the System as a tool of Treasury, and latterly State Department, policy—will be briefly treated. By shortly after the end of World War II the ends so boldly set forth by the earlier Roosevelt had been largely achieved; the Federal Reserve, along with the great mass of the electorate, had become inured to authoritarian controls, and docilely acquiescent to the edicts from Washington.

PART I

The Roots of Reform

1.

The Quality of the Times

T HE EVENT THAT MADE the money system the dominant public
issue and brought the Federal Reserve System into being was the
Panic of 1907. It occurred during the second term of Theodore Roosevelt. It is known as the "rich man's panic." It was essentially a credit crisis.
It may have been sparked by Roosevelt's attacks on big business (his
"trust-busting") which unsettled confidence and the security markets; if
so, it was fired by an ardent public speculation founded on business
expansion and prosperity, and a number of spectacular security manipulations and failures that shook investor confidence.

To understand these events we must recognize the quality of the times
—different, but perhaps in degree only, from our own. It was a time of
immense individualism in American life—an era in which the destiny of
the nation depended more upon the character of men than upon their
institutions, more upon private decisions than upon the fiat of law and
regulation; more upon the integrity of leaders than upon the force of
custom and tradition. It was an era when men took large chances and
demanded equivalent rewards, when they assumed large responsibilities
and exercised large liberties. For better or worse it was a time of the
"moguls" of industry, finance, and enterprise, rather than of the minions
of bureaucracy and administration. Upon this characterization of the
epoch, all historians seem agreed.*

---

*Titles like *Age of the Moguls* by Stewart H. Holbrook (New York. 1953); *The Masters of
Capital* by John Moody (New Haven. 1919), and *The Robber Barons* by Matthew Josephson
(New York. 1934), are illustrative.

3

An incident may be as revealing as a volume, just as a droplet serves for the analysis of a blood stream. The break-up of the Harriman-Fish entente in 1906 serves as an excellent introduction to a larger tale. Indeed these two men and their affairs are inextricably a part of the larger tale. For both are involved in the Roosevelt story and the Roosevelt-big business antagonism. In fact, the Roosevelt ferocity toward big business may have been influenced by happenings flowing from the Damon-Pythias relationship of Harriman and Fish, the rupture of that relationship, and its various consequences.

Edward H. Harriman and Stuyvesant Fish had been business acquaintances for nearly thirty years. Harriman, son of an Episcopalian rector, had begun life in Wall Street as a stockbroker's clerk, and was rising in the world as an investment banker. Stuyvesant Fish was the distinguished-looking son of a distinguished father* and protégé of William Henry Osborne, chief stockholder of the Illinois Central Railroad. Starting as a clerk in the general office of the railroad, he became secretary to the president the following year; after a turn at banking, he returned to his first interest and in 1877 was elected a director. In 1881, the railroad was having difficulties in selling its bonds following the assassination of President Garfield. Fish may have discussed this with Harriman. Harriman undertook to find a market in Europe and admirably succeeded. For that service he was elected to the railroad's board of directors on Fish's nomination. This was the beginning of an intimate business association. It lasted for a quarter century before it was ruptured with reverberations that shook the financial world.

Harriman was no novice in railway securities. He had married the daughter of a railroad president and had gone on his honeymoon in a special train provided by his father-in-law, with a locomotive painted with the Harriman name. In those days ownership of a railroad, however short or long, was somewhat equivalent to owning one's private plane today and every man of means had one or two. With his father-in-law's help Harriman purchased a small, run-down road of thirty miles with strategic possibilities in its Lake Ontario harbor. He rehabilitated it, and sold it to the Pennsylvania System. Now he had begun to take an interest in the Illinois Central, and after his election to the board in 1883 this was to become his plaything and obsession. Fish meantime had become vice-president, and a little later was elected president.

The Illinois Central had the reputation of being a "Society" road

---

*Hamilton Fish, who had been Grant's Secretary of State.

because of the conservatism of its management and the prominence of its directorate; its securities were highly popular abroad, particularly in the Netherlands. Under Harriman's influence, the road began a bold policy of improvements and expansion, and within five years increased its length by a thousand miles.

To be president of a road like Illinois Central was no little thing and Stuyvesant Fish continued as president longer than any other man—for twenty-three years before the final break with his long time associate and partner. He was a fine, aristocratic looking man—a tall, broad-shouldered figure whose bearing and distinction immediately attracted attention and cast into the shade his slight, bowed, bespectacled, and almost shabbily dressed associate.* In contrast to Harriman, who had the unfortunate faculty of arousing antagonisms, Stuyvesant Fish appears to have been universally liked. As Harriman more and more emerged in the public eye as a cold-blooded manipulator of high finance, and as the "Colossus of Roads," Stuyvesant Fish appeared as the genteel, strait-laced aristocrat, the image of financial conservatism.

Certainly Stuyvesant Fish had no need to seek the bubble reputation. His own was of the highest. When, for instance, the affairs of the Mutual Insurance Company came under question in 1905 on charges of loose lending for railway speculations, Fish, though a railway president himself, was named a member of a select investigation committee of three. And when he found himself at odds with his fellow members over their reticence, he resigned and issued his charges of malfeasance to the press. Unfortunately, Stuyvesant Fish enjoyed his position and prestige too fondly, and did not complain at the expensive and lavish parties which his socially ambitious wife Marian was fond of giving: some of them were enough to strain the purse of even a railroad president.

Mrs. Fish was tall, florid faced, with black eyes under high, arched brows; she had an imperious manner, was capricious and demanding. She was a highly successful hostess, partly no doubt because she was indifferent to caste or wealth; people, to amuse her, and gain her invitations, had to be either funny or handsome or brilliant or arrogant. She enjoyed

---

*The *New York Times* for November 19, 1906, reports that "Edward H. Harriman, master of 20,000 miles of railroad, valued at more than $2,000,000,000, was in Chicago for nearly an hour and a half this morning, and he worked hard most of the time. He had traveled as an ordinary passenger [but in his private car] . . . Mr. Harriman who is small and slightly built, was buried in the capacious folds of a rough steamer overcoat of loud pattern, such as can be bought for $15 to $16. He wore a derby hat well down over his forehead, and under it appeared his keen eyes looking through his spectacles."

entertaining actors, authors, and other celebrities. She was rivalled as a society leader only by Mrs. William Waldorf Astor of the "Four Hundred" legend; and when Mrs. Astor voluntarily abdicated as Society matriarch in 1908 following the famous ball in which that legend originated, the sceptre was seized and held by Mrs. Fish. Up to her death in 1915, it is said, her dicta were even more absolute than those of her predecessor.

By contrast to Stuyvesant Fish's opulence of manner and association, the diffident-mannered Harriman had established his domicile on a country place near Tuxedo, where Mary Averill Harriman devoted most of her time to rearing her five children. Still, it must not be assumed that they lived as recluses, or avoided their status as leading citizens.

Fish's fall may perhaps be traced to the pursuit of social distinction and Mrs. Fish's heavy entertainment involvements. Mrs. Fish, not content with dominating New York society, had successfully invaded the Washington scene. When Stuyvesant Fish attended the international railroad convention in Washington in 1905 she rented a house near the White House to which she brought all her servants, and gave a party for a reported thousand guests, serving delicacies such as pheasant, transparent aspic, beflowered salads, caviar, and tinted ices, without the aid of a caterer and with her own household staff.

Mrs. Fish's social invasion of Washington may have been the result of the intimacy that existed between her husband and Roosevelt. It is important to recall this camaraderie in any attempt to understand the tangle of subsequent events. Both were New York aristocrats; both were Republicans; they had a common fondness for rural estate life; they had gone together on hunting trips to the South. It is reported that during the Fish residence in Washington, Roosevelt, who was accustomed to early morning canters in Rock Creek, would ride over to the house and shout up, "Stuy!" and when the railroad president came to the window would joke with him for a while before continuing his ride.[1]

We must conjecture that Stuyvesant Fish's intimacy with Theodore Roosevelt had its influence in the intense hostility that Roosevelt later showed toward Harriman, and which began after the break-up between the two railroad executives.

While Fish had been content with the rewards of a railway presidency —its immense powers and emoluments and the opportunities it gave for side deals—Harriman's ambitions had been on a vaster scale. A master of the intricacies of finance, he was also an able and conscientious administrator with a fine sense of good public relations. Beginning with the

Illinois Central he had acquired strategic stockholdings in a number of systems with potentials for interconnection and expansion. During the financial crisis of 1893 he had gained control of the vast Union Pacific system. The road was in a shambles of neglect—"twin streaks of rust" it was called—with great stretches of worn, sun-warped, frost-bitten rails, stretching over small, rotten ties, on creaky trestles and hair-raising curves. The powerful firm of J. P. Morgan & Co. had refused to touch it and it was sinking into bankruptcy when Harriman, with the aid of Kuhn, Loeb & Co., acquired enough stock to take control.

We may ask how a man, starting in life as a stockbroker's clerk, and with no more assets than his wit, could acquire control of assets of such dimensions. In particular, how was it possible without chicanery, fraud, or corruption—or practices approaching such? While there may have been elements of sharp dealing, or worse—ethics then being what they were—the actual explanation of how fortunes were amassed lies on another plane. It is to be found in the practice of capitalizing earnings. To illustrate: assume a shop with annual sales of $10,000, annual costs of $9,000 with a net to the proprietor of $1,000, and buyers who are willing to purchase at $10,000, or 10 times the net earnings (formerly a rule of thumb in buying stocks). Assume that the new purchaser is able to reduce expenses to $8,000, or to increase sales to $12,000 with an increase of costs to only $10,000, then the net is doubled, and the value of the business accordingly doubled, with a gain of $10,000 to the entrepreneur. With these new values he is now able to buy another shop, either by mortgaging the increment in value, or by selling the shop and investing in a larger one.

Behind this financial process, it is obvious, must be the capacity to increase earnings of an enterprise, which is the basis of capitalization. Where earnings are rising, a shrewd and careful business man can multiply his capital many times. This is more apt to follow in the case of an expanding industry enjoying a steadily growing demand for its goods and services. This was the situation of the railroad industry during the years down to World War I.

Nevertheless, not all railroads were prosperous, and much of Harriman's success lay in his careful husbandry of his properties and his superb railroading management. He was like a good householder. If he milked his cow, he also fed it well. No sooner had he acquired control of the Union Pacific than he began a large scale rebuilding of tracks and stations, and modernizing equipment. He continually travelled inspecting his properties. He paid particular attention to public relations. He cultivated new customers by offering inducements to industries to establish themselves on his routes. In the only magazine article he is known to have written, he gave his creed of railway management: "The railroad that does not seek to build up the territory through which it passes by offering good service, pursues a policy that will only bring it grief in the long run."[2] When the Colorado River left its banks and flooded the Imperial Valley of California in 1907, Harriman sent Southern Pacific engineers to the area and he personally directed the work of relief and rehabilitation. Before the control of the river was achieved, the Southern Pacific had invested $3 million in the effort.

These may not be all the factors that made Harriman rich and powerful as a railroad "mogul," but they must be accounted as the principal.

By 1905, Harriman had achieved what no financier or enterprise has done since—control of a network of railroads stretching across the continent. He had gone even further. He held control of ocean steamship lines and was dreaming of—nay, planning; more, actually negotiating for—a 'round-the-world transportation system of railways and connecting steamship lines.

A main link in this enterprise would be the South Manchurian Railway which had just come under Japanese control as a result of the Russo-Japanese War. Harriman went to Japan and made attractive offers to the Japanese. The railway was in disrepair and the Japanese needed money. Premier Katsura was impressed. Unfortunately, Baron Komura, the minister for foreign affairs, had come home from the Portsmouth treaty negotiations with suspicions of U. S. policy and resentful at being frustrated in his pursuit of the fruits of victory by Roosevelt's mediation of the settlement. He interposed legal pretexts, and the negotiations were suspended—though never abandoned by Harriman.

The year 1905 may be said to mark both the high tide in the Harriman affairs and in those of Wall Street, and from then on the drift was toward decay and demoralization. The Harriman fortunes and the tenor of the securities markets were moving in harmony. The market took its tone from the "Harriman rails." When they moved up the market improved; when they fell the market declined.

In 1906, the Union Pacific unexpectedly raised its dividend from 6 to 10 per cent and the stock promptly shot up, making fortunes for many holders, but causing at the same time certain winds of dissatisfaction to blow in the Street, carrying gossip of insiders' profits.

About the same time rumors drifted in another region of Manhattan of a falling out between Harriman and his long-time associate Stuyvesant Fish. Tongues wagged that Marian Fish had declined to sponsor the debut of Harriman's daughter Mary, known more for her fondness for fox hunting in Virginia than for the Virginia reel in the ballrooms of New York.[3]

In October of 1906 Fish circularized the Illinois Central stockholders seeking proxies for the annual meeting of shareholders. The purpose of the solicitation was not made public, but rumors gathered that there had been a falling-out between the two financiers. The effect was a sensation in Wall Street that was promptly felt on the floor of the Exchange. The year that had started with such promise ended on a note of gloom.

2.

❧❧❧❧❧❧❧❧❧❧❧❧❧❧❧❧

The First Shock Wave

T HE SIGNIFICANCE of the Harriman-Fish rupture lies first in the shock it gave to the financial markets, and to public confidence in the integrity of the national financial leadership. More importantly, however, it served as the fuel that heated to the boiling point the Rooseveltian antagonism to Big Business.

Roosevelt, like so many Americans born to wealth and position who, since the appearance of *Das Kapital,* have been guilt-ridden over their blessings, early became a reformer and pursuer of causes. His antecedents went back to the Dutch patroons of colonial New Amsterdam, and his family had been prominently identified with banking and finance in New York. In his youth Roosevelt entered politics, became a State assemblyman but, his health failing, he went West for recuperation and took up ranching for a while. His speech and manners ever afterward showed more the gravel of the frontier than the polish of civilization. Returning to politics, he became famous for his fighting speech and his advocacy of the "strenuous life" and political reform. The episode in American history that is called the Spanish-American War became a further opportunity for flamboyant leadership, when he organized a regiment known as the Rough Riders and led them in his dashing charge up San Juan Hill. He was now a national figure and won election as Governor of New York in 1898. His reform administration alarmed his opponents who maneuvered quietly to inter him politically in the vice-presidency; but McKinley's death by an assassin's bullet in 1901 put Theodore Roosevelt in the seat of power. He promptly began his efforts to reshape the Republican Party in his own image.

McKinley had been elected President to his first term on a platform upholding the gold standard, high protective tariff, and a vigorous foreign policy; his Party manager was the Cleveland industrialist Marcus Hanna. McKinley's second election, in which Roosevelt was substituted for Garret A. Hobart on the ticket, was on a substantially similar program: the Republicans were regarded particularly as the party of the "moneyed East" in opposition to the agrarian South and West, and the campaign was between creditors on the one side and debtors on the other.

McKinley's assassination occurred at a moment when the public itself was becoming disturbed over the trend toward industrial combinations. In particular, anxiety arose over formation of the U. S. Steel Corporation under the influence of J. P. Morgan, by merging several independent companies into an integrated steel producing enterprise. The new company did not monopolize but it did dominate the important steel producing industry. The organization of the Northern Securities Company, also under Morgan influence, as a means of resolving the struggle between the James S. Hill and the E. H. Harriman railroad empires for control of the Northern Pacific railroad system, also bred public suspicions. (When it became apparent that neither of these rivals—one of whom controlled the Union Pacific, the other the Great Northern—had been able to capture enough stock to control the Northern Pacific, a compromise had been worked out by which the railroad would be controlled jointly through a securities holding company.) Roosevelt, who was nothing if not an opportunist, seized upon these in his first message to Congress, in December of that year, and recommended legislation to curb such combinations. Congress declined to act, whereupon Roosevelt ordered his Attorney General to file suit for dissolution of the Northern Securities Company, and three years later the Supreme Court sustained his action.[1] Meantime Roosevelt took his case to the people in a speaking tour in which he gave his campaign the slogan of a "square deal for all."

Roosevelt's attack on the corporations ("We do not wish to destroy the corporations, but we do wish to make them subserve the public good") was assisted by a public opinion aroused by a number of writings exposing corruption in politics and business practices. One of the first of these is Ida M. Tarbell's classic *History of the Standard Oil Company,* which began as a serial in *McClure's* in 1903. This work startled and aroused the public not only by its disclosures of business malpractices but by the obstacles, approaching violence, by which the author's efforts to collect her data were met. Lincoln Steffens' *The Shame of Cities* (1904), Thomas W. Lawson's *Frenzied Finance* (1902), Gustavus Myers' *History of the Great American Fortunes* (1910), Burton J. Hendricks' *Story of Life Insurance* (1907), and Charles Edward Russell's attack on the meat industry, *The Greatest Trust in the World* (1905), all contributed to an unsettlement of public faith in business and finance and in the leaders of industry, and encouraged Roosevelt in his anti-business policies.

In June, 1906, Roosevelt obtained passage of legislation (the Hepburn Act) greatly strengthening the powers of the Interstate Commerce Commission in regulating the railroad industry and it was under this authority, after the Fish-Harriman feud broke into the open, that Roosevelt early in 1907 directed an attack upon Harriman for his railway manipulations.

While Roosevelt was attacking big business in the press and in Congress it appears that he was not unwilling to have side deals with big business men. Unfortunately also, he allowed himself to play with fire in dealing with Harriman. Harriman, not unexpectedly for a man of his ambitions and in possession of his substantial resources, had found himself something of a political power, at least in New York State. This does not seem to have been of his conscious choosing, for as we have noted he was not an extrovert, but shy, retiring, and indifferent to appearances; if he interested himself in politics, it was because of his conviction that it was good for the railroad industry to have a powerful advocate in high councils.

Whatever the exact relations between Roosevelt and Harriman, there exists a considerable record of intimate correspondence between them in which Harriman's opinion on affairs of state was solicited, or at least welcomed, by the President. Whether this was from Harriman's desire, or through the influence of Roosevelt's closer friend Stuyvesant Fish or from other causes, by 1904 Harriman, now a key factor in New York State politics, was also a Roosevelt confidant.

During the final weeks of the 1904 campaign it appeared that New York State might be lost to the Party and that additional campaign funds were needed. Roosevelt's anxiety over the possibility of losing his own State prompted an exchange of letters in which Roosevelt wrote (on October 10, 1904) to Harriman:

> In view of the trouble over the State ticket in New York, I would like to have a few words with you. Do you think you can get down here within a few days and take either luncheon or dinner with me?

Roosevelt seems to have had second thoughts about the political wisdom of the invitation to a man so identified with his pet bogies and to cover his tracks he followed this up with a second letter in which he indirectly withdrew the invitation and threw on Harriman the initiative for the call. He wrote:

> White House
> October 14, 1904

Personal
My dear Mr. Harriman:

A suggestion has come to me in a roundabout way that you do not think it wise to come on to see me in the closing weeks of the campaign, but that you are reluctant to refuse, inasmuch as I have asked you. Now, my dear sir, you and I are practical men, and you are on the ground and know the conditions better than I do. If you think there is any danger of your visit to me causing trouble, or if you think there is nothing special I should be informed about, or no matter in which I could give aid, of course give up the visit for the time being, and then, a few weeks hence, before I write my message, I shall get you to come down to discuss certain government matters not connected with the campaign.

With great regard,

> Sincerely yours,
> Theodore Roosevelt

Harriman, no stickler for form, went to Washington and on his return to New York set about raising the $250,000 needed to meet the campaign deficit—contributing $50,000 of this sum himself.

Between 1904 and 1906 the relations between Harriman and Roosevelt cooled to the point of distrust, and Harriman practically withdrew from party politics by refusing to contribute to the mid-term Congressional campaign. The reason offered by Harriman's biographers is that Roosevelt reneged on his promise to Harriman, for his 1904 rescue, to appoint Chauncey Depew as ambassador to France, but it may have been Roosevelt's increasing hostility to big business.*

Roosevelt's reaction to Harriman's political defection was prompt and ferocious. When it was reported to him he sat down and wrote a letter to James S. Sherman, chairman of the Republican Congressional Committee, in which he charged Harriman with having attempted improper influence on the White House, called him "an undesirable citizen," "an

---

*Depew was chairman of the board of the New York Central System and also Senator from New York. It is said that Harriman's interest in obtaining the ambassadorship for Depew was to get him out of New York State politics, because of his growing unpopularity (he lost the election in 1910); but it may have also been for reasons of railway politics.

enemy of the Republic," and excoriated the financier for "cynicism and
deep-seated corruption" and as a "wealthy corruptionist."

The letter was written October 8, 1906, and coincided with the first
rumors of a falling-out between Harriman and Fish; but it was not until
April of the following year, at the time of the Interstate Commerce Commission investigation of Harriman's railway affairs, that the letter became
public.[2]

We must now say a word about the causes of the Fish-Harriman fight,
for it had its part in hastening along the debacle that became the Panic
of 1907. For several years, beginning at least in 1903, Fish had been using
corporation funds to his personal ends. It was learned that he had deposited half a million dollars of Illinois Central funds in a trust company of
which he was a director, to shore up the trust company's credit at the
expense of the railway; a little later he lent himself a million and a half
dollars from railway funds, we may guess to meet Mrs. Fish's extrava-
gances. The loan was theoretically secured, but Harriman, when he
learned of it, in order to avoid a scandal, personally lent Fish the money
to pay it off. (Some time later Fish complained about the interest rate
charged—5 per cent it appears to have been—protesting that he was
obtaining other credit for as low as 3 1/2 per cent.)

Meantime Fish continued to use railway funds to assist other enterprises in which he was interested. In those days such easy freedom with
corporate funds flavored more of the unethical than the immoral; in any
case these practices went on for some time before the directors felt
compelled to make an issue of them. It appears that the directors may
have been more resentful of the chief officer's autocratic ways than of his
misappropriations; it was not until 1906 that they concluded to remove
Fish from office. A persuasive factor may, of course, have been that
everyone lived in glass houses. Fish resented Harriman's use of Illinois
Central credit to expand the Harriman railway empire. Harriman was
then chairman of the board of the Union Pacific in addition to being
director and chairman of the finance committee of the Illinois Central. He
was a heavy stockholder in both roads. In a contest over a vacancy in the
Illinois Central directorate, Fish opposed Harriman's nominee, and it
appears also that he subsequently reneged on a compromise solution.

The annual meeting was now approaching and Fish began to solicit
proxies to strengthen his hand against Harriman. However, he did not
disclose the purpose of solicitation and the contest was kept within the
directorate. The meeting passed without incident, but at the board of
directors' meeting on November 7, 1906, Fish was summarily deposed as

president of the road he had ruled nearly a quarter century.

The reaction to this event came within sixty days—from the White House. On January 4, 1907, the Interstate Commerce Commission, at Roosevelt's direction, announced an investigation of the railway industry, and particularly E. H. Harriman's portion of it.

3.

The Lapping at the Dikes

T HE YEAR 1907 had opened in Wall Street with the usual consultation of oracles, among them Stuyvesant Fish. Whether or not his views were colored by his late humiliation by Harriman, they reflected a well-founded pessimism that was noted but dismissed by the press and that deserved perhaps more respect than was given it. Fish accused the age of "misfeasance," of "speculative excesses," of monopolism and manipulation, and proclaimed a general distrust of the future.

On January 3 the *New York Times* reported him as saying, "Wall Street is absorbing more than its share of the loanable funds. While our Western and Southern banks are lending more freely than usual at this season, that which they lend is instantly and persistently absorbed by Wall Street." He went on to charge the New York Stock Exchange with ceasing to be "a free market where buyers and sellers fix prices through the ebb and flow of demand and supply." It had become, he said, "the plaything of a few managers of cliques and pools to such an extent that for months past every announcement of increased dividends, of stock distributions and of rights has been met by a fall in prices." The investing public were staying out of the market, he declared, "because of the distrust which even those possessed of ample means have of the methods of corporate finance now in vogue in New York. That Europe shares this distrust of these methods is shown by its outcry against the misuse of American finance bills."

Fish's criticisms, however well-founded—"It has all been said before, and by men as competent to say it as Mr. Fish," commented the *Times*— were generally passed over as "the point of view of a man who has been beaten in an ugly fight." Equally ignored was the stiff renewal rate of 16 per cent for call loans reported the same day, as well as the rising premium on sterling and an urgent enquiry for bills. Moreover, the charge that the tight money market was due to Wall Street speculation was stoutly challenged by others who pointed out that the market generally —except for the Harriman issues—was lower than a year earlier, and that the bull market had reached its high point in January, 1906.

"The times are paradoxical," commented the *Times*. "The country is brimming over with material prosperity, and yet in Wall Street four in every seven men you meet are looking for the top of the bull market, bending their mental energies to the task of catching the psychological moment at which to lay out a bear campaign."[1]

The Interstate Commerce Commission investigation into the Harriman affairs opened on January 4, and its disclosures were meat for the stock market bears. Fish had announced his willingness to lay before the Commission all information he had, and it was assumed that he knew a great deal. There were other enemies of Harriman who could no doubt make things uncomfortable for the financier. "Mr. Harriman has always seemed to feel that he could afford to make enemies," gossiped the *Times'* "Topics in Wall Street," and mentioned in particular Mr. Stickney, president of the Chicago Great Western which Harriman had beaten out of the Omaha terminal by one legal maneuver after another. Union Pacific stock was under pressure all day long before the investigation opened. Nevertheless, the *Times* thought it could be overdone, since a stock yielding 10 per cent and selling at 177 must be regarded as cheap.

The first day's hearings confounded the pessimists on Union Pacific stock at the same time that they confirmed suspicions of railway manipulation. For the first time the actual grip of Harriman on the railway world was fully revealed. The Union Pacific was shown to hold large blocks of stock of railway companies as remote as the New York Central—all paid for, incidentally, from earnings and without recourse to borrowing.

The hearings continued until the end of February, reaching their climax on February 26. The chief inquisitor of the Commission was an attorney named Frank B. Kellogg who was later to become even more famous as Secretary of State.

The hostility of the Commission toward Harriman was so evident that the correspondent of *The Economist* (of London) commented: "The members of the Commission surprised many present by their manifestly hostile spirit toward Mr. Harriman . . . the Commission's lawyers acted toward Mr. Harriman and Mr. [Otto] Kahn quite as if they were prosecuting attorneys who had at last got before the bar of justice some well-known malefactor."[2]

Mr. Kellogg brought up the ouster of Fish, and sought to draw a connection with the sale of Illinois Central stock to the Union Pacific. Harriman seized the opportunity to explain and insisted on giving the story, over Kellogg's protests.

"Do you want me to tell you about that?" he demanded, and when Kellogg tried to close him off, snapped, "I will tell you how the Illinois Central's president was changed," and went on to spread on the record, for the first time publicly, the events which we have recounted above. He testified that the movement to remove Fish had started as early as 1903 with the discovery that Fish had deposited $500,000 of Illinois Central funds in the Trust Company of the Republic, of which Fish was a director at a time when the trust company was in financial difficulties and as a move to stave off bankruptcy. There was no connection, Harriman asserted, between this business and that of the sale of shares to the Union Pacific.[3]

Two days later, the hearings closed abruptly and were not resumed, and the Commission was compelled to report to the President that "no violation of law by Mr. Harriman had been discovered," and that legal proceedings against him would be inexpedient.[4] *The Economist* was led to comment sarcastically: "If they cannot put him [Harriman] through for railroad manipulation, why don't they charge him with carrying concealed weapons, or breaking the Sabbath, or shooting game out of season? Anything to catch him. It won't do to give it up in this weak way."[5]

On the same day that the Commission abruptly terminated its hearings Mrs. Stuyvesant Fish gave what the *New York Times* described as "the most novel and probably the largest luncheon of the Winter."

Several seemingly unrelated events of the weekend may have in their coincidence contrived to detonate the explosion in Wall Street that began on the following Monday. The *Times* reported an address by a Professor Clark before the Federation of Church Clubs, in which he contrasted the "soulless and criminal corporations" with "the individualism of commerce in bygone days." It also reported that Harriman had called on President Roosevelt at the White House, ostensibly "to show the sights to his ten-year-old son Rowland," but rumors went that he had gone to plead for respite from the government's harrowing of the railroads.*

---

*It appears, however, from subsequent revelations (at the time of the *World* exposé, in April, of the Harriman-Roosevelt correspondence) that Harriman's efforts to see Roosevelt were fruitless. See below.

On Monday the market opened weak, but there appeared little strain, and call money—funds borrowed to buy shares, repayable on demand—dropped to the low for the year—3 per cent. The apathy of the market was indicated by the low volume of transactions—some 38 1/2 million shares since the first of the year compared with over 60 million for the same period of the previous year.

This was the lull before the storm. On Tuesday came the deluge. Suddenly, unexpectedly, without warning, a flood of sell orders, mainly in "Harriman" stocks, demoralized the market. The *New York Times* gravely recorded that "the report that Mr. Harriman will retire from the world and enter a Trappist monastery has not been confirmed," adding that he did, however, call on the Interstate Commerce Commission, which was "a pretty prompt going to Canossa." The following day, a rumor that Harriman was buying control of Reading caused quotations for Reading shares to rebound ten points in ten minutes, carrying the whole market with it. Harriman also announced an end to his policy of silence in regard to railway affairs, declaring that, "the most important duty now confronting the managers of the railroads of the country is the development of more friendly relations between the railroads and the public and the government, and for my part I mean to devote myself to that work."

Liquidation continued, however, throughout the week and Harriman, in a further effort to restore confidence, gave an interview in his library in which he pleaded again for respite from government attacks on the railroads and for better understanding all around. Harriman's plea was now seconded by the bellwether of Wall Street, J. P. Morgan. On Monday the great financier himself went to Washington, going directly from his private car to the White House where he remained closeted with the President for two hours, urging him to take some action to "allay the public anxiety now threatening to obstruct railroad investments and construction." James Speyer, another leading figure in Wall Street, following up Morgan's cue, hurried to Washington the next day.

These moves had some influence in steadying the market, but on Wednesday the avalanche began again, with the market in the greatest crash since the panic of 1901. Call money went to 15 per cent while leading shares plummeted. Toward midday support appeared in the market but as the afternoon wore on selling resumed, and the day closed with stocks at their low. Nevertheless the decline was orderly, the total volume of sales falling short of the previous Wednesday's total. Monetary stringency—the need of funds to meet the first installment of the $60 million Pennsylvania Railroad issue and the $15 million Standard Oil dividend

—was assigned as the cause of the collapse, rather than any fundamental weakness in the economy. It was also remarked that for the first time values were no longer dependent solely, or even chiefly, upon economic factors, but that the powerful influence in the market was that exerted by "a group of bearish speculators whose drives against prices were accompanied by the usual grist of disquieting rumors."

One of the things that attracted the attention of the market—or at least that of the editors of the *Times*—was the assault upon Harriman stocks. Trading in one Harriman stock alone—Union Pacific—totaled 440,000 shares, accounting for over a fifth of total transactions on the Exchange. It was also noted in this connection that of the three leading influences in Union Pacific affairs—Jacob Schiff, Otto Kahn and E. H. Harriman—only Harriman was in the city, Schiff being in Palm Beach and Kahn on the high seas en route to Europe.

The following day quotations plunged again, led by a 25 point drop in Union Pacific—now down to 110 from 177 earlier in the year—and bringing lows unequalled even in the panics of 1901, 1873 or the Black Friday debacle of September 24, 1869.

Nevertheless, there were no great failures, and commentators remarked that it was a rich man's panic, that the public was not in the market, and that "it was the rich men who were suffering the losses entailed by the day's declines."* The rumors went around that Harriman was being forced to sell his holdings, but this he vigorously denied, and on being asked the cause of the decline remarked ominously, "I would hate to tell you to whom I think you ought to go for the explanation of all this."

Friday, the market rallied, after two days of disastrous selling, and at the close of the day, when it was realized that the week had passed without a failure, a spontaneous cheer arose from the floor of the Exchange. The recovery continued into the following week; Morgan sailed for Europe—perhaps as a symbol of confidence—and the headlines turned to other subjects such as the announcement of Miss Fish's engagement and Roosevelt's quest for delegates—except for a front page headline "Cullom Would Put Harriman in Jail—Senator after Talk with Roosevelt, Calls Railroad Man a Rascal"—which brought Harriman to comment: "If Cullom said that, he couldn't have been sober."[6]

New York Times. March 15, 1907. Three rich men—John Jacob Astor, Robert W. Goelet, and Cornelius Vanderbilt were reported to have lost between $8 and $9 million in Union Pacific stock which they had bought the year before on a tip from Harriman. (New York *World,* March 31, 1907.)

It was at this point in the decline that Washington concluded to abate its campaign against the railroads. Morgan had cabled Roosevelt from London urging consideration of the railway problem, and now with the threat of a widespread strike on the Western roads—an event that would have stopped traffic on 95,000 miles of track and made 50,000 men idle —Roosevelt exerted pressure on the trainmen and conductors and on April 1, issued a reassuring statement that he was not hostile to the railroads.

It was just as this truce was having a moderating influence on sentiment that the New York *World* published, on April 2, a letter written by Harriman to his friend Sidney Webster in 1905, which the *World* had acquired from a disgruntled former secretary of Harriman's. The letter was like an explosion. In it Harriman complained that Roosevelt had asked him to save him and the Republican party in the New York State campaign in 1904, and that Roosevelt had not rewarded this effort with the political appointment he had promised.

The Administration forces were thrown into confusion. Roosevelt called his cabinet into session and issued a defense in which he accused Harriman of having deliberately told an untruth, of being "an enemy of the Republic," of being "worse than men like Debs and Moyer and Haywood." He said that Harriman's statement justified the use of "a shorter and more ugly word" than untruth. Accompanying the statement were copies of correspondence between Roosevelt and Harriman that seemed to justify the President's assertions. Harriman responded with a statement of his own, that while he regretted the publication of a private letter he did not retract any statement—by implication passing the lie back to Roosevelt—and adding that the correspondence published by the President omitted certain significant letters. These he now made public on his own part.

The Harriman-Roosevelt controversy has been examined at length by scholars and others,[7] with mixed conclusions. The incident is of significance in the financial history of the period as evidence of the widening breach between business and government, and the antagonism toward big business by Washington bureaucracy that, regardless of the party in power, and despite periods of truce, was to intensify during the following half century.

4.

⊰∾⊱∾⊰∾⊱∾⊰∾⊱∾⊰∾⊱∾⊰∾⊱∾⊰∾⊱∾⊰∾⊱

The Rich Man's Panic

T HE STOCK MARKET now entered a period of apathy, but not of recovery. The Administration renewed its anti-monopoly campaign and filed suit against the Reading Company and others, alleging monopoly in the anthracite industry.

So passed the spring and summer. After early June Washington had gone into summer hibernation, and no cabinet meetings occurred until late in October, after the Panic. Toward the end of summer it was announced that the President would go game hunting in Louisiana and Oklahoma around the first of October. In September, Stuyvesant Fish opened his campaign for return to power in a circular to Illinois Central stockholders, soliciting their proxies, in which he insinuated that Harriman's support was from directors who had made money through Harriman's stock rigging. Fish's successor to the Illinois Central presidency, J. T. Harahan, promptly countered with a letter to stockholders, made public, in which he disclosed for the first time publicly that Fish, in addition to his loans of Illinois Central funds to favored banks, had lent $1 1/2 million from the corporation to himself on inadequate security.

The contest between the parties for proxies at the annual meeting was a much more public affair than such contests today. In Hartford, Connecticut, a meeting of local stockholders was convened and the merits of the case were discussed by a member of the clergy, the Reverend Francis Goodwin. After counselling against personal feelings, he outlined what he regarded as three great evils in the management of the railroad. First, he said, Fish had admitted that millions were loaned to him as president of the road, and although the road had suffered no loss, yet stockholders should make it felt that they held this practice wrong, and one that might lead to disastrous results. Second, as the road was presently managed, the board of directors was practically impotent. The chairman of the executive committee (Mr. Harriman) was in absolute power, and if the stockholders remained silent, they would be responsible. Third, Harriman's career was such that no confidence could be reposed in him. He was in it for his own profit and to carry out his own vast schemes.

Among Harriman's misdeeds, spread before the meeting, was his juggling of Southern Pacific accounts to manipulate the stock. Thus, he had charged cost of improvements to operating expenses, thereby showing reduced earnings, and so depressed the stock, but later, desiring to enhance the stock he transferred these same accounts to surplus, which would be distributed to stockholders.

The consensus of the meeting was that Fish was the lesser of two evils and that the stockholders should give their proxies to the Fish nominee, Charles M. Beach.[1]

The climax of the fight came just before the annual meeting, which opened on Tuesday noon, October 15, when the Fish forces obtained a court injunction forbidding Harriman to vote the Union Pacific holdings of Illinois Central stock. About 400 persons attended the meeting in Chicago, and it was reported that Fish was greeted by applause as he entered the room, but that Harriman, because of his small stature, entered unobserved—in any case, without recognition by those present. Fish affably approached Harahan, his successor in the presidency, and attempted to lay his hand on his shoulder, but Harahan was not to be placated, and almost returned the gesture with a blow. Fish, it is said, merely smiled and returned to his seat. Harriman, however, noticing Fish's son, went over and shook hands with him.

The meeting ended in a draw, and a motion was accepted to adjourn until December 18.

The day before the Illinois Central meeting the telegraph services reported that Roosevelt had stalked a bear in the Louisiana swamps, but had failed to bag it.

The same week brought more earth shaking events in Wall Street. The first of these involved the fortunes of a copper mining figure, F. Augustus Heinze. Heinze, born in Brooklyn and educated as a mining engineer, had made a fortune as a mining promoter in Montana, and a reputation as an opponent of the copper "trust." His battles with the big companies ranged from court conflicts over mining claims to miners' brawls fought with hose and pick deep in the earth. In 1906 he beat a retreat by selling

out for a reputed $10 1/2 million, only to re-open the attack in Wall
Street with credit as his ammunition and the complexities of stock issues
as his strategy. With associates he organized a concern named the United
Copper Company, with an authorized capitalization of $80 million; and
to finance its expansion bought control of a bank, the Mercantile National. Quotations on United Copper rose from 37 to 60, but fell as
suddenly—under the influence, it was said, of Heinze's financial enemies,
the Standard Oil interests.[2]

The pricking of the United Copper bubble collapsed the assets of
Mercantile National, and when suspicious depositors started a run of
withdrawals, the company appealed to the Clearing House for help,
where it met with the demand that Heinze and his partner Morse be
removed from the bank directorate. This was done but it did not halt the
run. The week ended with rumors that all was not well with another big
bank.

Uneasiness grew and spread, but like fire eating through a bale of
cotton, it was not yet ready to burst into flames. Only those market
operators whose perceptions were trained to such smolderings were sensitive to the portents.

Among these was the financier, J. P. Morgan, often an opponent of the
railroad magnate Harriman. Morgan, regarded by many as a buccaneer
of finance, was a devout Episcopalian and was at the time attending the
triennial Episcopal convention in Richmond, Virginia, and playing host
to a company of bishops in the Rutherford mansion which he had rented
and refurbished for the occasion. As the news from Wall Street darkened,
the old man—he was now over seventy and semi-retired—grew more and
more preoccupied with the affairs of this world; but when one of the
bishops commented on the bad news, Morgan, it is said, shot him such
a glare that the subject was not mentioned again. But Morgan was, in a
sense, Wall Street in person, and the financial world awaited his nod. He
remained to the end of the convention on Saturday; but then called for
his private railway car and hastened north—not overlooking the courtesy
of carrying a delegation of clergy with him in a second car. Arriving in
New York Sunday morning, he neglected church and went directly to his
new marble library on East 36th Street that Stanford White had designed,
where his associates of the world of finance were awaiting him and where
he spent the rest of Sunday until toward midnight in conference and
studying balance sheets.[3]

Monday, October 21, was a day electric with omen. Wall Street braced
for a storm, not knowing in what quarter it would strike. The Knicker-

bocker Trust Company, an uptown bank with 18,000 depositors and $67 million in deposits, was the first to feel the force of the blast. There was no apparent run—no visible panic in the streets, but all day long the bank was paying out cash to depositors who wanted their money. The Knicker-bocker was not a member of the Clearing House Association, and at the day's end the National Bank of Commerce notified the Clearing House that it would no longer act as Knickerbocker's clearing agent. That evening the Knickerbocker directors called on Morgan for help, meeting him at his library where the conference went on until 9 P.M., and then the directors with some of Morgan's men adjourned to a private dining room in Sherry's restaurant where, amid the coming and going of waiters, they continued their discussions until 2 o'clock of the following morning.

Morgan had little confidence in the Knickerbocker management, but a stake in its solvency. It is said that he himself, or his firm, was a substantial stockholder. He eventually agreed to find some support for the bank on condition of the resignation of the Knickerbocker president, C. T. Barney.* Financial support—understood to be to the extent of $12 million —was guaranteed. The news was too tardy to stem anxiety and the public-ity of the Sherry Restaurant meeting did not help. When the bank's doors opened the following morning the lines stretched along Fifth Avenue for a block, and the bank had to open seven paying windows. It had $8 million in cash, and hoped that would serve, but at noon a runner from the Hanover Bank presented a check for $1 1/2 million. The draft was met, but that was the end; the till was empty. The windows rang down, and the Knickerbocker Trust Company was in insolvency with $52 million of liabilities.

Panic now spread in Wall Street, throughout the nation. On the Stock Exchange call money went to 70 per cent and quotations tumbled. The ticker brought news from Pittsburgh of the triple failure of the great Westinghouse interests—the Westinghouse Electric and Manufacturing Co., the Westinghouse Machine Co., and the Securities Investment Co., along with the closing of the Pittsburgh stock exchange. As the day wore on reports came in of bank closings and business failures throughout the land. Like fire leaping a break strip, a run started on the Trust Company of America, and by closing time the bank had been drained of $13 million.

The country was now in the cold grip of crisis.

While this was going on, Roosevelt had been winding up his Louisiana hunting trip, with comments on the relative merits of possum and bear

---

*Who committed suicide a few weeks later.

meat, and had started leisurely toward Washington. Along the route he found time to praise Confederate heroes, and in Nashville made a speech in which he finally took note of the financial disaster, defended his role ("All I did was turn on the light") and excoriated the manipulators of securities, particularly railroads. It was a speech, of course, which did nothing to restore confidence.[4]

The general who directed the strategy to control the crisis was J. P. Morgan—whose leadership in Wall Street had been successfully challenged only by E. H. Harriman. Morgan was the personification of all that Roosevelt and his reform party opposed. So violent was the antipathy between the two that at a Washington Gridiron dinner earlier in the year, which both men attended, Roosevelt in the course of his speech savagely attacked the financier, striding to where he sat and thrusting a clenched fist under his nose as he berated him for his opposition to the Roosevelt policies.[5]

Morgan, now at the helm, had gotten in touch with George B. Cortelyou—Roosevelt's Secretary of the Treasury—and Cortelyou had come to New York, leaving on the four o'clock train, Tuesday afternoon. Cortelyou was not a financial expert. He had begun his career as a stenographer, and his skill at shorthand had brought him to President Cleveland's service. Later he became a private secretary to President McKinley. When the Department of Commerce and Labor was created in 1903, Cortelyou obtained the secretaryship. Later Roosevelt made him Postmaster General, and it was only shortly before the Panic that he had been elevated to the Treasury.

Tuesday evening, after a day of continuous conference at his offices, Morgan and a group of financiers went uptown, where Morgan's secretary had engaged a suite at the Manhattan Hotel, to await Cortelyou. Among those with Morgan were James A. Stillman of the National City Bank, representing the Rockefeller interests; John A. Stewart, president of the United States Trust Company, who presided; Henry C. Frick and Elbert H. Gary of the steel "trust"; Thomas F. Ryan, the speculator; August Belmont; and Hamilton Fish, brother of Stuyvesant Fish. Not least in the company was the railway magnate E. H. Harriman.

It was not until toward midnight that Cortelyou arrived.

Meantime, the urgent question was the condition of the Trust Company of America, where a run was expected on the morrow. Its balance sheet indicated that it could meet its obligations, given a breathing spell. The group agreed to advance $13 million. Would the Treasury assist?

Roosevelt was not due back until Thursday, the twenty-fourth. Cortelyou hesitated, but in the end agreed to deposit $25 million of government funds in various New York banks.* Having gained this much, Morgan went off to bed, leaving his partner, George Perkins, and Oakleigh Thorne, president of the Trust Company of America, to draft a formal agreement on the undertakings. Somewhere around 1 A.M. on the morning of Wednesday, October 23, Perkins gave out a statement that read in part:

> The chief sore point is the Trust Company of America. The conferees feel that the situation there is such that the company is sound. Provision has been made to supply all the cash needed this morning . . . The company has $12 million cash and as much more as needed has been pledged for this purpose. It is safe to assume that J. P. Morgan and Company will be leaders in this movement to furnish funds.[6]

It was not a diplomatic statement, or as reassuring as it was intended to be. The reference to the Trust Company of America as the "chief sore point" was not one to allay distrust among the bank's depositors, despite the promise of support. When the bank opened, the street before the bank was jammed with depositors with their pass books. The line continued to grow and at one o'clock extended east to William Street and down almost to Exchange Place. On the Exchange a frantic selling was going on, and call money reached 90 per cent, but the Exchange did not have to close. Fresh money came in—$5 million from the National City at around two o'clock—and quotations steadied. All day long the Trust Company continued to pay out cash, preserving as much as possible the routine of a normal day. Three o'clock came, and to accommodate those who had not yet been able to present their drafts, the bank kept its doors open a little longer.

Two hours after closing, porters from J. P. Morgan & Co. carried a big tin box and several bags into the bank. No explanation was made; none was needed. Vice president Babcock announced during the evening:

"After one of the most remarkable runs in the history of banking, we will open our doors as usual tomorrow. We paid all checks today as fast as they were presented, and will do so tomorrow. The Trust Company of America is perfectly solvent. . . ."

---

*A niggardly amount considering the fact that the Treasury at the time held over $300 million in free gold (not required for the redemption of gold certificates) and nearly $50 million in other forms of money—sums equal to more than 20 per cent of all gold in the country, 10 per cent of the total money stock and well over a third of the total deposit liabilities of all the New York clearing house banks.[7]

The crisis had been met, the peak of the storm was over; but the waves of panic continued to beat, and the winds of disaster to howl. A call began uptown at the Dollar Savings Bank; when a headline reported the run on "a Harlem savings bank," a scramble began at the Harlem Savings Bank. Some three other banks in Harlem were involved.

Downtown, when Morgan, accompanied by his son-in-law, Herbert Satterlee, arrived in Wall Street by brougham, following his late conferences of the night before, he was met with the news that the Stock Exchange was in collapse due to the drop in stock values and the inability of brokers to find call money. The president of the Exchange, R. H. Thomas, called Morgan with the news that the Exchange would have to close unless funds were found. It was then 1:30 P.M. and less than an hour remained for settling accounts. Morgan promptly summoned the leading bankers to his office and notified them that $25 million was needed within fifteen minutes. The meeting produced $27 million, and the *Evening Post* headline ran, "MORGAN AND COMPANY SAVE MARKET."

There followed that evening another long conference in the Morgan library that lasted until 1 A.M. The problem was the disappearance of cash into safe deposit boxes. Even the sound banks—sound so far as balance sheet preponderance of assets over liabilities to others was concerned—were in an illiquid state: they had exhausted their cash. Everywhere ready money was disappearing into safe deposit boxes, shoe boxes, coffee cans, stockings and mattresses.

What emerged from that conference was the decision to utilize the well-tried device of clearing house certificates—a technique to which we will give attention in a subsequent chapter.

The storm continued to blow: on Friday the stock market again felt the shock of heavy selling; since Monday nine great banking houses in New York had succumbed, and throughout the country, from the great cities of Chicago and St. Louis and San Francisco to the smallest hamlets, the shock waves caused the crumbling of countless little banks and business firms with insufficient cash. But the main disaster was in the financial centers, New York most of all.

For a fortnight the storm continued to lash. On Monday a run began again at the Trust Company of America, so narrowly saved the week before. Night after night Morgan was awake, holding conferences in his opulently furnished library, until daylight showed through the portiered windows and fell upon the Italian marble and the Renaissance treasures with which it was filled. By the end of the week, however, the blasts were subsiding.

Reassuring statements from Morgan and other Wall Street leaders like Stillman and Vanderlip helped. The issuance of clearing house certificates provided a form of cash that restored some liquidity to the banking system and to business.

Roosevelt had arrived in Washington from his western trip about four o'clock in the afternoon of the violent Wednesday, October 23. He had gone directly from his train to the White House, where it was announced he would see no callers. The *New York Times* reported that all efforts to see him, or obtain some expression from him regarding the financial situation, failed.[8] He responded, however, to the interest shown in the trophies of his hunting trip. After a bundle of umbrellas and a pile of storm coats had been handed out, and a couple of pairs of antlers followed, the reporters of the *Times* observed that "there was a lot of comment because one pair was white and bleached, showing that it was not obtained by any bullet fired on this trip." There followed a deer hide, "perhaps the one that had belonged to the buck which wore the pair of fine antlers tied up with the old one, a rough shaggy hide. . . ."

"I had a delightful time," the President declared in a brief acknowledgment of the reporters. "I am extremely gratified over the fact that I got a bear as the result of my hunt, and nonetheless so that I had to work twelve days to get it . . . The entire twenty-four days have been full of both profit and pleasure. . . ."

The following day a cabinet meeting was held—the first since early June—that lasted two hours and a half, and while "the financial situation was discussed at some length," the principal preoccupation was an accumulation of routine departmental matters, as well as naval matters—the latter probably the projected display of the naval forces in foreign waters.

The Panic of 1907, as we noted earlier, has been called the rich man's panic. If it was the product of the open market, the natural outcome of the private enterprise system, the fruit of the misdeeds of the financial community, it was in these areas that the issue was met and mastered, the problem solved, the penance paid and the battle won. The panic may have been precipitated by financial manipulators, but they assumed the responsibility and leadership for arresting its spread and restoring stability. There was no hesitancy. And among them all, authorities agree that Morgan was chief. Abroad, his leadership was universally acknowledged, while French editorials caustically commented on Roosevelt's hunting trip during the crisis.[9]

Winkler, in his *Morgan the Magnificent,* may be somewhat overcome by his subject, but his comment is of interest:

> Overnight Morgan became a towering, heroic figure. There was something elemental in this dogged, scornful man's appearance in his old age (he was six months past seventy) after years of unanswered criticism; in this crisis he gathered strength and courage from the weakness and timidity of others, while the leagued wealth of a nation called on him for leadership, and immense systems of banks and trust companies, stock exchanges, multitudes of brokers listened humbly, gratefully for his word and depended for salvation upon his judgment and force.[10]

The financial markets gradually regained stability, but the general effect of the crisis was like that of a four-minute earthquake: the economy of the country was crippled and hobbled throughout the following year.

Agitation now mounted for currency or banking reform, or some government action that would prevent such debacles in the future.

5.

ᲐᲡᲐᲡᲐᲡᲐᲡᲐᲡᲐᲡᲐᲡᲐᲡᲐᲡᲐᲡᲐᲡᲐᲡᲐᲡᲐᲡᲐᲡᲐᲡ

A Measure of Expediency

W HEN CONGRESS CONVENED in December following the panic,
it was universally agreed that the earliest object of attention
should be the monetary system. But there was bitter argument as to what
should be done. The White House offered no leadership. President
Roosevelt boasted that he knew nothing of economics, and that he was
essentially a moralist in politics; he had ideas as to the regulation of the
corporations, but none to offer on the money system.

Sentiment was agreed, however, that his proposals, in his State of the
Union message, for federal incorporation of companies engaged in interstate commerce and income and inheritance taxes were less urgent than
the restoration of banking and commercial confidence. And everyone, it
seemed, was agreed that the cure lay somewhere in the money system.
As the *New York Times* argued with indisputable logic, there was no other
explanation for the debacle. "In 1907," it reasoned, "we had neither war,
pestilence, nor famine, earthquake nor conflagration."[1]

Surveying the events of the year the *Times* came to the retrospective
conclusion—which may not have been unbiased, considering its political
complexion*—that government intervention in the economy, at the state
as well as at the federal level, was a principal cause, leading as it did to
loss of confidence in business and among businessmen. To support this
view, it pointed out that the year had opened with anxiety over Federal
regulation of railway profits in accordance with what it called "erratic

---

*The *Times* was, as today, Independent Democrat, but this, as we have noted, meant
something far different in 1907 from what it does in 1980.

views of the effect of capitalization upon rates." So great was this anxiety that J. P. Morgan had visited the White House to protest, and the President had dismissed as "utter nonsense" any supposition that he contemplated anything prejudicial to railway investments. Nevertheless, such superficial approach to the problems of big business as that displayed by Attorney General Bonaparte in his proposal, as the *Times* reported it, "to bag trusts miscellaneously by shooting into a covey and to institute receivership for solvent concerns, unconvicted of violating any law,"[2] did not allay disquiet. The *Times* cited the Presidential proposals for income and inheritance taxes, and noted especially the marks of a persecution complex which Roosevelt had manifested in a recent speech at Providence (R. I.) in which he attributed the stock market collapse to a conspiracy to discredit his policies entered into by certain "malefactors of great wealth."

The cleavage between those who prefer to trust their liberties to a centralized government functioning through an authoritarian bureaucracy, and those who would rely upon the operation of individual freedom curbed mainly by an increasing sense of individual responsibility, appeared in the various proposals for monetary reform. As so often in history, the staunchest defenders of the people's freedom were most vocal in demanding more authoritarian government. William Jennings Bryan—the "boy orator of the Platte," the "Great Commoner" who had twice been the standard bearer of his party and twice the defeated candidate for President—urged a central bank issuing currency secured by government bonds and a government guarantee of bank deposits; but his views, seemingly, were not given much weight.

A poll by the *Times* of ninety members of Congress, on the eve of their convening, indicated three main bodies of opinion.

There were those who favored some form of "asset" currency—which meant presumably notes issued by individual banks and secured by bank assets, though the specification was not clear as to what assets might be included. Another substantial group advocated a currency issued by a central bank, and secured by government bonds. A third group favored only an emergency currency to be issued within limits by the national banks (as distinct from state banks or other banking institutions) on other than bond security, and to be subject to a sliding tax that would force its redemption as soon as the urgency had passed, and hence confine the circulation to a normal level of requirements.

None of the various schools was clear as to the details or effects of their proposals. It was nevertheless a general consensus, the *Times* found, that any changes in the currency should be in the direction of an "intimate connection between the currency and legitimate trade"—that is, an "elastic" currency fluctuating in accordance with the commercial demand for circulating media.

It was Senator Nelson W. Aldrich of Rhode Island, as head of the Senate Finance Committee, who came forward with a concrete legislative proposal for debate. Senator Aldrich was the accepted leader of the conservative wing of the Republican Party in Congress. He was then sixty-seven years of age and had been a Senator for twenty-seven years. He had started life as a poor boy whose parents had been able to give him no more than a common school education and a year in the East Greenwich Academy. He went to work at the age of seventeen, starting in the grocery business, but soon entered politics as a local councilman. He happily married into wealth, acquired more from shrewd operations in spinning and railways, and became allied with the Rockefeller interests through the marriage of his daughter Abby to John D. Rockefeller, Jr. In Washington his influence was identified with tariff and silver legislation —though, paradoxically, his tariff views were more liberal than those of many Democrats. He seems to have had only a cursory knowledge of monetary matters, however, until the subject was forced upon him by the Panic of 1907. The story is told that in the fall of 1907 Aldrich called on Jacob Schiff, of the noted firm of Kuhn, Loeb & Company, to inquire about certain technicalities of German note issue and that Mr. Schiff, not being familiar with the matter, introduced a younger partner who had only come to this country from Germany six years before. This was Paul Warburg who was to have important influence later in shaping the Federal Reserve Act. The German was impressed with the Senator, and when the Senator walked out of the office is said to have commented to himself, "There marches national bank currency and there goes currency reform." Warburg had strong convictions on currency matters and he asked his senior partner whether he might write a personal letter to the Senator on the disadvantages of note issues secured by government bonds. Schiff, aware of Aldrich's opposite convictions, warned his partner to be cautious and not to precipitate that issue.[3]

The bill which Aldrich introduced called for the appointment of a national monetary commission to examine into the whole monetary and banking question and to bring in recommendations. As an interim measure it authorized a currency to replace the clearing house certificates that were still outstanding. The bill would, in effect, replace these certificates by national bank notes. It would authorize an emergency issue of currency to the total of $250 million secured by bonds approved by a Trea-

sury Department board. In addition to government bonds, however, the
bill authorized the use of certain types of railway bonds as security. Over
this stool his bill fell and something of Aldrich's influence. For railways
were in bad odor politically, and Democratic opponents as well as some
Republicans were prompt to make political hay of this aspect of the bill.
We shall come to the debate presently.

Meanwhile, a word about clearing house certificates. They were, as
remarked, notes payable to bearer issued by the clearing house of the city
or district, the notes being secured by notes, bonds, or other assets of the
individual banks that received the certificates.* The process worked as
follows: a bank with insufficient cash to meet its depositors' drafts would
deposit with the clearing house such notes or other assets as the clearing
house authorities considered acceptable, and receive in turn the certificates of the clearing house. These certificates, which were the obligation
of the clearing house, would be accepted in lieu of cash by all member
banks of the clearing house association, and consequently they were a
limited currency. As rapidly as the banks were able to liquidate their own
"frozen" assets, by obtaining payment of notes and bills owing by customers, they were able to pay off their own obligations to the clearing
house and reclaim their collateral; at the same time the clearing house
retired its certificates.

This whole operation, of course, depended upon the existence somewhere in the economy of sufficient cash to pay off this circle of obligations. The chain of reactions necessarily depended upon the success of
the individual borrower in laying hands on sufficient cash to pay off his
note to the bank; until he did so the bank could not pay off its note to
the clearing house, and the clearing house could not retire its certificates.
But where was the individual to find the cash in this period of stringency?

What added difficulty to the process was the unwillingness of those who
had cash to release it except under pressure, for fear of another and
greater stringency. This was especially true of the Western and country
banks. Formerly they had been willing to send all their spare cash to the
centers—to their big city correspondent banks—for the sake of the interest it would earn. The suspension of redemption—actually the default—
of the central city banks during the Panic now made their country cousins
more cautious. They were keeping this cash in their own vaults and hang

---

*A "clearing house" was simply the association of banks that used a common agency or
facility to clear their checks or drafts on each others' banks. The clearing house matched
debits and credits arising from these checks or drafts and then credited or debited the
account of the particular member bank accordingly. This procedure economized time and
cash in settling accounts.

the expense! Thus, enormous sums of money that normally were in circulation were now locked up in bank vaults all over the country. How to loosen up the flow of this cash was the monetary problem that Senator Aldrich hoped to solve by his bill.

Such was the theoretical argument and situation, and at the time the available banking statistics were too limited to permit a critical analysis of the case. Subsequent studies made by the National Monetary Commission indicated that the so-called country bank absorption of cash was less significant than it appeared at the time. Thus, the Commission tabulated the weekly movement of money from the interior into, and out of, New York City banks for the years 1899 through 1909. The figures showed that the movement was normally inward throughout the year, except for the months of September through November and the first half of December. The weekly movement ranged between $1 1/2 million and $6 million. This pattern was broken in 1906 when a heavy withdrawal by interior banks occurred in the latter part of April and the early part of May, coincident with the stock market decline of that year, with $42 million going out in two weeks, and with the drain persisting until the end of the month. Thereafter an inward movement resumed until the fall withdrawals began—this year somewhat earlier, beginning the first week in August. The spring of 1907 saw a resumption of interior withdrawals, though neither heavy nor consistent, and a renewal of an inward movement beginning in May and continuing, with some breaks in August, until the first week of September. The movements remained modest, however, but nevertheless inward, until the stock market crash, the first tremors of which began on October 16. Thereafter, between October 18 and the end of the year, New York City bank balances were drawn down by interior banks to the extent of $124 million. With the New Year, however, a heavy return movement of funds began and $68 million was recovered by the end of January.*

During the three years 1905–1907, the net annual outward movement of funds to the interior had been $37 million, $85 million, and $106 million, respectively. In 1908 the movement abruptly reversed and the net inward flow accumulated to the amount of $156 million by the year end.

A further item illuminating the nature of the October crash was the

---

*National Monetary Commission, Vol. XXI, *Statistics for U. S.* pp. 229 ff. It should be noted that this inward movement reflected a restoration of confidence in the banking system just as the similar indices in 1932 showed a revival of confidence and trade well before any new legislation or administrative reforms had been enacted or even agreed upon.

disclosure in January, 1908, that the total number of clearing house
certificates that were issued between October 22, when this emergency
measure was adopted, and the end of December, totaled only $97 million,
or about 5 per cent of total deposits. By comparison, the issue of clearing
house certificates in the 1893 crash amounted to $41.6 million, or about
10 per cent of the deposits then outstanding.

Senator Aldrich's bill came under immediate criticism, on the grounds
that it did not provide for a currency supply that would respond to the
seasonal demand and fluctuate in accordance with the volume of trade.
It made the condition of the bond market the determinant of the money
supply rather than the state of trade. Even those who favored bond-
secured currency found the bill objectionable. They pointed out that the
restrictions in the bill upon the acceptability of certain types of bonds
were so stringent—railways, for instance, had to have paid 4 per cent
dividends for four years for their bonds to qualify—as practically to
render the bill meaningless.

The argument for a flexible currency was counter-argued by the *Times*
with an analogy from railroading. It took up the hypothetical question as
to what a central bank should do with its funds when money was not
required for moving the crops, by pointing to the 200,000 idle freight
cars which, it said, had been built to move the fall crops at a cost of $124
million. "That large sum is now earning nothing and the cars are depreciating while unused," the *Times* commented. "Yet it was but the other
day that laws were being passed providing fines and imprisonment for the
neglect of the railways to provide cars—as they would have been glad to
if they could."[4]

The moral was obvious. The attempt to increase bank earnings to the
maximum by reducing cash reserves—in the case of country banks, by
sending them to the central city banks where they would earn interest—
was as unwise banking and monetary policy as to destroy or sell off
equipment not in immediate use.

"There is no remedy for an alternate excess and deficiency of cars,"
continued the *Times*. "They cannot be extemporized for nothing and
burned up when not wanted. But that is exactly what a central bank exists
to do in the case of bank notes. It creates them at a profit to itself, and
at a cost to borrowers of nothing more than a fair price for the use of
capital. And when the notes are in excess they are burned, again at no
cost."

Obviously the questions left hanging were deeper, lying in the realm
of moralities and metaphysics, but none the less real and imperative on

that account. They were: Is there a moral justification for confusing "circulation" with "capital," that is, of treating as equal and tangible, both banknotes that are the fictitious creation of a financial institution and money, which is a form of tangible capital (or the certificate of title thereto), such as gold and silver or gold and silver certificates? What were the economic and juridical effects, upon the relative ownerships of wealth, of the process of creating purchasing power through fictitious money issued by a central bank? If one man may buy in the market only by the exchange of goods won at the cost of some human labor and effort, while another need only rub the Aladdin's lamp of banking and thereby draw purchasing power from the air in the form of crisp banknotes, what are the effects upon the prices of goods in the market, the distribution of ownership of these goods, and the state of contentment or discontentment among the several classes of the citizenry as they are affected by this process?

Various alternative proposals now began to appear. Congressman Charles N. Fowler of New Jersey, a close associate with Aldrich on other matters, proposed a comprehensive reform including the retirement of the bond-secured circulation as well as the remainder of the Civil War greenbacks (which had no specific backing) and the issue of "national bank guaranteed credit notes" secured by reserves, in the form of "lawful money," of 25 per cent for central city banks and 15 per cent for other banks. The American Bankers' Association recommended a currency expanding and contracting with the needs of business and secured by "the property for the exchange of which they were issued."

During the following months the Treasury applied every pressure and influence to induce the banking system to increase the circulation—a campaign that recalls that exerted by the government upon the steel industry in the late forties to increase steel production capacity. The bankers resisted, as the steel industry did later, for so rapidly had confidence been reviving that money was returning from the countryside into the city banks in such quantities as to create a plethora.

Among the more influential voices heard above the din of argument was that of Paul Warburg, whose views gained more and more adherents, and which we will look at further on.

Andrew Carnegie and William Jennings Bryan debated the issue extemporaneously when they jointly addressed the New York Economics Club—Carnegie roundly damning the existing system as "the worst in the world" and Bryan retorting that time did not permit an "answer to all the heresies that have been presented by Mr. Carnegie," or allow him "to defend the honest dollar from all the attacks that have been made upon it." Of one thing he was certain, he asserted with a wry reference to his own political defeats, the conditions described arose from nothing with which he had anything to do. Bryan, oddly enough for the moralist and humanitarian that he was, seemed to play into the very hands of those who would manipulate the money system to their profit, by deriding the view that currency should be backed by gold. There was not sufficient gold for the purpose, he declared, and implied that the system of issuing money against only government bonds was both adequate and honest.

Opposition to the Aldrich bill also came from the Merchants Association of New York which began a concerted campaign against it, condemning "as essentially unsound the principle that a currency should be based on fixed securities of any description."[5]

More violent opposition to the Aldrich proposals came from the Wisconsin firebrand and "liberal," Senator Robert M. La Follette, whose position was grounded in the prevailing antipathy to the railroads. He urged that the bill gave them an indirect subsidy by making their bonds legal reserve for note issue. It was dangerous, he argued, to legalize railroad securities as a basis for currency unless the actual value of the property which the bonds represented were established.* He held correctly that without such valuation and without strict control over "capitalization" (i.e. the issue of new securities), a vast inflation of railway securities would ensue which would in turn impede any effort to reduce railroad rates. His point was that the attractiveness of railway bonds as a backing for note issues would run up the market price on all railway issues, both bonds and stock, and that investors paying such higher prices for the issues would in turn demand higher dividends, which in turn would compel the maintenance of high freight and passenger rates.

To placate La Follette, Aldrich agreed to accept an amendment to his bill to this effect, but he stipulated that the valuations should be limited to the physical valuation only of the properties securing the particular bonds used as note issue reserve. La Follette declined to accept this compromise, since he had long been agitating for an appraisal of the entire railway system.

The La Follette attack served to raise the deeper issues in the Aldrich

---

*The attempt to evaluate the physical assets of the railways as distinct from the valuation of their earnings subsequently became a mammoth and ineffectual project that gave a career employment to a corps of economists and accountants.

proposals, and it soon became apparent that, emergency or not, no bill could expect an easy passage. For all his great influence, Aldrich found himself and the Senate playing second fiddle to Congressman Foster and the House.

Not the least of the frustrations of the able and sincere Senator from Rhode Island was a sudden assault upon his bill by one of his freshman colleagues, Senator Robert Latham Owen of Oklahoma. Oklahoma had been admitted to statehood only the year before and Senator Owen had taken the oath as Senator only two months earlier. Though Owen had been born in Virginia, son of a prosperous banker, he had Cherokee blood in his veins and there were some private jokes in the corridors that his chief service would be to keep Senator Curtis of Kansas, who was a member of the Kaw tribe, from growing lonesome.

One of the cherished Senate traditions is that a new senator should avoid speechmaking during his first session. Jefferson Davis had tried to break that tradition with disastrous results. For two months the lithe and handsome, black-eyed and square-jawed young man from the West kept an Indian taciturnity to the proceedings, and was, as someone commented, "a good Indian."

Suddenly the "Oklahoma Indian" came to life. "In the course of three days in February," the *New York Times* feature writer reported, "the young member not only galvanized the Senate into astonishment, but he managed to upset a whole rack of senatorial traditions." As the *Times* reported:

> Owen's dramatic and spectacular transformation from the silent and saturnine Indian of the council fire to the rampant warrior of the warpath took place on Tuesday [Feb. 24, 1908]. He liked the change, evidently, for on Thursday he again whetted his oratorical tomahawk and dashed forth to garner a few more senatorial scalps in debate. . . .
>
> On Tuesday the Senate received a twist that it will not recover from in some time. Owen had given notice that he would speak on the Aldrich currency bill. . . . The new Senator had not gone far in his speech when his hearers began to sit up. Here was eloquence, but here also was the argument of a man who knew what he was talking about. Certain of the leaders began to stir uneasily, and it was evident that the hazers were about to begin the inquisition.

But the young representative of the sovereign State of Oklahoma forestalled them. Sensing that he was about to be challenged, he paused suddenly in his reading and announced, enquiringly, "If any Senator wishes to interrupt me . . ."

When no one accepted the dare and the silence became painful, he resumed his speech.

Eventually the supporters of Aldrich rallied. Senator Reed Smoot of Utah undertook to defend the New York banks, but was overpowered by Senator Owen's trenchant rejoinder and mastery of his subject. After several members attempted to answer Owen, Aldrich himself rose to the defense of his bill. But he fared no better.

"Why this discrimination against United States bonds?" Owen thundered. "Why should railroad bonds, the value of which is never stable, take precedence over the bonds issued by the government?"

Aldrich, suave and conciliatory, made lengthy reply, but there was in fact no answer. Neither party seemed to grasp that the root of the problem lay elsewhere—not whether government promises to pay were better backing for money than railroads' promises to pay, but whether either offered a sound basis for a monetary system.

Owen's early entry into the monetary controversy is of interest because of the influential part he was to play in the enactment of the Federal Reserve Act—a part, incidentally, which has never been properly appreciated.

Aldrich's bill came under attack also from some of those who favored his theories but objected to his application of them. It was pointed out that the legislation was discriminatory in that of some $6 billion in railway bonds outstanding, only some $2 billion would be eligible as reserve for currency.[6]

Senator La Follette renewed his opposition to the bill, charging that it would encourage panics rather than prevent them.

Despite the opposition the Aldrich bill, much amended, passed the Senate on March 25, 1908, with a vote of 42 to 16.

Meantime, on the House side, the effort was being made to work out a satisfactory bill through the process of Party caucus rather than committee hearing and finding. Representative E. B. Vreeland of New York offered a bill that attempted to meet a consensus of opinion among the Republican membership, eager to redeem Administration promises of a currency bill. Some currency legislation was imperative, and the powerful Speaker of the House, Joseph Cannon, who wielded unprecedented influence but who was known to be at odds with Roosevelt, let it be known that he would use his prestige toward the Vreeland bill.

At a private hotel room meeting in the Arlington House, on April 14, between Aldrich, Cannon, and Vreeland, a compromise was worked out to accept the Vreeland bill as a substitute for the Aldrich bill.

But the powerful Speaker of the House was no more successful in forcing his views than the influential Senator Aldrich. Three weeks after its introduction the Vreeland bill had been radically changed by amendments. As the *New York Times* commented, "Nothing could be more admirable than Mr. Vreeland's industry, unless it is his readiness to oblige. Day after day he produces fresh versions of his bill. Mr. Vreeland of the Salamanca Trust Company, Cattaraugus County, wastes no time over objections. He simply offers a new bill."[7]

The *Times* went on to say:

> Nobody knows what the bill will be tomorrow, or even what it is today, for that matter, for it exists as yet only in Mr. Vreeland's mind. Only two things are sure—it will not be the Vreeland bill unless it provides for the issue of some large part of a billion dollars of emergency currency, or if it does not provide some method of getting in the currency after it is put out. The omission of adequate methods of redemption is quite as characteristic of the bill as its ample, not to say excessive, provision for issue.[8]

The *Times* took occasion to charge President Roosevelt with obstruction of monetary legislation. Recalling his promise at the beginning of the session that Congress would enact a currency bill, it wondered whether the declaration could have been redeemed if the President had mastered the subject and given it the attention it deserved. "Instead," the *Times* complained, "he has dragged so many red herring across the currency trail that he must share responsibility for the fact that nothing has been done that is worthy of respect."[9]

Finally, on May 11 after a stormy meeting lasting until midnight, during which one of the Congressmen is reported to have shaken his fist under the nose of the Speaker, the Republican membership agreed 128 to 16 on a currency bill that endorsed the principle of commercial paper as an asset of the currency reserve. In the compromise the name "Clearing House Association" was dropped from the bill, but the provision for note issuing associations open to membership by any bank was retained. No machinery was provided by which to discipline the member banks (as was the case with the clearing houses), a defect which opponents immediately used to advantage.

On May 14 the House passed the Vreeland bill by a vote of 184 to 145, but when it was sent to the other House, Senator Aldrich unexpectedly killed it. He moved "to strike all after the enabling clause," to amend it by substituting a new bill of his own draft, to refer it to the Committee which he headed, and without moving from his seat reported the bill favorably and called for a vote. Such in those days was the control of the leadership over their respective Houses! The bill was adopted 47 to 20 and again a struggle for a compromise began.[10]

Eventually, after several White House conferences marked by the faithful cooperation of Speaker Cannon, who for the first time joined forces with the White House on an important item of the Administration program, a compromise was accepted which left open the question whether currency issues should be backed by bonds or commercial paper. To obtain support of reluctant Congressmen for this hermaphroditic measure, the *Times* charged that it would be coupled with a $23 million public works or "pork barrel" bill.[11]

On May 27 the compromise squeezed through the House under Speaker Cannon's whip, 166 to 140, but in the Senate confronted a new and formidable attack by Senator La Follette. The "La Follette Filibuster" is one of the most famous in the annals of legislative debate. Only the currency bill held up adjournment and the members were eager to leave for home. In such circumstances a filibuster, holding the Senate in session, can be a powerful weapon. The La Follette filibuster was defeated by circumstance of the blindness of one of the La Follette coterie, Senator Thomas P. Gore of Oklahoma, combined with the unceasing watchfulness and consummate strategy of the opposition. Senators La Follette, Stone and Gore were taking turns speaking so as to prevent the bill from coming to a vote. The blind Gore had taken the floor on the understanding that at his signal Senator Stone would relieve him. But Senator Stone had stepped into the lobby at the moment the blind Senator, unaware of his absence, gave his signal. As Gore paused in his speech Senator Gallinger rose and demanded a roll call and the cooperative Clerk began calling the names beginning with Aldrich. The La Follette group shouted a point of order but Vice President Fairbanks ruled that the roll call was in order. La Follette had lost the floor, the bill passed by a vote of 43 to 22, and was signed by the President on the same day, May 30, 1908.[12]

6.

The Aldrich-Vreeland Bill

THE ALDRICH-VREELAND BILL, as the Emergency Currency Act of May 30, 1908, was known, embraced the principles of an "asset currency" which represented a revolutionary innovation in U. S. currency practice, and prepared the way for the theories and practices later embodied in the Federal Reserve System.

The bill took a step toward centralization of the note issue by conferring control over the issue upon associations of banks, and by widening their discretion as to the acceptable reserves behind the currency. Recall that the reserve for the principal paper money—the national bank notes —was narrowly restricted to government bonds, but that within this restriction the determination of the amount of notes to be issued lay with the individual bank and the play of economic and other forces that affected their decisions.

Under the new act, any ten national banks having aggregate equity funds* of at least $5 million could organize themselves into an association with power of note issue, subject to an overriding but nominal

---

*A prevailing misunderstanding—paradoxical in such a period of sophisticated financiers —was as to the nature of "capital." The bill insisted that only banks with "surplus" equal to 20 per cent of "capital" were eligible for membership in an association. No one seemed to realize what a later generation did, that capital and surplus are simply accountants' descriptions of the forms of stockholders' equity, that is, the excess of corporate worth over corporate liabilities to others. Later, it became common to create "surplus" or to cause it to disappear by stockholders' action. A better term would have been "earned surplus," but it is common today to capitalize earned surplus and absorb it into "capital." Likewise, surplus is frequently created by issuing stock for consideration in excess of par and treating the excess as "surplus."

control of the Treasury. That is, the associations were authorized to receive, to validate, and to hold for note issue purposes, certain kinds of security or collateral, and in return to issue to the depositing bank an equivalent amount of circulating notes which the association in turn received from the Comptroller of the Currency.

The mechanics of this process need not detain us. The essential features of the system were: (a) Banks could obtain and issue legal tender paper money secured by a wide range of collateral, including state and municipal bonds, corporation bonds, and commercial paper. (b) The kinds of acceptable security were within the discretion of the associations, within certain limits. For example, "commercial paper" was defined simply as notes representing actual commercial transactions, bearing the endorsement (guarantee) of two responsible parties, and having a maturity not exceeding four months. (c) Note issue privilege was limited to banks that had already outstanding notes secured by government bonds to the extent of 40 per cent of their capital. (The purpose of this provision was to restrict the additional issues to "emergency" needs.) The amount of the additional notes was further limited to 75 per cent of the cash value of the securities or commercial paper deposited (but 90 per cent in case of state and municipal bonds). These additional issues were also restricted to a finding by the Secretary of the Treasury that business conditions in the locality required the issuance of the additional notes.

Although commercial paper was qualified as acceptable security for note issue, it was apparent from the bill that the general expectation was rather that the principal reserve would be state and municipal bonds and other bonds.

An additional deterrent to over-issue of notes, and incentive to their prompt retirement, was the heavy tax laid upon the emergency issues. While the regular national bank notes were taxed at 1/2 per cent to 1 per cent per annum of the notes issued (depending upon the coupon rates of the securing bonds), notes secured by other forms of collateral were to be taxed up to 10 per cent per annum.

A final provision of the act was the creation of a National Monetary Commission composed of nine Senators and nine Representatives, with the duty to enquire into and report to the Congress at the earliest date practicable upon whether changes in the monetary and banking systems were desirable and necessary.

The act decreed its own expiry on June 30, 1914; but by that time the Commission had reported and the Congress had enacted the Federal

Reserve Act which came into effect December 23, 1913. This act extended the life of the Emergency Currency Act to June 30, 1915. The subsequent events relating to this legislation are bound in with the story of the Federal Reserve Act and the outbreak of World War I and will be related in that connection.

Here we may note only that the act remained moribund until the outbreak of World War I. The immediate effects of the 1907 Panic had passed and the necessity for the organization of currency associations did not appeal to the banks. In fact, while the National Currency Association of Washington was organized very speedily, on June 18, 1908, it was not until 1910 that any other action was taken. In that year associations were formed in New York, Philadelphia, Louisiana, Boston, St. Louis, St. Paul and Minneapolis, Detroit, Albany (counties of Rensselaer and Schenectady), Kansas City and St. Joseph, Baltimore and Cincinnati. In 1911 associations were formed at Dallas, Texas, and in Alabama, and for Denver, Colorado Springs and Pueblo. In 1912 the Los Angeles Association was formed. Only three were formed in 1913, at Louisville, San Francisco, and Pittsburgh. Thus, at the close of 1913, there were in existence twenty-one National Currency Associations, representing 352 national banks, with combined capital of $381,184,710 and surplus of $329,-300,510. While the number of banks represented was less than 5 per cent of the total in operation, they represented over one-third (36 per cent) of the total capital and about 45 per cent of the aggregate surplus of the national banking system.[1]

However, no additional currency, that is, emergency currency, was issued throughout this period until the outbreak of World War I.

In retrospect, the Aldrich-Vreeland Act fulfilled its function of creating an emergency currency power. It continued the system of fiat money of the old National Bank Act, which permitted the issue of paper notes secured only by government bonds. It introduced one novel feature in U. S. currency practice: it gave validity to the view that if fiat money was to be issued at all, sound promissory notes of short maturity made for commercial transactions were good collateral for such a purpose.

7.

An Interlude for Debate

A FTER THE PASSING of the Panic of 1907 the demand for business credit and for circulating money abated. For six years, as we
have noted, until the outbreak of war in Europe in August, 1914, not a
single dollar of emergency currency was issued. On the contrary, the
press complained of the plethora of money and credit. Public interest
turned to other events—the election of William Howard Taft to the
Presidency and the retirement of the controversial Roosevelt to the hunting wilds of Africa, and to other topics—that of the tariff, and the agitation for an income tax, and the mounting European tension.

Meantime, the issues in the money debate began to clarify—if their
underlying meaning remained foggy. Oklahoma, admitted to statehood
in 1907 as the 46th State, had adopted a constitution with a number of
novelties, including the initiative and referendum, and some laws that
caused reactions from laughter to consternation in the older sections of
the country. Among them was one prohibiting the common drinking cup;
another required hotel keepers to use bed sheets nine feet long—the
"nine foot bed sheet law"; and another authorized a system of bank
deposit guaranty.

Under the Bank Guaranty Act, passed in February, 1908, state banks
were required, and national banks permitted, to contribute one per cent
of their deposits to a fund to meet the claims of depositors of defaulting
banks. Despite a ruling of the U. S. Atrtorney General that national banks
could not lawfully participate in the program, the idea attracted the
attention of politicians: William Jennings Bryan, the perennial Democratic Party candidate for president, enthusiastically endorsed it, and the

Democratic Party adopted a plank in its platform favoring a national bank guaranty system.

Unfortunately, in September, 1909, long after banking had returned to normal throughout the country generally, the Columbia Bank and Trust Co. of Oklahoma City failed with deposit liabilities of $2.9 million and cash and liquid items of less than $1.2 million. The guaranty fund then had less than $260,000 of assets and despite special assessments of another $250,000 the fund was soon exhausted. Many of the member banks, to avoid further assessments, transferred from state to national charters.

Although a few other Western states followed the Oklahoma example and although the constitutionality of the system was sustained by the Supreme Court, the idea lost popularity and faded from interest until revived by the Great Crash of 1933.

Among the Eastern financial community, and in Congress, discussion turned upon the use of gold and the nature of the reserve. It was about this time that the phrase "economizing gold" began to appear as the latest novelty of economic sophistry. The *New York Times* editorialized on the subject with naïve solemnity. The occasion was an address by Secretary of the Treasury Sherman in which he had admiringly pointed to the nearly $1 1/2 billion of gold in the Treasury, in addition to the $200 million in national bank vaults, and had emphasized that the Treasury's holdings alone exceeded those of the three richest powers of Europe.

"Mr. Sherman seems to think that it is a good thing to waste abundance of resources" commented the *Times*. "The nations whose supply of gold is so scanty support a commerce larger in the aggregate than the commerce of the United States. . . . By making one gold dollar do the work of four in the United States they save the burden upon industry of supplying three unnecessary dollars."*

Despite its captivation by the idea of "economizing" gold, the *Times* correctly saw the evils in a system of bond secured money, as one of monetizing the public debt, and stated the fundamental objection as admirably as it has ever been stated:

"It is no proper function of a central bank to support the public credit. A central bank may very well be the Government's banker, and give it banking accommodations, but the maintenance of the Government's

---

*September 28, 1908. From the gold miners' viewpoint, a procedure that permits the banking or monetary authorities to create, with a stroke of the pen, three dollars each having a purchasing power equivalent to the dollar of gold extracted from the earth at cost of labor and equipment is nothing short of iniquitous.

credit is the business of the Government, and of the people who support the Government."[1]

Meantime, the National Monetary Commission, authorized by the Aldrich-Vreeland bill, with a broad grant of investigative power and unlimited funds, had begun its studies under the chairmanship of the industrious and able Aldrich.

Aldrich, however, as chairman of the Senate Finance Committee, was heavily involved in the controversial tariff legislation that later became law as the Payne-Aldrich Tariff Act. It was not until the following year, 1909, that he was able to give personal direction to the activities of the Monetary Commission.

Undoubtedly, the most influential intellect in shaping the course of public opinion was that of Paul M. Warburg, a Jewish newcomer to the United States, member of the distinguished banking house of Kuhn, Loeb & Co. and formerly a member of an equally distinguished German banking house. Paul Warburg came to the United States in 1902, when he was thirty-four years of age and successfully established as a banker. In November, 1907, he published a pamphlet, "A Plan for a Modified Central Bank," that attracted wide attention and that strongly influenced the direction of discussion, and impelled the course of the National Monetary Commission investigation toward German experience.

The trouble with the U. S. monetary system, Warburg explained, was that it was inflexible. Circulating money was limited mainly to gold and silver coins, and certificates of deposit therefor, or to the remnants of the Civil War greenbacks (United States notes) and to national bank notes. The greenbacks were no longer being issued, and national bank notes had to be secured by U. S. government bonds. Because of the frugality of the government, surpluses rather than deficits were the rule, and the amount of bonds which could be used as backing for currency was steadily diminishing. The debt, that had stood in excess of $2 billion following the Civil War, had been reduced to a little over $1 billion by 1900, and to less than $900,000,000 at the time of the Panic.

The net effect of the currency laws in force and the fiscal tendencies in effect was that there was no "elasticity" in the money supply. Thus, as Warburg argued, in times of great seasonal movement of merchandise, as when the wheat was in harvest and the great American plains were yellow with the ripening grain, the merchants and millers were straitened for ready cash with which to buy and store this abundance of nature's wealth. The consequence was that farmers, unable to find buyers with ready cash, dumped this grain for what it would bring. There were great fluctuations in price, and the farmer and the basic producer took the loss. The solution to this dilemma, the German banker-economist pointed out, was a money supply that would fluctuate in accordance with the rise and fall of business demand. The question was, how to achieve this desirable result?

Warburg argued that the proposal to create an emergency currency was dangerous for the reason that if a bank were involved in difficulties, as happened in the case of the Trust Company of America and the Knickerbocker Trust Co., if it had notes outstanding, the run of the depositors would have been carried into the ranks of the note holders, to the disaster of the entire money system.

The solution, he urged, was that discovered abroad and most highly developed in Germany, of issuing money (circulating notes) against the security of good commercial paper (notes of hand) made in the course of trade and business. Such notes would meet the urgent demand for circulating money when crops were moving, and the amount would naturally contract as the obligations behind them were paid off.

As a provisional measure to meet the shortage created by panic Warburg proposed a modified central bank, to be called for convenience the Government Bank, endowed with a capital of from $50 to $100 million, possibly to be paid up only in part; the shares to be owned, if possible, half by the government, half by the national banks; the management to be by a president, named by the board of directors and enjoying indefinite—and unlimited—tenure. The Bank would act as depository for the Treasury, and would in turn redeposit Treasury funds in the member national banks. The Government Bank would be authorized to issue legal tender notes, not to exceed a certain multiple of its capital and gold reserves. These notes would find their way into the bloodstream of commerce through the process of exchanging them for commercial paper— short term promises to pay given by merchants and others and held by the member banks. To limit the privilege such notes would have to be guaranteed by endorsement of the member bank.

Warburg had commented in an article published nearly a year earlier[2] that it was a strange fact that, despite the commercial development of the United States, it had progressed so little in the form of its commercial paper. The United States, he declared, was in fact "at about the same point that had been reached by Europe at the time of the Medicis, and by Asia, in all likelihood, at the time of Hammurabi."

"Most of the paper taken by the American banks," he explained, "still consists of simple promissory notes, which rest only on the credit of the merchant who makes the notes, and which are kept until maturity by the bank or corporation that discounts them. If discounted at all they are generally passed on without endorsement, and the possibility of selling any note depends on the chance of finding another bank which may be willing to give the credit. The consequence is that while in Europe the liquid assets of the banks consist chiefly of bills receivable, long and short, which thus constitute their quickest assets, the American bank capital invested in commercial notes is virtually immobilized."

Warburg's idea was that this commercial paper, if doubly or triply secured by the endorsement of banks, could be made an acceptable medium of payment and could circulate like money. Actually, the veritable documents themselves would not circulate but they would be deposited with a central institution which would issue its own promissory notes secured by its holdings of endorsed commercial paper. The promissory notes would be issued in standard denominations and in pieces of uniform size, and would be declared by law to be legal tender in payment of debts and taxes.

This is the essence of the idea that eventually became the foundation of the Federal Reserve System.

The theory now advanced differed from that of the *assignats* of the French Revolution and the *rentenmark* of the Great German Inflation in that the security of the proposed circulation was not land but the produce of the land in trade. In this respect it differed only in degree from the system proposed by John Law to the Regent of France, by which he would restore the credit of France, ruined by the excesses of Louis XIV, and which became the basis of the charter of the Banque Générale in 1716.

The conditioning view of Paul Warburg, which in turn was ultimately to govern the procedure and direction of the Federal Reserve System, was admirably stated in his article written after the Panic, in which he proposed his new currency system.

"We need some centralized power," he wrote, "to protect us against others and to protect us from ourselves—some power, able to provide for the legitimate needs of the country and able at the same time to apply the brakes when the car is moving too fast. Whatever causes may have precipitated the present crisis, it is certain that they never could have brought about the outrageous conditions, which fill us with horror and shame, if we had had a modern bank and currency system."*

---

*A Plan for a Modified Central Bank. Mr. Warburg did not live long enough to see his assurances confounded by the Crash of 1929, the Debacle of 1933, and the Break of 1962.

With a central bank such as he proposed, the "inelasticity" of the prevailing system would have been remedied. The prevailing system, as Warburg rightly pointed out, depended primarily upon stock exchange loans, while the most legitimate business, that of the purchase of commercial paper, caused a dangerous locking up of capital in single name promissory notes, which under normal conditions were unsalable. By creating a central bank, after the European pattern, such commercial paper would be converted from a non-liquid asset into the quickest asset of the banks.

What Warburg neglected to point out, however, was that such commercial paper, while gaining increased liquidity—that is, wider acceptability and marketability—was not thereby rendered more substantial as a base for money, particularly if the endorsing banks were careless of their credit and endorsed more notes than their own assets could possibly cover.

Warburg's proposal was, undoubtedly, an improvement over the existing system which permitted the unlimited issue of circulating notes against government bonds, though as we will notice later, the system eventually adopted did not remove this evil.

Warburg's ideas, cogently phrased as they were, were profoundly influential, perhaps because they seemed to offer such an easy solution to the problems besetting the country.*

Because of the influence exercised by the German system in the ultimate framing of the Federal Reserve System, a brief description of its features is appropriate.

The defeat of France by Prussia in the War of 1870 and the collection of a war indemnity of 5 billion francs in gold made possible the formation of the German Empire and with it the establishment of a new currency system and standard. The condition of the currency had been one of near-chaos. Six different systems were legally in force, and in addition an uncounted number and variety of coins were in circulation. Both gold and silver were legal standards. Currency reform began with the Acts of December 4, 1871, and July 9, 1873, which established the standard as the gold *mark* equivalent to 1/1395 of a pound weight of fine gold (5.531 English grains) and proclaimed the formal acceptance of the gold stan-

---

*The National Monetary Commission spent a great deal of time in examining the workings of European banking systems, particularly the German, to the exclusion of a study of monetary history, the question of coinage, or the standard, or the qualities and requisites of legal tender. Of the twenty-four volumes of reports produced by the Commission, five dealt exclusively with the German banking system.

dard. The acts permitted coinage for individuals, or what is known as free coinage, subject only to the mint charges or brassage, and provided for the gradual retirement of the circulating notes outstanding. The note issue was gradually to be concentrated in the Reichsbank, a new institution that took over the charter of the Prussian state bank.

What was unique in the German system was the allowance of a note issue secured by "good commercial bills," as the act described them, provided that the bank held in vault cash equal to one third of the notes issued. A limit was also placed upon the total amount of such notes that could be issued, and the bank would be taxed at the rate of 5 per cent per annum on the amount of notes issued in excess of this maximum. The theory of this was that in times of financial emergency, additional notes could be issued to prevent a monetary stringency, but because of the tax to which they would be subject, there would be every incentive to reduce the amount the moment the emergency had passed.

A limit of 385 million marks was prescribed for the total free, or nontaxable, notes that could be issued, of which 250 million marks were assigned to the Reichsbank and the balance allocated among the various banks whose charters still permitted them to issue notes.*

Not unexpectedly, the amount of the "contingent" issue was enlarged periodically, and by 1910 it had been increased to 618 million marks, most of which was by now concentrated under the note issue power of the Reichsbank.

Nevertheless, at the time of the Panic of 1907 German currency enjoyed a prestige rivalled only by English sterling, and was actually more strongly fortified with gold than the English pound.

---

*In addition, of course, the banks could issue circulating notes secured 100 per cent by coin. These would be in the nature of warehouse receipts for gold and silver. It is the "fiduciary" or "contingent" issues with which we are concerned here.

8.

$\sim\!\!\sim\!\!\sim\!\!\sim\!\!\sim\!\!\sim\!\!\sim\!\!\sim\!\!\sim$

The Great Investigation

T HE NATIONAL MONETARY COMMISSION considered its subject for
nearly four years; it sent its investigators throughout the civilized
world studying banking and monetary systems; it concluded its work on
January 8, 1912, with the presentation of twenty-four volumes of reports.
These are a mine of research that includes much esoteric information but
that strangely omits treatment of the most important elements of a monetary system—such, for instance, as the definition of the standard, the
nature of the coinage, and the integrity of the reserve. There are volumes
on banking and banking practices, but there is very little on money, and
the reports offer neither historical perspective nor prophetic insight into
the fundamental problems of currency, the media of payments, the nature
of legal tender, or the qualities of money. In fact, of the twenty-four
bound volumes into which the numerous reports were assembled, only
one bears a title relating it to the subject of money.[1]

Characteristic also of the prevailing confusion regarding the nature of
money is the circumstance, reported by the *New York Times,* that during
the 1907 Panic gold certificates were refused as legal tender in the settlement of real estate obligations.[2] The Act of March 14, 1900, had effectively founded the U. S. monetary system upon gold, by declaring that
"the dollar consisting of 25.8 grains of gold nine tenths fine . . . shall be
the standard and unit of value, and all forms of money issued or coined
by the United States shall be maintained at a parity of value with this
standard." The act also provided that nothing contained in the act "shall
be construed to affect the legal-tender quality as now provided by law of

53

the silver dollar, or of any other money coined or issued by the United States." Despite this provision, the gold certificate, representing gold deliverable on demand at the Treasury, carried only limited acceptance. This was due in part to the fact that the certificates, as originally issued under the wartime Act of March 3, 1863, gave them only limited legal tender quality; that is, they were declared legal tender only for duties on imports. Subsequently, by the Act of July 12, 1882, upon the resumption of specie payments, the certificates were made legal tender for customs, taxes, and all public dues. While the certificates nominally represented warehouse receipts for gold they were in fact a form of fiat currency, since the Act of March 3, 1863, authorized the issuance of certificates up to 20 per cent *in excess of* the amount of coin and bullion held by the Treasury.[3]

Actually, gold certificates were not declared full legal tender for all debts, public and private, until 1919,[4] although legislation to that effect had been proposed following the Panic of 1907.

The recommendations of the Commission are of interest in comparison with the legislation finally enacted. Like many political documents it straddled the main issues. Nevertheless, by admitting divergent viewpoints and giving them recognition it did propose basic changes in the organization and administration of the money system and in the quality of the money.

On the principal issue of whether currency should represent a monetization of public debt or private debt, the Commission boldly adopted the views so lucidly advocated by Paul Warburg: its proposals provided in effect that the substantial backing of the note issue should be commercial paper rather than bonds, whether private or public.

Thus, banks participating in the proposed new organization would be permitted to obtain money (in the form of circulating notes) through the sale or rediscount of "notes and bills of exchange arising out of commercial transactions; that is, notes and bills of exchange drawn for agricultural, industrial, or commercial purposes, and not including notes or bills issued or drawn for the purpose of carrying stocks, bonds, or other investment purposes."[5]

The strictly commercial character of this new backing for paper money was assured by the stipulation that such notes and bills have a maturity of not more than twenty-eight days, and that they must have been made at least thirty days prior to the date of discount. In exceptional cases, bills running up to four months would be accepted as collateral for note issue, if they were guaranteed by the endorsement of the local bank association in addition to that of the member bank.

At the same time, as a concession to advocates of a bond backed currency, the Commission's proposals would authorize the issue of notes against the pledge and deposit of satisfactory securities up to 75 per cent of the value of such collateral. The character and quality of the "satisfactory securities" was left open—a provision that tacitly allowed the use of corporate bonds as note issue reserve. Notes could also be issued against U. S. government bonds and also against notes of one year maturity or less of states and even of foreign governments.

Ordinarily, circulating notes and demand liabilities of the proposed central issuing authority (the National Reserve Association) were to be secured by gold to the extent of one-half, but a technical provision would permit U. S. government bonds to be counted at par as reserve, and provision was made for a tax upon the note issue when the reserve fell below 50 per cent, with a minimum reserve in any case of 33 1/3 per cent. An additional limitation was that notes issued in excess of $900 million should be covered 100 per cent by gold or be subject to a graduated tax.

On the question of the locus of authority, whether control of the banking and monetary system should be centralized in one institution with autocratic powers, or dispersed throughout the banking system, the Commission again offered a compromise. Control over the quality of the note issue, that is, of the reserves supporting the notes, would be vested in a central authority called the National Reserve Association. This institution alone would have the power to issue notes through the rediscount process, and to assess the quality of the collateral offered. It would also have the right and the duty to examine into the condition of member banks—although, curiously, the draft bill gave no disciplinary authority to the Association beyond publishing the reports.

The quantity of the note issue was to be governed by the market demand for money. That is, as member banks needed cash to meet calls from depositors or to extend credit to customers, they would obtain the means from the National Reserve Association by rediscounting their commercial paper with the Association.* As demand for credit diminished, and the discounted paper matured, the circulating notes would be retired. The procedure represented an essential democracy in the money system whereby the economy, working through the mass of individual transactions, would make its will manifest in regard to the money supply.

---

*Rediscounting technically is the sale of a promissory note at a discount representing the amount of interest, with the guarantee of the offering bank—indicated by "endorsing" the note—to pay off the note at maturity if the maker defaults.

Such was the admirable theory. The structure, however, had a fault that did not become apparent until much later when the scheme was taken over essentially in the Federal Reserve System. This was the provision that would permit the National Reserve Association, of its own accord, to purchase acceptances* from bankers or financial houses. This little provision, inserted for use in emergencies, became the seed of the "open market" operations of the Federal Reserve System, by which the central authority took upon itself to determine the amount and flow of liquid assets (money and credit) into the economy, and which eventually became a major instrument by which the central authorities sought to manage and control, not only the credit stream, but the direction and pulse of the entire productive activities of the country.

The administrative mechanism of the National Reserve Association need not detain us. The Commission proposed that the Association function through fifteen branch banks which would become regional money centers, and that the operating units of the systems be local associations of banks. Such associations could be formed by any ten banks serving contiguous territory. Such local associations would perform normal clearing house functions. Government of the National Reserve Association was to be through the member banks through a representative system moving upward through the local association to its corresponding branch to a board of directors, but the national interest was preserved by the requirement that the top executive, the governor of the National Reserve Association, be selected by the President of the U. S. from nominees presented by the board, and by the requirement that the Secretary of the Treasury and three other high officials serve ex officio on the board of forty-six directors. Provision was also made that the board membership reflect the principal economic interests of the country.

Finally, the Commission set forth the mechanism by which outstanding national bank notes should be retired and replaced by notes of the National Reserve Association—provisions that need not delay our story.

Senator Aldrich, in presenting the Commission's report, drew up a seventeen-point criticism of the existing monetary-banking system. He began by declaring that in examining the printed literature of banking, the Commission was struck by the meagre information available on any

---

*Another form of commercial paper, being a "draft," that is, an order upon one person to pay to a certain other person such and such sum of money, which the drawee has agreed to honor by "accepting" by writing his name, or "endorsement," upon the face of the draft preceded by the word "Accepted."

aspect of banking except the history of the note issue privilege. By contrast, as we have noted, the Commission's report dealt almost entirely with banking operations to the neglect of the theory or the history of money.

The Commission's attitude toward this subject is evident from the seventeen points. Point 1. states: "We have no provision for the concentration of the cash reserves of the banks and for their mobilization and use wherever needed in time of trouble."

From this it is apparent that the Commission accepted assumptions which it should have been its prime duty to question and analyze. Probably no question is more germane to the theory of individual (that is, personal) sovereignty and of representative government exercising delegated powers, than that of where the reserves of a nation are to be kept. To deprive an individual of his liquid reserves and to concentrate them in the hands of a central bureaucracy is, of course, the ultimate negation of individual liberty and responsible citizenship, and the substitute therefor of autocratic and irresponsible government. We shall have more to say about this as we go along, but the cleavage in political and economic philosophy should be clear at the outset: human liberty is co-extensive with the right of property. The simplest and most usable and marketable form of property consists of a piece of intrinsic money—a coin of good metal. When, by whatever means, the individual is deprived of the possession of that piece of metal—that intrinsic substance of worth—whether by the subtle sophistries of "mobilization of reserves" or other phrase, we witness the first steps on the road to serfdom and submission to an all-powerful state.

The second item in the Commission's summary states that "antiquated Federal and State laws restrict the use of bank reserves and prohibit the lending power of banks at times when, in the presence of unusual demands, reserves should be freely used and credit liberally extended to all deserving customers."

In this statement the Commission neglected to consider the function of money. For when the proposition is stripped to its bones it means that regardless of the condition of business, the individual, or the economy, the individual should always be able to convert his property into money. (For the moment, of course, the proposition limits itself to notes of hand represented by property in the course of movement from hand to hand; but the theory is the same.) The logical meaning of this is that the *quantity of money should always be potentially or actually co-extensive* with property—at least with movable property in the course of trade. (Later it would mean all property when subsequently bonds and mortgages were made eligible for rediscount.)

Now, obviously, if money must be co-extensive with goods in trade, or potentially so, any notion of a stable value of money—or any value whatsoever—must be abandoned. For the unique quality of money—that which gives it meaning above other forms of wealth—is this, that it is the most liquid of all forms of wealth, being generally infinitely divisible, readily transmitted, and universally acceptable. Now, if this liquidity be nullified by equating it to all other forms of property (at least property in course of trade) then its uniqueness as money ceases and its worth diminishes. In short, any idea of stability in the value of money must be surrendered.

At the same time, the theory upon which the notion of bank liquidity rests requires the negation of the theory of profits and rent. For the essence of profit is compensation for risk; but the commonest risk of enterprise is its illiquidity—that is, the inability to convert goods of trade into money. (The risk of loss from natural or other disaster is commonly covered by insurance.) Now if goods in trade (or even capital goods) can be converted into cash at any time—through the mechanism of note issue as proposed by the Commission—then enterprise is relatively without risk, and the incentive of and reason for profit disappears.

The remaining fifteen points need not detain us. They are, in one form or another, elaborations of the argument discussed above, that the defect of the banking system, which monetary legislation should attempt to remedy, was that it lacked the means to provide cash to all customers in time of need—that is, to discount their notes of hand, and provide them money in exchange for a claim on their goods.

Whether there should be, in monetary practice, allowance for emergencies and provision to relieve business in time of credit crisis, may be left for further consideration. We need only note here that the theory, apparently endorsed by the Commission, that it was the responsibility of a monetary system—or rather the managers of the monetary system—to provide practically unlimited liquidity to trade—is one that leads down the path of economic chaos if not annihilation.

Senator Aldrich's presentation to the Senate (January 8, 1912) was followed by an address to the House, on February 6, by Congressman Edward B. Vreeland, joint chairman of the Commission. His report is an extensive, sometimes impassioned, argument for a paper money system secured by commercial power.

"Mr. Chairman," he declared, "I stand here to say that, in the opinion of all intelligent men who have studied the question, both here and abroad, these money panics are entirely due to a defective banking and currency system. . . .

"I say it, Mr. Chairman, because when we turn to every other great nation on the face of the earth . . . we find that no one of them has had a money panic for more than fifty years."

Observing with perspicacity that while "elasticity of cash is important," "elasticity of credit is of vastly greater importance," Vreeland pointed out that 95 per cent of business transactions were done with instruments other than currency. "The banking part of our problem is vastly more important than the currency part of it."

Proceeding from these premises he argued against the minimum reserve requirements of American banking practice. "Go to England, Austria, France, Germany—any great country abroad," he exhorted— "Not one of them by law requires a bank to keep a dollar of reserve on hand."

To illustrate his meaning he cited the practice of the French Crédit Lyonnais, at the time the greatest bank in the world, with over $300 million of deposits and upwards of $80 million capital funds. He reported that he asked the governor how much cash he kept in the vault against these deposits. The governor called his bookkeeper, who announced that it amounted to about 5 1/2 per cent of the demand liabilities. In surprise, the Congressman asked if they did not have runs upon banks in France, and did the people never become excited? The governor conceded that the French did indeed become excited. "With the most excitable people on earth," asked Vreeland, "how do you feel safe in carrying this small reserve of 5 1/2 per cent?" The explanation which the Congressman reported from the governor was that the bank could take to the Bank of France up to $150 millions of paper bearing three solvent names and obtain notes "as good as gold." "If I could not do that," added the governor, "I could not sleep nights."

Vreeland summarized his conclusions in two points.

First, the note issue should be centralized in one institution, with the issue to rest upon gold and commercial paper, not less than one-half of the reserve to consist of gold.

Second, the mobilization of part of the cash reserves of the banking system in one institution, this institution to carry large reserves, and to have the right to expand its note issue and credit liability based upon gold and commercial paper.

Congressman Vreeland, had he been gifted with prophetic foresight, might have curbed his enthusiasm for European monetary and banking systems by the knowledge that in the course of the following half century the German mark would twice disappear in a bottomless gulf of inflation, carrying with it the commercial structure of Germany and reducing trade to a barter basis in which—during the second experience—a cigarette would obtain more value in trade than a bundle of paper money. Had he lived through the following decades, he would have seen the practical disappearance of the French franc as he knew it, and a repeated devaluation of the English pound. He would also have discovered that the flexible currency system which was subsequently adopted for the U. S., following the main recommendations of the Committee, of a commercial paper security for the note issue, would not save this country from what history has set down as the most devastating panic and depression in modern annals, nor would it save the currency from a major devaluation of 40 per cent.

9.

The Setting of the Current

T HE NATIONAL MONETARY COMMISSION had been composed entirely of members of Congress—on the theory, apparently, that they would be more influential thereby in promoting enactment of the Commission's recommendations. As a result of the 1910 elections, two-thirds of the Commission lost their seats in Congress and were thereafter disrespectfully called "lame ducks," while still others faded from the scene after the 1912 election.

The general political currents of the time require our attention because their conflicting tendencies are reflected in the monetary legislation subsequently enacted. Beneath the particular issues that rose and found attention lay deeper issues that emerge even more clearly today, more insistently demanding resolution—of the state versus the individual, of the locus of sovereignty, and of the range of individual liberty. Contrary to today's colorations, the Republican Party was then probably more authoritarian, in demanding more powers for the Federal Government, than was the Democratic Party, traditionally the party of states' rights—though this coloration may not be evident in respect to individual issues before the public.

Under Theodore Roosevelt, for instance, the campaign against industrial monopolies had resulted in 44 antitrust suits; under Taft 90 proceedings were initiated against monopolies. Taft had also formally proposed legislation requiring federal incorporation of companies engaged in interstate commerce, and the establishment of a Federal Corporation Commission to supervise companies holding national charters, but these proposals were rejected by Congress. Other legislation of the Taft Administration in the direction of centralization of authority were the Mann-Elkins Act, which placed telephone, telegraph, cable, and wireless companies under the jurisdiction of the Interstate Commerce Commission and authorized the Commission to suspend rates pending a court decision; a postal savings bank system which put the Federal government in the banking business, and a tariff act (the Payne-Aldrich Tariff Act of April 9, 1909) which lowered duties from an average of 57 per cent to around 38 per cent.

Despite these evidences of "progressivism," dissatisfaction with Taft within his own party became pronounced, and during the debates on the Payne-Aldrich tariff bill open dissension emerged under the leadership of Senator Robert M. La Follette. Opposition to Taft mounted when, in a speech at Winona, Minnesota, he termed the tariff bill "the best bill that the Republican Party ever passed."[1]

Theodore Roosevelt returned from a year of big game hunting in Africa and a triumphal tour in Europe to find again an opportunity and a demand for his political talents. Drawn by an appeal to public service, and perhaps to a considerable degree by ambition,* he began to angle for the leadership of the insurgent wing. In a speech at Osawatomie, Kansas, on August 31, 1910, on "The New Nationalism" he backed the Supreme Court's attitude toward social legislation and announced the political doctrine "that every man holds his property subject to the general right of the community to regulate its use to whatever degree the public welfare may require it."

The speech was interpreted as an open break with his protégé, Taft. Opposition to Taft within the Party was further strengthened by the election losses in the fall of that year and in the following January Senator La Follette instigated the formation of the National Progressive Republican League for "the promotion of popular government and progressive legislation." Among its objects were: direct election of U. S. Senators; direct primaries for the nomination of elective officers; direct election of delegates to the national conventions; amendment of state constitutions to provide for the initiative, referendum and recall; and a corrupt practices act. The president of the new organization was Senator Jonathan Bourne of Oregon, and the obvious objective was to gain control of the Republican organization, block the renomination of Taft and choose their own candidate, Senator La Follette.

---

*This is vigorously denied by his biographers.

Well before the convention in June of 1912, it was apparent that La Follette did not command the strength to win the nomination, and the Progressives began to sound out Roosevelt on his receptivity. The stage was set for his acceptance by a letter addressed to him and signed by seven Republican governors declaring, "A large majority of the Republican voters of the country favor your nomination, and a large majority of the people favor your election as the next President of the United States." This letter was sent on February 10, 1912. In an address on February 21 before the Ohio Constitutional Convention at Columbus, Roosevelt reaffirmed the principles which he had announced in his Kansas speech, and a little later responded to the governors' letter by stating that "I will accept the nomination for President if it is tendered to me, and I will adhere to this decision until the convention has expressed its preference." His followers now set out to gather delegates.

When the Party convention convened at Chicago on June 18, however, the credentials committee refused to seat the Roosevelt delegates and President Taft was renominated. Immediately, the Roosevelt delegates withdrew and issued a condemnation of the nomination, and on August 5 reassembled in Chicago as the Progressive or "Bull Moose" Party and nominated Roosevelt for President and Senator Hiram W. Johnson for Vice President.

At the same time, the Democratic Party, long dominated by William Jennings Bryan and still under his influence, was also seeking other leadership. The principal rivals who emerged were Beauchamp ("Champ") Clark of Missouri, who had succeeded Joseph Cannon as Speaker of the House after the Democratic victories in 1910, and Governor Woodrow Wilson of New Jersey. Despite an unfortunate reference by Wilson to Bryan that was reported and publicized—"Would that we could do something to knock him into a cocked hat"—Bryan preferred Wilson to Clark and gave him his support. Wilson was nominated, but only after 46 ballots, and the Republican split gave him the Presidency with a total of 435 electoral votes to 88 for Roosevelt and 8 for Taft, although he received only a minority of the popular vote (6,286,214 out of a total of 15,028,521, with 4,126,020 for Roosevelt and 3,483,922 for Taft).

The Democratic platform plank on the money question, written under Bryan's influence, was confusing and contradictory. It called for "such a systematic revision of our banking laws as will render temporary relief in localities in which such relief is needed, with protection from control or domination of what is known as the 'money trusts,' " and it opposed "the so-called Aldrich bill," or the establishment of a central bank.

The President-elect appeared equally vague as to what he wanted. Sometime before, in addressing a convention of Democratic clubs, he had used such expressions as "the control of credit dangerously concentrated in this country" and had referred to the "money monopoly" as being "the greatest monopoly in this country." Later, his tone became more moderate, and he declared from time to time that he was "as was his wont" keeping his mind open and guarding himself from too definite or possibly premature conclusions. He had spoken from the same platform with the now former-Senator Aldrich, who had announced his general agreement with Wilson as to existing conditions and measurably as to the remedy for them. The *New York Times* concluded that it was safe to assume that the final and formal expression of Governor Wilson's views would be "clear and tempered."

There was little difference between the major party platforms in their common advocacy of conservation measures, a corrupt practices act, and banking and currency reform. The Republicans, however, called for a stricter regulation of trusts and for a milder protective tariff, whereas the Democrats asked for virtual abolition of monopolies, proposed a tariff for revenue only, and promised "immediate downward revision."

The "New Freedom" proclaimed by Woodrow Wilson could be distinguished from Roosevelt's "New Nationalism" mainly on the issue of monopoly control. Roosevelt proposed to regulate the monopolies while Wilson wanted their abolition.

Wilson came into office under considerable popular momentum toward centralization of government. Ten days before his inauguration the Sixteenth Amendment to the Constitution, which had been proposed only three years before, was finally ratified and declared in effect. This revolutionary fiscal measure, authorizing a tax on incomes, vested in the Federal government almost unlimited taxing power and gave it the financial means by which it could dominate and eventually overwhelm the state governments. On February 28, 1913, the Pujo Committee investigation into the "money trust," which had been authorized the February before,* reported an unwholesome concentration of money and credit through bank consolidations, company mergers, interlocking directorates, security syndicates, and increased banker representation on the boards of insurance companies, railroads, public utilities and industrial corporations.

---

*A Subcommittee of the House Committee on Banking and Currency, headed by Representative Arsène Pujo of Louisiana.

The public state of mind toward Wall Street favored Federal absorption of power. Shortly after the election Wilson declared that he would build "a gibbet high as Haman's" for any man who dared to start a panic. In a speech to the Southern Society he served notice on those who "hold the machinery to breed panics."

"I know that certain men make artificial panics," he proclaimed, with the assurance of authority, "in order to impress the country that something about to happen is going to happen wrongly. I don't fear such men. I don't believe any man alive dares to start the machinery of such a panic. But if any man does I promise him I will build a gibbet for him as high as Haman's."[2]

The *New York Times* reproved him editorially for his loose charges and looser thinking.

"The mind of the President-elect," the editorial stated,

> is apparently occupied by some notions regarding panics which would probably be less perturbing if they were clearer. . . .
>
> . . . especially he would have done well to avoid even "figurative" reference to the gibbet of Haman. When he gets into the White House he will find, first, that he will have many things of real importance to attend to, and, second, that he has no power and no authority to exercise the art of executioner, and, third, that there is not and cannot be any such offender as he has allowed himself to conjure up.
>
> Mr. Wilson says, rather loosely, but with some approach to justice, that "a panic is a state of mind." That is so far true that the state of the public mind may necessarily make a panic far worse than it otherwise would be. . . . It is peculiarly unfortunate for such a man to talk on this subject without fullness of knowledge and the greatest deliberation and care. The former, Mr. Wilson acknowledged that he does not possess; the latter, he does not manifest.[3]

Events in the international field were also of a nature to encourage centralization of power. In 1910 a revolution broke out in Mexico, led by Francisco I. Madero, which succeeded in forcing out President Porfirio Diaz who had ruled that country since 1877, but the assassination of Madero plunged the country into new upheavals. The loss of American investments and the expropriation of others, along with Wilson's strict ideas about *de jure* and *de facto* governments, eventually led this country to military intervention.

In Europe, the Young Turk revolution had forced concessions from the Sultan, but had weakened the government and invited war with Turkey's Balkan neighbors.

Next door, in Persia, a similar discontent with monarchy had brought a constitutional regime and political anarchy, and the country was saved from extinction only by the rivalry of Great Britain and Russia. To restore order, and perhaps to obtain American influence against dismemberment, the young government invited in an American, Morgan Shuster, as Treasurer-General, to reform the fisc of the country. Shuster's activities revived Persian morale and patriotism, but on that account displeased the Russians, who issued an ultimatum demanding Shuster's resignation and occupied Resht and Tabriz in the north, during the course of which some five hundred Persians were slain.

In the Far East the collapse of the old Manchu Dynasty and the establishment of a republic (1911) produced further unsettlement which became Russian opportunity, and parts of Mongolia and Turkestan passed under Russian influence, if not under Russian authority.

The war between Greece, Bulgaria, and Serbia on the one hand and Turkey on the other began in October, 1912, and although it was practically ended by the first of November, it unsettled the already precarious balance of power in Europe, and on December 3 Germany gave a warning to Russia that it would go to war in support of Austria if Russia should support Serbia. The prospect of war became a common preoccupation, and in 1913 France instituted a new regime of universal conscription.

Political unsettlement brought evidences of a "money famine" in Europe and the hoarding of gold. All these events gave new urgency to the U. S. monetary problem.

10.

❧❧❧❧❧❧❧❧❧❧❧❧❧❧

The Bill Considered

IN COMMENTING UPON THE DIRECTION of currency reform under
the new Democratic Administration, the *New York Times* pointed out
that William Jennings Bryan, whom Wilson had named Secretary of State,
would exercise an important influence upon the shape of coming legislation, and analyzed for its readers the essentials of Bryan's monetary
philosophy:

> Under Mr. Bryan's leadership the doctrines of the Democratic Party in
> respect to banking and currency have been perfectly well understood. The
> Party has insisted upon cheap and unsound money, the cheapest and un-
> soundest it could get the country to accept. In 1896, the year of Mr. Bryan's
> first candidacy, the Party demanded the free, unlimited and independent
> coinage of silver, denounced gold monometallism, condemned the issue of
> circulating notes by banks, insisted that all currencies should be issued by the
> government, and it further demanded that United States bonds be paid in
> silver or gold at the option of the Treasury. The country's opinion of these
> Democratic banking and currency doctrines was expressed in the electoral
> vote, McKinley 271, Bryan 176.
>
> In 1900 Mr. Bryan was again the candidate, and his platform denounced
> the Act of March, 1900, establishing the gold standard, condemned the issue
> of notes by national banks, demanded their retirement as fast as the govern-
> ment could redeem them in gold or silver certificates, and again declared that
> the government should issue all currency. Once more the country expressed
> its opinion of the Bryan money doctrines in the electoral vote, McKinley 292,
> Bryan 155.
>
> In 1908, Mr. Bryan once more presented himself as the candidate. His
> platform belabored Wall Street, the stock gamblers, and the banks, and

67

pledged the Party to enact a law for the guarantee of bank deposits. The country was still unconvinced, as shown by the electoral vote, Taft 321, Bryan 162. At length in 1912, the Party on quite other issues came into power, upon a platform making no very definite declaration of banking principles, but condemning the Aldrich Bill, and promising such a revision of banking laws as would give temporary relief where it was needed, "with protection from control or domination by what is known as the money trust."

What Mr. Bryan really means by his declaration that banking and currency reform "must be along lines in harmony with Democratic history and doctrine" is, as we pointed out the other day, the recall of the decisions taken by the people in 1896 and reaffirmed in 1900 and 1908, the decisions against his money doctrines. It is important, it is of the highest importance, that the country should understand, that all businessmen should understand, that the controlling purpose in Washington now is to enact a banking and currency law in conformity with the Democratic doctrine. That it should be a safe, sound, and practicable measure is secondary. The proof is in the bill itself. It takes from the banks the power of control over their business, invests that control in a board whose members are to be appointed by the President—political appointees. It permits no issue of circulating notes by the banks: for their notes government paper money is to be substituted. These are all Democratic "doctrines." The well-nigh unanimous condemnation of the plan by the banks proves that these are not banking doctrines, not business doctrines. It is a plan for Democratic banking, for Bryan banking, that is in preparation.[1]

Following the passage of power to the Democratic Administration, the principal protagonists of currency legislation in the Congress were Carter Glass, chairman of the House Banking and Currency Committee, and Robert L. Owen, chairman of the corresponding Senate committee, along with academic figures like H. Parker Willis (who served as an assistant to Glass) and A. Piatt Andrew, who had served as special assistant to the National Monetary Commission.* William Gibbs McAdoo, a New York lawyer, had been named Secretary of the Treasury and the spokesman of the Administration on monetary matters.

Despite the urgency of currency legislation, despite the importance given to it by the new Administration, it was not until three and a half months after Wilson's inauguration that the Administration's proposals were presented to the country. Congress had been called into special

---

*Owen, as noted, had been a member of the Senate only since the admission of Oklahoma to statehood in 1907. His appointment to a position of such rank is partly due to his previous membership on the Senate Committee on Committees. Following the Democratic victory at the polls, this Committee divided the Committee on Finance into two committees (one being the new Committee on Banking and Currency) with Owen named as chairman of the new committee. Owen, of course, had eminent qualifications for the post.

session for two limited purposes—revision of the tariff and currency legislation. While the Administration debated among themselves the form of the currency bill they could agree on, Congress devoted its time to the tariff.

On June 18, 1913, after numerous White House conferences, the Administration released the text of its proposed bill. The Bryan influence was evident. Instead of a currency based upon commercial paper, fluctuating with commercial demand, and controlled by bankers, as proposed by the National Monetary Commission, the bill provided for a currency that rested almost entirely on government fiat. That is, while it proposed a Federal Board of Reserve of nine members, six of the members would be government appointees and only three would represent the banking system; moreover, notes would be issued by the U. S. Treasury to banks against the deposit of acceptable collateral, but the notes would be obligations of the U. S. Government. In addition, the bill would terminate the national bank note issue and the circulation privilege which national banks had enjoyed since 1864.

The news provoked an immediate reaction in the banking community, sufficient to cause a number of modifications before the bill was formally introduced in the two houses on June 26. The opposition now became an uproar, with a threat from banks of wholesale surrenders of their national charters and transfer to state charter if the bill were enacted.

Almost at once, the *New York Times* declared that the Administration's banking and currency bill in its present form was "dead and done for." "Even the enactment of the measure would not modify this judgment," the journal declared, "for it is now perfectly evident that it should not be put into practical effect."[2]

The immediate objection of the banks, of course, was to the termination of the circulation privilege. Banks were principal holders of the government two per cent bonds outstanding, eligible for security of notes. Of the $731 million outstanding, $700 million were held to secure circulation and deposits. The demand for these obligations by banks served to keep the bonds at par despite the low interest rate they carried. The proposal to abolish the circulation privilege promptly caused a drop in the quotations and threatened loss to the holders.

Faced with this unexpected development, the Administration gave assurances that the bill would be amended to continue the circulation privilege for twenty years. Before the end of July the banking bill had come under the influence of more temperate views and a number of suggestions of the American Bankers Association relating mainly to tech-nicalities of the note issue were incorporated in the draft bill. Chief among these was the provision that the notes issued by any reserve bank would bear their own distinctive letter and serial number, and when these notes were paid into any other reserve bank they would not be again paid out but would be returned to the issuing bank. A Federal Reserve note would thus be treated exactly like a bank check, which always returns to the bank upon which it is drawn. This was an anti-inflation deterrent since the note would automatically disappear when it had done its work.

Another amendment accepted by the Administration was one to pro-vide for 33 1/3 per cent reserve against the note issue, to be kept entirely in gold rather than in gold and lawful money as was provided in the draft of the bill. The question of the political control of the institution re-mained in contention. Meantime, the idea of a currency based upon trade rather than monetization of the public debt began to acquire new respect and one of the proposals that gained some attention was for three kinds of money—$300 million to be called "commercial currency"—a gener-ous nod to the commercial interest; $200 million to be called "industrial currency," to be issued to States and Territories on the security of their bonds and to be used for building roads, bridges, and paying the costs of other public improvements; and a third class called "agricultural cur-rency" in the amount of $200 million, which would rest upon the security of farmers' warehouse receipts for their cotton, wheat, and corn.

In the Senate Banking and Currency Committee Senator Owen carried on a running battle with banking opinion. He introduced a bill, which he described as a supplement to the existing bill rather than a substitute for it, which would have defied the bankers by basing the proposed note issue almost entirely upon government bonds. Banking opinion now became more vocal and at a banking conference in Chicago towards the end of August strong resolutions were adopted in opposition to the proposed bill. A good deal of the merchant sentiment of the country rallied to the bankers, provoking the Committee to agree to a wider exchange of views on the proposed measures.

On August 29, Carter Glass introduced a new version of the bill. It was reported from his committee on September 9, and passed the House September 19.

In the Senate, the bill languished in the Senate Banking and Currency Committee. The Administration could not muster more than half the members of the Committee to report a bill. Wilson, though he frequently pleaded his ignorance of monetary questions, threatened to carry the question to the public, and the Committee continued to hold hearings in a well nigh futile attempt to resolve its differences. The American Bankers Association convened in Boston that year on October 8, but the day before the formal opening a pre-convention conference of small bankers —banks with less than $250,000 capitalization—was held with about six hundred country banks represented, and this conference adopted resolutions of protest against the bill. These protests were seconded by the full convention, representing some two thousand banks, and the Currency Commission of the Association brought in a resolution "that the bill in its present form imposes unwise hardships upon the banks and equally unwise hardships upon the general public." In his opening address the acting president of the Association, Arthur M. Reynolds of Des Moines, declared:

> We are facing proposed legislation which I can hardly regard as less than an invasion of the liberty of the citizen in the control of his own property by putting under government management enormous individual investments and a branch of the country's business which should be left to individual effort. . . . No nation in the world has ever found it necessary to assume such broad powers as are contemplated under the new bill.[3]

The *Times* in an editorial stated the case:

> After the proceedings in Boston it will require hardihood to maintain that only the big banks are opposed to the pending banking bill. . . . Big banks would not be listened to in arguing that their profits would be prejudiced against the counter proposition that the country would be benefited. The country is thinking of larger things than the bankers' commissions, large or small. The issuing and redemption of currency, the control of banks by government as administrator rather than as regulator, the trusting of credit accommodations to distant sub-treasurers rather than to neighborhood bankers . . . these are all topics larger than the rate of bank dividends.[4]

It was now apparent to the Administration that further changes would be necessary. Among those demanded by the banking community were: a reduction of the proposed regional reserve banks from twelve to not more than five; the note issue to be an obligation of the banks rather than of the government and the notes to be redeemable in gold rather than in "gold or lawful money"; finally, that small banks should be relieved of compulsory subscription to the capital stock of the reserve banks.

Unfortunately, the bankers' drive was blunted by a division among some of the leading bankers. Frank A. Vanderlip, president of the National City Bank of New York, came forward with a proposal for a single central bank with a board of directors all appointed by the President and with capital stock provided by the government—a proposal that would have nullified the concept of banking control of the system. Jacob Schiff of Kuhn, Loeb & Co., the firm with which Paul M. Warburg was associated, suggested that the Owens-Glass bill would be preferable to the Vanderlip substitute. The division caused the *New York Times* to comment that the public "may as well abandon its foolish dread of a Wall Street bankers' conspiracy against the Administration measure."[5]

The Administration had counted largely on the support of the country banks and their antipathy to "Wall Street" to carry the currency bill, but as it stood the Administration no longer dominated the Senate on this question, and in the Banking and Currency Committee the division was even and the Committee unable to report out a bill. At this juncture William Jennings Bryan, whose job as Secretary of State did not cover monetary matters, took the ball from McAdoo by writing a letter to Carter Glass, declaring the Administration position that on two "triumphs of the people" there could be no surrender now: (a) government issue of notes and (b) government control of the issue.

As we shall see later, neither of these provisions was accepted in the final legislation, but the advocates of government control have never conceded the case, and the pressure persists for government control over the Federal Reserve System.

Congress, as we have noted, had been summoned to extra session limited to consideration of a tariff bill and the currency bill. So firmly was the Democratic Party in control, that one hundred and fifty new Congressmen with portfolios full of private bills had found themselves facing an unscalable wall in the Party caucus, and a sphinx in their appeals to the President. Especially after the off-year elections that November had demonstrated renewed strength with the electorate, Wilson began to display the indifference toward politicians that was later to defeat him and to reduce him to a helpless paralytic in the great crisis of his career six years later.

"The relations between President Wilson and the members of the Senate and House are ideal—simply for the reason that Mr. Wilson doesn't see them," commented the *Times* tartly. "Mr. Wilson sees no Congressman except on the same terms on which he sees everybody else. You may be a Congressman or a greengrocer; it makes no difference; you call up Secretary Tumulty and make your appointment, and the President sees you, Congressman or greengrocer. He will only see you between the hours of 10 and 1."[6]

Congress meantime had completed its action on a tariff bill. The Payne-Aldrich Tariff of 1909 had recognized the public demand for freer trade by scaling down the rates set in the Dingley Tariff of 1897 (averaging 57 per cent) to around 38 per cent. The Underwood Tariff now reduced duties another 8 points to an average of 30 per cent. It put iron, steel, raw wool and sugar on the free list. The bill was signed October 3.

The Congressional whips now had difficulty in holding the House in session while waiting for the Senate Committee to make its report on the currency bill. "An illness seemed to sweep over the House of Representatives today, to judge by the number of requests from members to be excused from attending on the ground that indisposition kept them from Washington," reported the *Times*,[7] and added, "The House laughed derisively as those requests were made."

Finally, on October 20, President Wilson was compelled to agree to a recess until the bill could be reported out, but for not later than November 15. At the same time he let it be known that he would not oppose amendments to reduce the number of reserve banks and to remove the Secretary of Agriculture and the Comptroller of the Currency from the Federal Reserve Board. His Republican opposition, nettled at the long delay, now announced that they would oppose any recess.

At this point Frank A. Vanderlip appeared before the Senate Banking and Currency Committee with a draft of the plan he had enunciated earlier. The proposal threw the debate into even greater confusion. Here was a Wall Streeter cutting the ground from under the radicals by proposing even greater government control, and exclusion of banker influence, than the most radical member of the Committee had ever contemplated. He had gotten his ideas, he admitted, from Senators Bristow of Kansas, Reed of Missouri, Hitchcock of Nebraska, and O'Gorman of New York.

At the same time, his proposal for a single central bank, instead of twelve or more, was the very item that the Democratic platform of the previous year had blasted as the invention of the arch-conservative, Nelson Aldrich, and was the thing that the Democratic Party had opposed since Andrew Jackson had killed the second Bank of the United States in 1832, when he vetoed the renewal of its charter.

Nine of the twelve Committee members indicated their approval of the Vanderlip plan, but as the House was effectively under Presidential domination, enthusiasm cooled when Wilson issued a statement reiterating his warm endorsement of the pending bill. At the same time he declined to receive Vanderlip and Henry P. Davison at the White

House, on the ground that banking was a subject with which he was not familiar.*

Meantime, Senator Owen, smarting no doubt under the loss of prestige from his inability to control his Committee, began to feel the need of accommodating his Wall Street antipathies for the sake of action. He now showed a refreshing willingness to accept amendments suggested by bankers, and within the next few days the Committee made a number of changes to mollify their opposition. Among them was one to open the regional reserve banks to public ownership—though not at the expense of government control. There was still no agreement on the main issues of the composition of the governing board—whether government or banker controlled—and the character of the note issue.

On November 7 a major concession was made to banking opinion when the words, "or lawful money" were deleted from the references to redemption of the note issue. The effect of this was to require that whether the notes were issued, redeemed, or guaranteed by the banks or by the Treasury, they would be redeemable in gold, and hence would be a gold backed currency. This was a major defeat for the Bryan wing of the Democratic Party.

In waving the editorial flag over this triumph the *New York Times,* which in those days was pretty much the spokesman for Wall Street, fell into the error of disputing the popular view that "government money" was better than "bank money."

"This is an American idea," the *Times* announced, "due to the traditional belief that our government is better than our banks, whereas the experience of the world is that banks as good as ours will be more stable than governments." It went on to cite the experience of the Bank of France, which continued to make payments after the Germans had captured Paris.[8]

It was the view of the *Times* that a currency backed by gold, even to the extent of only one-third, along with commercial assets was intrinsically sounder than a currency backed by government bonds, since the latter reduced the currency to the status of a fiat money, the value of which rested entirely on the good faith and credit of the government. The deeper issue eluded discussion—namely, the *quality* of the commercial

---

New York Times, Oct. 24–26, 1913. There may have been an element of pique in Wilson's reluctance to see Vanderlip. As a trustee of the Carnegie Foundation, Vanderlip had been one of a committee that had rejected Wilson's application for a pension, and though Vanderlip had been in favor of the grant, he was accused of having gossiped about the matter to Wilson's discredit.

assets and the *quality* of the government promises to pay. Neither possesses an intrinsic value above the other, but the value of each depends upon factors deep in the economic and moral structure of society.

It was at this point that the question again emerged, which later was resolved into settled policy of the monetary authorities, of the main and basic function of the money system. The question appeared in an editorial of the *Times* in the following reference: "The reason for looking at the phrase 'lawful money' which is alternatively in and out of the pending currency bill is that it is urged by those who think it a benevolent function of government to regulate prices by regulating the amount of money in circulation."[9]

As we shall note further on, the matter of the price level was to become the preoccupation of the Federal Reserve authorities to the reduction, if not actual exclusion, of almost every other issue.

By the end of November, the Senate was showing restiveness and also threatening to recess, and only by making it an issue was Wilson able to hold the body in session. There were now before that body three different currency bills—the Glass version (the bill reported out by the House committee of which he was chairman and passed by the House); the Owen bill, being the version which he and five of his colleagues on the Senate Banking and Currency Committee favored; and a bill drafted by Senator Gilbert M. Hitchcock, Democrat of Nebraska, and supported by the Republican members of the Committee. The principal feature of the Hitchcock bill was its elimination of the "lawful money" provision and a stipulation for note redemption in gold. The Hitchcock bill also provided for public ownership but government control of the regional reserve banks. The Democratic caucuses continued to favor the Owen version.

Finally, on Sunday night, November 30, the Democratic caucus reached agreement on the text of the bill, and the following day it was presented to the Senate.

The bill, now on the Senate floor, was again subject to debate, and it was not for two weeks, until December 15, that any vote was taken. This was on an amendment by Senator Hitchcock to provide for popular subscription to the capital stock of the proposed regional reserve banks, rather than compulsory subscription as directed by the Owen bill, and to reduce to four the number of regional reserve banks from the eight to twelve fixed in the bill under debate. The amendment was tabled by a vote of 40 to 35, the result indicating the sharpness of the division.

The bill now came under a devastating attack by Senator Elihu Root of New York the effect of which, either because of the Senator's logic or his influence, compelled a major retreat on the part of the Administration. Senator Root had attacked Senator Owen's claim that the notes issued under the pending bill would be amply guaranteed, since there were at least twelve different kinds of security supporting them. Root pointed out that it was not a question of the security, but the volume of the note issue. A note issue based on gold and commercial paper, he argued, had natural limits, since the supply of basic collateral would be the exact measure of the needs of business. In a note issue secured by government bonds, there was no limit to the volume, since the appetite of a government for funds is voracious, money being a form of power, and, since legislatures are reluctant to tax, a constantly available market for the promissory notes of the government is a convenience of unimaginable possibilities.

Root objected not only to the nature of the reserve under the bill, but also to the reduction in the required reserves to be held by the member banks. He cited the case of a bank with, say, $100 million of deposits. The current requirement as to cash on hand was 25 per cent, or $25 million. Under the Owen bill this required reserve would be reduced to $18 million, but of this amount the bank need keep only a part in its own vault, with the effect of reducing required reserves by about a half from the previous standard. The end result would be a release of new credit into the market with temptations to expansion greater than the business community could resist, and an inflationary push greater than human prudence and banking judgment could withstand. Root demanded, in conclusion, that a gold reserve of at least 50 per cent be stipulated.

Alarmed at the breach caused by the Root assault, the Democratic leaders hastily reconvened a Party caucus and agreement was reached to meet Root's views, at least to raise the gold requirement from one-third to 40 per cent, and to impose a progressive tax upon any deficiency in the reserve.

On December 19, 1913, the amended Owen bill passed the Senate, 54 to 34 with the support of six Republicans, and went to conference with the House over the amendments made by the Senate.

The conference moved with speed under White House pressure. Most of the Senate changes were accepted, but one important decision was to eliminate the provision for the guarantee of bank deposits which had been a pet project of the liberals, particularly Bryan and Owen. The Senate provision for a number of regional reserve banks between eight and twelve prevailed over the House minimum of twelve. On December

22, the conference report was accepted by both House and Senate, and on the 23rd the bill was signed by President Wilson and the Federal Reserve Act came into effect.

The public acceptance, between relief and enthusiasm, of the resolution of the currency question was reflected in the full page advertisement in the *Times* run by the United Cigar Co., at the time one of the leading retail store chains of the country and one of the larger users of credit for expansion. The advertisement was headlined: THE NEW CURRENCY LAW A FORERUNNER OF BETTER TIMES.

Probably the best summary of current opinion was that offered by Paul M. Warburg in an interview given the following day:

> There cannot be any doubt that the enactment of this legislation will inaugurate a new era in the history of banking in the United States. While it is to be regretted that some important suggestions made by the business community could not be adopted, the fundamental thoughts, for the victory of which some of us have worked for so many years, have won out. That is to say, from now on we shall witness the gradual elimination of the bond-secured currency, of scattered reserves, of immobilized commercial paper, and of pyramiding of call loans on the Stock Exchange. The ship is headed right, and nothing will ever turn her back into her old course. . . .[10]

PART II

The Great Reversal

11.

◇◇◇◇◇◇◇◇◇◇◇◇◇◇◇◇◇◇

Advent of Storm

ISTORY ALLOWED THE ADMINISTRATION seven months to
construct its new financial ark before the deluge of the First World
War. The immediate task was purely political—where to locate the regional reserve banks provided by the Act. The Reserve Bank Organization Committee, which meant, in short, Secretary of the Treasury William
Gibbs McAdoo and Secretary of Agriculture David F. Houston,* was
provided with $100,000 for its investigations.

The two officials fitted out a special car, organized a corps of secretar-
ies, and right after the New Year began a country wide tour to study the
advantages and disadvantages of each proposed reserve center. Hearings
were held in eighteen cities and concluded on February 18. Over two
hundred cities requested that their claims be heard. Certain decisions
were foreordained. The influence of New York City would be cut down
by lopping off New England and creating a reserve bank in Boston and
another in Philadelphia. Pittsburghers, led by Andrew Mellon,† protested
loudly at being neglected, urging the importance of their city as the
center of the steel industry. Baltimore was disappointed to lose out to
Richmond, Va., but this was inevitable considering Carter Glass's origins.

The grand tour was headline news subordinate only to such items as
Henry Ford's profit distribution of $10 million among his employees[1]—

---

*The Comptroller of the Currency was also a member, but he kept to a passive role.
†Head of the Mellon National Bank, and later to become "the greatest Secretary of the
Treasury since Alexander Hamilton."

81

then a revolutionary innovation in business; by Constance Bennett preparing her way for later renown as a motion picture queen by steeplejacking and painting a flag pole 480 feet above the street;[2] by the British Prime Minister opening a "peace campaign";[3] by the J. P. Morgan & Co. partners relinquishing some thirty board directorships in the interest of abating anti-trust hostility;[4] by the Kaiser stripping the Crown Prince of his authority in punishment for his having intervened politically in the Zebern affair;[5] by the lifting of the arms embargo on Mexico;[6] by Wilson winning repeal of the Panama Canal tolls bill that favored U. S. ships;[7] by police battling I.W.W. (Industrial Workers of the World—a pre-Soviet workers' movement) in Union Square, New York;[8] by Rockefeller's embarrassment over the strikes in his Colorado mines—the "Rockefeller War"—that eventually led to intervention by U. S. troops;[9] by the intervention in Mexico and landing of marines at Vera Cruz.[10]

For thirty-seven American cities, however, the principal preoccupation was their claims to be selected as a reserve city. The Committee stretched its authority to the maximum and chose twelve, and announced its decision on April 2. New Orleans was passed over in favor of Dallas; the Committee ignored the claims of Senator Owen's home state and chose Kansas City instead of Oklahoma City, at the same time passing over Denver and Omaha. The twelve cities selected were: New York, Boston, Philadelphia, Richmond, Atlanta, Chicago, Cleveland, St. Louis, Dallas, Kansas City, San Francisco, and Minneapolis.

Meantime, another issue arose over appointments to the governing board of the new institution. McAdoo, as Secretary of the Treasury, and John Skelton Williams, as Comptroller of the Currency, were ex officio members. On May 4, it was reported that the President would propose the following for membership: Richard Olney of Boston, Attorney General and Secretary of State in the second Cleveland Administration, and now seventy-eight years old; the New York banker Paul M. Warburg; Adolph Caspar Miller of Berkeley, California, forty-eight years old, educator and economist and at the time assistant to the Secretary of the Interior; W. P. G. Harding, president of the First National Bank of Birmingham, Alabama; and Harry A. Wheeler, a Chicago banker and former president of the U. S. Chamber of Commerce.

Olney, however, declined the appointment because of his age, and Wilson found it expedient to make other changes in his list. He nominated instead Thomas C. Jones, head of the International Harvester Company—who immediately became a controversial figure because of his association with what had come under attack as a monopoly of farm machinery manufacture—and Charles S. Hamlin, a Boston attorney.

The Senate Banking and Currency Committee, after some reservations regarding his connections with the Boston and Maine railway, accepted Hamlin, and it also made no obstacle to confirming Harding and Miller, but it wanted to examine Jones and Warburg—Warburg because of his banking connections with the railway industry, but more because of his strong views on central banking theory.

Warburg was promptly offended that the Committee had not required the other nominees to appear before it, and declined to present himself. President Wilson, equally offended at what he regarded as an impertinence on the part of the Senate, raised his hackles and announced his intention of forcing acceptance of his nominees.

Jones, however, willingly appeared and made a spirited denial of his alleged disqualifications; the Committee nevertheless withheld confirmation. Wilson demanded the confirmation; the Committee remained obdurate, and finally broke with the President by rejecting the nomination July 9.

Wilson was now more determined than ever to obtain confirmation of both Jones and Warburg. At the same time Warburg, now more sensitive than ever, continued to decline to appear before the Committee.

While this was going on, the press reported the front page news that the heir to the Austrian throne had been assassinated in an obscure city of Eastern Europe, in the realm of the little kingdom of Serbia, where he had been making a state visit. Condolences were sent by the German government to the Emperor Franz Joseph on the death of his nephew, but the German Emperor, Kaiser Wilhelm, after it had been announced that he would go to Vienna to comfort his neighbor and war ally, made excuses to remain in Berlin. This allayed any uneasiness over the possible political consequences of the tragedy, and the affair passed over to the inside pages of the American press, or was ignored in favor of the three-cornered tussle over Warburg's nomination.

On July 23, Wilson conceded defeat on Jones and withdrew his nomination in a letter that the *Times* characterized as captious and one to "put him in the category of irritable and querulous losers." It added that "if he had had a cool headed literary adviser he never would have published the letter."[11] Wilson had complained that the action had been made only by the minority Party members of the Committee aided by two majority members, and that it did not reflect the attitude of the Senate. However, the burden of Wilson's plea was that men should not be condemned merely because they belonged to the class of big business.

What may now have caused Warburg to change his mind and consent to appear before the Senate Committee was the mounting crisis in Europe, followed swiftly by ultimata, mobilizations, invasion, and declarations of war—all of which hastened the urgency for completion of currency reform. Two days after Wilson's defeat on his nominee, on July 25, the Austrian envoy left Serbia, and Russia began mobilization. On July 27 Austrian troops crossed the Serbian frontier, and war became inevitable. On July 30, Warburg telegraphed Senator Owen that "in deference to the President's urgent request, and in view of the seriousness of the present emergency . . . I have decided to waive all personal considerations and am prepared to appear before your committee at the earliest convenient date."[12]

Amid the declarations and cross-declarations of war among Russia, Austria, Germany, and France, Paul M. Warburg was confirmed as the seventh member of the Federal Reserve Board, along with Frederic O. Delano (whom Wilson had named in place of Jones), and on August 10 they took the oath of office. The President designated Hamlin as governor and Delano as vice governor of the board.

It was not until October 25, however, that the Secretary of the Treasury, in accordance with the law, was able to announce the formal establishment of the Federal Reserve System. The effective date for the opening of business and for the application of the new reserve requirements was November 16, 1914. Two days before this the Comptroller of the Currency had signed the charters of the twelve reserve banks, and two weeks earlier (November 2) the initial installment of one-sixth of the capital subscription to the banks had become payable.

The inauguration of the new banking and currency system was accompanied by exorbitant promises of the benefits that would flow from it, a typical statement being that issued by the Comptroller of the Currency, that among these benefits, "it supplies a circulating medium absolutely safe" and that "under the operation of this law such financial and commercial crises, or 'panics,' as this country experienced in 1873, in 1893, and again in 1907, with their attendant misfortunes and prostrations, seem to be mathematically impossible."[13]

In the light of the terrible financial catastrophe and debacle of 1933, the consequences of which are still with us, charity requires that such statements be read as another of the fond delusions into which mankind is periodically led by an incurable optimism or an inner necessity for hope.

The full statement, which sets forth some of the more modest gains in banking and currency practice, is as follows:

Among the principal direct benefits which the new act confers are these:

First, it supplies a circulating medium absolutely safe, which will command its face value in all parts of the country, and which is sufficiently elastic to meet readily the periodical demands for additional currency, incident to the movement of the crops, also responding promptly to increased industrial or commercial activity, while retiring from use automatically when the legitimate demands for it have ceased. Under the operation of this law such financial and commercial crises, or "panics," as this country experienced in 1873, in 1893, and again in 1907, with their attendant misfortunes and prostrations, seem to be mathematically impossible.

Second, it provides effectually and scientifically for the mobilization of bank reserves in the 12 Federal reserve districts, where these funds are not only available for the member banks of each respective district, but, under wise and well-guarded provisions of the law, the surplus moneys of any one district become available for the legitimate needs of any other districts which may require them.

Third, it eliminates the indirect tax of many millions of dollars annually upon the commerce and industry of the country, heretofore imposed in the shape of collection or "exchange" charges on checks, and inaugurates a system of clearances by which it is expected that every check or draft on any member bank in any one of the 12 Federal reserve districts can be collected ultimately free of the exchange charges heretofore exacted and may be charged on the books of the Federal Reserve bank to the account of the bank upon which drawn, in most cases, within 24 hours or less after it is deposited with a member bank. This provision renders available many hundreds of millions of dollars heretofore carried in transit in the mails in expensive and tedious processes of collection, sometimes absolutely useless during weeks when much needed, held in transit moving from point to point.

Fourth, it furnishes a discount system by which every well-managed member bank may have the opportunity of converting into money by rediscounting, to such extent as may be necessary or desirable, all commercial paper having not more than three months to run which it may have taken in the ordinary course of its business. The new law removes, so far as borrowing money from a Federal Reserve bank is concerned, the limitation which prevented a national bank from borrowing an amount in excess of 100 per cent of its capital. The significance of this release may be appreciated when it is realized that some national banks have deposits amounting to 10 times their capital or more. The ability to borrow only an amount equal to capital would be wholly insufficient, in many cases, to enable banks to meet the demands which arise from unexpected runs, or in financial crises, or other extraordinary demands.

It removes from prosperous and well-managed banks penalties hitherto imposed on their very prosperity and success.

It relieves the well-managed bank from the limitations of original capital invested and gives it the legitimate advantages of its own enterprise and the business it has built up and actually does.

Fifth, by making it possible for any well-managed bank to convert its assets readily into cash to meet unexpected contingencies or runs, the necessity for the large reserves heretofore required ceases. It is estimated that by this reduction in the reserve requirements alone more than four hundred millions of dollars of money or credits heretofore held in reserves and inert, will become available for commercial purposes and the legitimate demands of business.

Sixth, the new law also makes it possible for national banks to lend money on improved, unencumbered farm property, thus enabling farmers, the most numerous and in many respects most important portion of our population to participate directly in the beneficent provisions of the new law.

Seventh, the new law provides that national banks may establish branches in foreign countries, these branches to be under the jurisdiction and subject to the rules, regulations, and examinations of the comptroller's office. These branch banks should be material aids in building up our foreign commerce.

Eighth, the former system of paying national bank examiners by fee is abolished; and the examinations of all member banks, both National and State, are now placed upon a basis which necessarily will insure a thoroughness and efficiency hitherto impossible.

Under the provisions of the new law the failure of efficiently and honestly managed banks is practically impossible and a closer watch can be kept on member banks. Opportunities for a more thorough and complete examination are furnished for each particular bank. These facts should reduce the dangers from dishonest and incompetent management to a minimum. It is hoped that national-bank failures can hereafter be virtually eliminated.

Ninth, the establishment of a system of bank acceptances and an open market for commercial paper, which, it is believed, will aid and facilitate this country in obtaining a larger share of international trade and of the world's commerce.

12.

<del>ᔕᔕᔕᔕᔕᔕᔕᔕᔕᔕᔕᔕᔕᔕᔕ</del>

The First Inundation

I T WAS A FORTUNATE CIRCUMSTANCE —we can hardly call it foresight—that the Congress included in the Federal Reserve Act a provision extending until June 30, 1915, the Aldrich-Vreeland emergency act of May 30, 1908. That act had been due to expire June 30, 1914. It permitted, as will be recalled,* national currency associations to issue emergency currency.

It was the operation of this act rather than the Federal Reserve Act that permitted the monetary system of the country, such as it was, to meet the shock of the outbreak of World War I.

The Aldrich-Vreeland Act had been on the books more than five and a half years, but up to the signing of the Federal Reserve Act only twenty-one currency associations had been formed under its terms, and no currency had ever been issued nor had any individual bank applied for the issuance of currency notes. One reason, of course, was the prohibitive tax on such issues (as were secured by other than government bonds) imposed to discourage their issuance except for extreme emergencies. This tax was at the rate of 5 per cent per annum for the first month, with the rate increasing at the rate of one per cent a month to a maximum of 10 per cent per annum.

The Federal Reserve Act, in extending the Aldrich-Vreeland Act, reduced this tax to a minimum of 3 per cent per annum and a maximum of 6 per cent per annum.

---

*See Chap. 6.

87

The immediate effect of the war tension in Europe had been an unprecedented demand for gold from abroad. As the crisis mounted the gold flow increased. On Friday, July 31, 1914, the S.S. *St. Louis* of the American Line left New York carrying the largest cargo of gold ever to have been shipped from that port in one bottom—over $11,025,000. Earlier in the week the S.S. *Kronprinzessin Cecilie* carried out $10 million.

At 9:45 A.M. on July 31, the New York Stock Exchange authorities, facing a day of certain demoralization, ordered the doors of the Exchange to remain closed—for the first time since the panic of 1873. London, earlier that morning, had taken similar action, and had doubled the bank rate, from 4 to 8 per cent. J. P. Morgan—the junior*—perhaps recalling his father's calming influence in the 1907 panic, issued a reassuring statement that, "alarming as the news is from Europe, I am still hoping there will not be a general war,"[1] but history had already traveled beyond recall by either bankers or statesmen. The issue was now in the hands of the general staffs. As the *New York Tribune* reported, in horror, on August 1:

> Although Russia and Germany have not yet come to the breaking point, all the developments yesterday indicated the swift approach of a crisis. The Kaiser declared all Germany except Bavaria to be in a state of war, Bavaria being allowed under the constitution of the empire to make such declaration herself. Mr. Asquith told the House of Commons that Russia had mobilized her army and navy and that Germany would answer with a similar mobilization.
>
> The world looks on in a stunned, incredulous way while Europe is rushing forward to a stupendous catastrophe. . . . We have been told again and again that the financiers of the world, largely denationalized in their sympathies and interests, would never permit the great nations to impoverish themselves by a general war. A tightening of the screws of credit, it has been said, would bring most chancelleries to their senses. . . .

On Saturday, August 1, 1914, Germany took the irrevocable step of declaring war on Russia. Under the treaties by which they held themselves bound, France and Austria were thereupon involved, but Great Britain not until August 4 when Germany invaded neutral Belgium, while Italy, though bound by alliance to Germany, managed to avoid war for the time being.

The effect of the war declarations changed the nature of the financial panic. During the week the reserves in the New York banks had dropped

---

*Morgan senior died March 31, 1913.

$43 million, and there was a deficiency of over $17 million. Stock market selling had been mainly for European account, to raise cash, but when exorbitant insurance rates for the shipping risks made the export of gold prohibitive, this liquidation died down. On Monday morning, August 3, the Secretary of the Treasury announced that it was prepared to issue $100 million of emergency currency to the New York banks, under the Aldrich-Vreeland Act, and in the same way to assist banks throughout the country. The following day, the Congress with remarkable celerity removed the limitations upon the total emergency currency that could be issued.

New currency associations were now formed throughout the country, and during the following two months another twenty-three such associations were organized, with member banks in nearly every state.

During the critical month of August some $208,810,790 of emergency notes were issued under the terms of the act; during September the total rose to $326,789,380; and during October to $369,558,040, and the issue reached its maximum of $381,530,000 during November.

The total issue power of the banks, under the Emergency Currency Act and the old National Bank Act, was approximately $2,230 million (125 per cent of combined capital and surplus). Of this, some $740 million had been used in the issuance of national bank currency. The $386 million issued under the emergency powers therefore represented about one-fourth the maximum issuable. The aggregate amount of outstanding national bank circulation reached a maximum in the middle of November, 1914, at $1,126,039,600.[2]

Thereafter, the demand for currency fell off, and by the end of the year 60 per cent of the emergency note issue had been retired, and by the following May all but $6 million had been redeemed.

In addition to the emergency currency, some twelve clearing house associations found it necessary during the height of the crisis to issue clearing house certificates.

The New York Clearing House Association began its issue on August 3, and made various issues until October 15. The total amount issued was $124,695,000, and the largest amount outstanding at any one time was $109,185,000.

Cancellations of clearing house certificates began on August 26, and the last of the entire issue was canceled on November 28.

The collateral put up by member banks to secure certificates issued to them by the clearing houses is of interest. Some $234,465,000, or 50.7 per cent, consisted of commercial paper; $163,873,000, or 35.5 per cent was in bonds and securities; and collateral loans provided $63,836,000, or 13.8 per cent. The maximum amount of collateral in the hands of the clearing house committees at any one time was reported at $158,327,000.

The total issue of clearing house certificates by all the clearing house associations was $255,536,300.[3]

On December 1 the Comptroller of the Currency declared the termination of the monetary crisis in the following announcement:

> Telegraphic advices received from the clearing house associations throughout the country show that all clearing house loan certificates have either been paid off or called for redemption.
>
> Chicago wires that the banks there are ready to pay off the comparatively small balance still outstanding and are only delayed by the required notice of redemption which prevents the last of them from being paid for a few days longer. The Baltimore banks have given notice for redemption of the last of their loan certificates not later than the 15th instant. New York, Boston, Philadelphia, St. Louis, New Orleans, and all other cities throughout the country which issued any clearing house certificates report all now paid in full.
>
> This encouraging fact is an acknowledgment and important evidence of the almost complete return to normal financial conditions in this country and marks our safe exit from the disquieting conditions which so recently confronted us.
>
> The total amount of additional currency issued under the provisions of the Aldrich-Vreeland Act to date is $381,530,000, and of this amount $127,-272,000, or more than one-third has already been redeemed. Very few new applications are being received, while redemptions are large and steadily increasing.[4]

Meantime, the crisis had passed from the financial to the commodity markets. The war scare had driven shipping to port, and exporters of wheat and cotton were unable to find bottoms to carry their merchandise. The problem was further aggravated by the demoralization of the foreign exchanges. Prices plummeted, particularly for cotton, and farmers throughout the South were in distress. The large mail order house of Sears, Roebuck & Co., whose trade was largely with farmers, offered to accept all cotton offered at 10 cents a pound.

On August 14, Secretary of the Treasury McAdoo convened a conference of leading bankers, business men and steamship and railroad managers to consider the grain export and foreign exchange and shipping situation, and on August 18 a similar conference convened to deal with the cotton problem. The cotton crisis was the more severe, for the war had broken out just at the beginning of the cotton picking season, and at a time when an exceptional crop brought upon the market the largest crop in the history of the country.

The wheat problem was largely solved by the War-Risk Insurance Act, but to meet the needs of the Southern farmers the Treasury agreed to accept warehouse receipts for cotton or tobacco, not having more than four months to run, as eligible security, at 75 per cent of their face value, for emergency note issue.

As an additional measure, Secretary McAdoo summoned a conference of bankers to form a loan fund to tide over the cotton farmers—and to provide a fund of cash by which to redeem the emergency notes issued against cotton. A loan pool of $100 million was the result.

A third emergency measure was a gold fund to support the dollar in the foreign exchanges. The war found the country with a short term foreign indebtedness of more than $500 million, and foreign creditors were eager to convert these claims into cash. Some $450 million was owing by business men and bankers and the City of New York had notes of $80 million payable abroad and coming due.

Sterling exchange in consequence was rising in relation to the dollar, and was now over $5 to the pound that at par was worth $4.87. Later, of course, the movement would set in the other direction; just now some means were needed to meet these maturities. The Treasury formulated what was known as the gold-fund plan by which leading banks, especially those in reserve and central reserve cities, were to contribute $150 million in gold, or gold certificates, to a gold fund to be used to buy foreign exchange as needed. The fund was to be managed by a select committee with authority to arrange for shipment of the gold abroad to acquire foreign exchange and in turn to sell the acquired exchange in the domestic market as needed to stabilize the market. The contributions of the participating banks would be in the form of deposits for which they would be issued depository receipts.

The plan was initiated early in September and came into operation on September 21, and a shipment of $10 million gold to Ottawa, Canada, was promptly arranged, with immediate effect on the market, and the need for gold was written down to $100 million.

By now, export trade was beginning to revive, and by the middle of November when the New York Federal Reserve Bank officially opened, exchange had returned to normal.

On November 23 the Chicago Stock Exchange reopened, with prices of leading stocks trading at quotations higher than at the closing on July

30, and as the *New York Tribune* observed, "Prosperity, who has had her foot in the stirrup ever since the Federal Reserve Bank was opened, leaped in the saddle today and went galloping off full tilt for normal conditions."[5]

The re-opening of the Chicago exchange was followed by the reopening of the Philadelphia exchange on November 24 for limited transactions (by an auction, with the sellers setting minimum offering prices), and bond trading under similar limited conditions was resumed on the New York Stock Exchange on November 28. Full trading in the New York Exchange returned on December 13. By then the crisis of 1914 was past, resolved largely by the vitality of the economy, the initiative of the business and financial community, and the operation of conventional governmental power, rather than any new monetary mechanisms.

The test of the effectiveness of the Federal Reserve System in meeting panics and shocks to credit would come later.

13.

~~~~~~~~~~~~~~~~~~~~~~~~~~~~~~~

Collapse of a Theory

THE SPLENDID THEORY of central banking championed by Paul Warburg and adopted into the Federal Reserve System did not survive the first strain to which the System was put. This came from the entry of the United States into the European conflict in April, 1917, and the immediate need for large sums not only to meet the U. S. war costs but to finance our European allies. While the war appears as the overt cause of the profound change that now came about in Federal Reserve policy and operations, a deeper cause was the fissures within the System itself, the cleavages of principle and theory that were merely compromised and never fused.

In addition, there were two other weaknesses that would inevitably cause collapse or transformation. Both of these are traceable to Paul Warburg, the leading exponent of central banking theory and practice, an original member of the Board and its vice governor after Delano's resignation on August 9, 1916. Some further notice of Warburg's background and outlook is therefore in order.

Paul Moritz Warburg was born at Hamburg, Germany, August 10, 1868. He was graduated from the University of Hamburg in 1886, and spent the following two years in business apprenticeship with a Hamburg commission firm. He then entered his father's banking firm for a further period of seasoning. This was M. M. Warburg & Co., which had been founded in 1798 by Paul's great-grandfather. Subsequently Warburg studied English banking methods while working with a prominent London discount and brokerage house. In 1891 he extended his studies to

French banking methods, and in 1892 and 1893 traveled through the Orient and around the world. During these journeys he visited for the first time the United States where he was later to migrate and become one of its distinguished citizens and bankers. After these journeys he re-entered his father's banking firm as a partner, a relationship he continued to hold long after he came to the United States.

For a decade Warburg engaged in banking and public affairs in his native city of Hamburg, eventually becoming a member of the Municipal Council; but in 1902 he moved to New York to accept a partnership in the firm of Kuhn, Loeb & Co. This was another banking house with German-Jewish antecedents that became influential in New World finance by means of its access to Old World capital. Much of the business of this and similar firms was in finding capital for U. S. industrial expansion through the sale of securities in the European markets. Kuhn, Loeb & Co., in particular, acquired a reputation as a leading banker for the railroads and, as we have noted, helped Harriman acquire control of the Union Pacific when J. P. Morgan & Co. declined to assist.

Warburg's intimate experience with, and study of, banking methods abroad led him inevitably into the debate on the reform of the American currency system, especially after the Panic of 1907. In December, 1906, when anxiety ruled the financial markets, Warburg was invited by the *New York Times* to write an article on the banking situation. The piece, published January 6, 1907, entitled "Defects and Needs of our Banking System," became at once the lodestone toward which all subsequent discussion turned. It was followed by other essays and addresses. Warburg became the leading exponent of monetary reform. At the same time he was increasingly active in civic affairs, and particularly in politico-fiscal questions. He was a member of the Merchants Association Committee on Currency and Finance, and also of a similar committee of the Chamber of Commerce of New York. He was active in various philanthropic and educational enterprises and was one of the founders of the National Child Labor Committee, and he took a deep interest in settlement house work.

Warburg's views exercised profound influence not only upon the actual form of legislation that emerged, but upon the subsequent policy and administration of the Federal Reserve System. He was an indefatigable and persuasive advocate. He argued first that the gold holdings of the country should be concentrated in one central institution (or group of institutions) where they would be employed as the ultimate reserve of the money system. Second, he advocated a circulating medium that should consist mainly of paper currency, or note issue, the amount of which should be regulated both in relation to the quantity of gold in reserve and the demand for payments media represented by commercial notes and bills. That is, the actual quantity of money in circulation at one time would be determined by the volume of commercial bills and notes available to secure the notes (in addition to the gold) and the need for circulating notes as evidenced by the amount of commercial bills which the banks were willing to discount (sell) to the central reserve institution for the purpose of obtaining notes.

It was these two tenets that were adopted as the basis of the new monetary system, and this triumph is largely due to Warburg's skill and logic, his influence as a banker and philosopher, and his persistence in arguing his views.

What Paul Warburg overlooked, or at least failed to take account of, was the absence in this country of any commercial bills of the sort required as reserve for note issue. Warburg was not alone, of course. No one in Washington seems to have thought of this aspect of the new system. The Federal Reserve Act contemplated (and so provided) that the main base of the note issue should be "notes, drafts, and bills of exchange arising out of commercial transactions."[1]

In Europe, where Warburg had learned his banking, the customary form of commercial obligation was the acceptance, which, as we have noted earlier, was a document in the form of an order to such an one to pay such an one a certain sum at a certain date. It was commonly used by a seller of goods. When he sent the invoice for the goods he would also send a draft on the buyer for the amount of the invoice. This was simply an order to the buyer to pay, after so many days, the sum designated. The buyer would accept the obligation by writing across the face of the draft the word "Accepted," together with the place at which he wished to pay the draft when it came due, sign it, and return it to the seller. Commonly in international trade, the draft would accompany the invoice and shipping documents and would be sent through a bank. Upon acceptance by the buyer the bank would release the shipping documents to the acceptor, thus permitting him to take delivery of the goods from the transport company.

The acceptance was a convenient form of financing trade with traders of small capital, since they could have time to re-sell the merchandise before they had to meet their acceptance obligation. The seller also was able to do business with limited capital since he could discount (sell) the acceptance to a bank and recoup the cost of his merchandise. From the banker's standpoint it was an advantageous form of lending its capital since (a) it indicated on its face a prime requirement of sound lending, namely, the purpose for which the money was being used; (b) it was a "self-liquidating" form of obligation; (c) it carried a double guarantee of payment ("two-name" paper), the buyer ("acceptor") being the primary obligor, and the seller the secondary obligor; and (d) it was a readily marketable form of obligation in case the bank wished to strengthen its own cash position. The rediscount privilege conferred upon such paper by the Federal Reserve Act, by which a commercial bank could in turn sell the obligation to a Reserve bank, enhanced this marketability. A further advantage conferred by the Federal Reserve Act was that it imposed no limits upon the amount of credit which member banks might extend through the acceptance mechanism. (Loans on straight promissory notes, to any one lender, were limited to 10 per cent of the bank's capital and surplus.)

Unfortunately for Warburg and his theories of a flexible currency based on commercial credits, he failed to take into account the inherent differences between the way business was conducted here and abroad. Acceptances were practically unknown in the American market. The *New York Times* estimated that not more than one per cent of commercial paper was endorsed, that is, two-name paper.[2] In most cases, where a buyer needed credit he would go to his bank direct and give his promissory note, either secured by such collateral as the bank required, or simply on the basis of a financial statement of his assets and liabilities. In some cases the buyer would obtain his credit from the seller, again by means of a straight promissory note. The seller might, in turn, endorse (guarantee) this note, thereby making it "two-name" paper, by signing his name on the back, but as the note might or might not indicate the purpose for which it was drawn it was not paper that was eligible for rediscount under the general theory of the Federal Reserve System.

Actually, the dominant practice was that of open account purchases, whereby the buyer settled periodically for his purchases (generally on the first of the month) or cash purchases, under which the buyer was allowed a discount from the invoice price for immediate or prompt payment. Some firms allowed a discount on open accounts settled within ten days after the account was rendered.

Leading bankers had pointed out that the theory of the Federal Reserve System was defective in the U. S. market, since it would force an inferior type of credit into the banks. If paper available for rediscount must be two-name paper, they asserted, the banks would be dealing with debtors of poor risk. If the new system was to rest on the best basis it should take such paper as was issued by traders strong enough to finance themselves without a guarantor, that is, on their own name. Every day the newspapers carried long lists of single-name promissory notes issued by industrial firms for commercial uses, and accepted as final payment by their suppliers. Such notes, payable to bearer, passed almost like money, without endorsement. This was a system almost unknown in Europe.

Following passage of the Federal Reserve Act, however, bankers undertook to popularize the use of acceptances and for a time a lively acceptance market grew up.

"What we need," said J. E. Gardin, vice president of the National City Bank, discussing the subject in an article in *Trust Companies* magazine, "is a standardized instrument, carrying the guarantee of the makers, acceptors, and endorsers in a natural automatic manner. This instrument is to be found in the bill of exchange, and is the instrument that is permitted by the law to be used by the Federal Reserve banks in their open market operations.

"If we are to have a discount market in this country, we must have an instrument that is recognized the world over, for it must be borne in mind that the benefits of a discount market in the United States will be freely taken advantage of by foreign institutions once we enter into the concert of nations financial. We have done this politically and there is no reason why we should not do it financially. It is essential that this should be the case in view of the very vulnerable position in which our gold supply will be placed; and when trade balances, created either through the exchange of commodities or the return to us of our securities, call for settlement, and when conditions are right, our evidences of indebtedness will be taken in preference to gold."[3]

Warburg himself undertook to promote an acceptance market by organizing the International Acceptance Bank of New York, and becoming a director of the Westinghouse Acceptance Bank and several other acceptance houses. He also became a chief founder and chairman of the executive committee of the American Acceptance Council, a trade organization formed to promote the greater use of acceptances as a form of financing. Due to his influence—as he was later glad to point out—the Federal Reserve broadened the eligibility of commercial paper, and adopted a policy of buying acceptances at a preferred rate above the rate for rediscounts. Warburg's primary interest in the acceptance business subsequently brought his integrity into question.[4]

Despite these efforts to popularize acceptances, they never became a significant element in Federal Reserve credit. The fact is, as we shall note in more detail further on, the idea of paper money substantially backed by commercial paper never got off the ground. This was partly the result of the war, and the availability of the Federal Reserve mechanism to finance its costs, but it was also due to the second arm of the Warburg theory of central banking.

This was his idea that the system should be under the firm and absolute control of the government.

In this aspect, Warburg was not alone. An influential political element of the country that stood, paradoxically, for the people and the people's rights, was most vociferous in demanding that the institution be under government control. William Jennings Bryan—the "Great Commoner" —was the peerless leader of this wing, but, as we have noted, he was ably assisted by leading bankers like Frank A. Vanderlip and Paul Warburg. Vanderlip's defection from the body of Wall Street opinion is a bit of a mystery, but Warburg was, of course, only reflecting the Prussian theories of state absolutism in which he had been reared. As Warburg testifies in his book, *The Federal Reserve System,*[5] he opposed Carter Glass on this issue.

Glass had drafted a bill that avoided a central bank with branches, and provided for twenty Federal Reserve district banks under control of a Federal Reserve Board with forty of the forty-three members chosen by the member banks. Warburg had finally persuaded Glass to reduce the governing body of the proposed system to seven, of whom four members would be appointed by the government, but that still was not enough to suit Warburg.*

Wilson received Glass and Warburg one night in the Cabinet Room of the White House. After a two-hour discussion, the President, Warburg reported, "coincided with my contention that the government should control every member of the Board on the ground that it was the function of government to supervise the system and no individual, however respectable, should be on the board representing private interests."[6]

The Glass draft had also provided, following the Monetary Commission proposals, that all moneys of the general fund of the Treasury should, after six months, be deposited in the national reserve banks and disbursed through such banks. Warburg, true to his authoritarian convictions, opposed this, "believing that the government should retain com-

---

*Warburg had been called into administrative councils on the bill as early as April, 1913, when Col. House (Wilson's intimate adviser) sent him a digest of a bill which had been drafted by H. Parker Willis.

plete control of its receipts and disbursements as a further check on the reserve banks by the government."[7]

The bill, as finally passed, failed to meet all of Warburg's ideas, as we have seen, but it left enough vagueness as to the ultimate power and influence of government to provide a handle for a firm and aggressive administrator to guide the agency in that direction, and bring it under authoritarian domination.

Warburg was such a personality, and he was now in a strategic position to mould the institution to his ideas.

Unfortunately for the complete success of his theories, Warburg's loyalties had led him to maintain his German connections, and in 1913, only a year before the outbreak of the war in Europe, he had accepted the Order of the Cross, second class, from the Emperor Wilhelm.

When the U. S. entered the war, in 1917, all things German were suspect. Public feeling against Germany was much more fanatic than in World War II. The Metropolitan Opera, for instance, dropped German operas from its repertory (some said because this country had no singers capable of the demands of German opera), and many persons of German extraction found it convenient to anglicize their names.

Warburg, because of the importance of the Federal Reserve in war finance, also came under a cloud, and resigned from the board on August 9, 1918.

Warburg's influence did not end, however. He continued as chairman of the influential Federal Advisory Council* and what he urged and counselled the necessities of war seemed to confirm.

---

*The group of advisers created by Sec. 12 of the Federal Reserve Act.

14.

~~~~~~~~~~~~~~~~~~~~

The Path of Retreat

W INDS ALWAYS RISE in the unexpected quarter. This is true of the early years of the Federal Reserve. All the monetary intelligence of the country, all the debates in Congress and in the pages of the journals, were devoted to devising a monetary system that would meet unexpected monetary stringency, a shortage of cash. That sort of crisis arose and was solved well before the new institution had gotten its sea legs. The problem it now had to deal with was of the very opposite—an unexpected plethora of funds.

The panic that had overtaken the markets with the outbreak of war had been followed by a dazzling recovery and boom as the U. S. became the supplier of all sorts of war materials to the Allied combatants. Merchandise exports, which had amounted to $2.6 billion in the year just preceding the outbreak of war, rose to $6.3 billion in the year ended June 30, 1917. U. S. exports went not only to meet European shortages but to fill the gap created by the withdrawal of European exporters from other foreign markets. Within three years the U. S. had piled up credits from exports of $6 billion. Some $2 billion of this was met by sales by Europeans of their holdings of American securities; of the balance, some $1.1 billion was settled in gold. Thus, the year 1914 had seen an export of $165 million of gold but in 1915 the tide returned with $420 million. Most of this went to the banks and from them in turn to the Federal Reserve banks, whose gold stock increased from $227 million to $542 million. At the end of 1916 the total gold stock was $2,556 million, of which $1,574 million was in circulation in the form of gold coin or gold certificates, and $736 million in the Federal Reserve banks.

Under Warburg's influence steps were taken to move the gold in circulation from the hands of the public into that of the Federal Reserve System. Initially, he says, "This was accomplished by devising a plan to pile up in the hands of the Federal Reserve agents some hundreds of millions of dollars of gold or gold notes which, however, as a technical compliance with the law, had to be held as having redeemed outstanding Federal Reserve notes. . . . The plan, in brief, was to allow the issuance of notes backed by 100 per cent gold cover instead of by 40 per cent gold and 100 per cent commercial paper. This enabled the Reserve banks, in case of heavy rediscount demands, to substitute discounted paper and to use the 60 per cent gold so withdrawn as a reserve for further note issues."[1]

Actually there was no demand for rediscounts. On November 17, 1916, the member banks of the Federal Reserve System held some $2,536 million of reserves, or something like $1 billion more than they actually required. This is shown in the following table:

Reserve Position of Member Banks
November 17, 1916[2]

Reserves held:

In vault	$ 813,600,000	
Balances with Federal Reserve banks	674,200,000	
With approved Reserve agents	1,048,300,000	
Total reserves held		$2,536,100,000

Required reserves:

In vault	$ 576,100,000	
Balances with Federal Reserve banks	606,400,000	
Optional—in cash or with Federal Reserve banks	151,700,000	
With approved Reserve agents	175,900,000	
Total required reserves		$1,510,100,000
Excess reserves		$1,026,000,000

To accomplish this concentration of the gold reserves of the country, the Federal Reserve Board submitted to Congress in December, 1916, an amendment to the act seeking to concentrate further the gold supply of the country in the Federal Reserve banks.[3] The Board proposed to advance the date on which balances with correspondent banks would no longer count as reserves and to increase the required reserves to be maintained by member banks at the Reserve banks, but to reduce the maximum amount of reserves to be carried as vault cash. The significant item was the provision that Federal Reserve notes held in the vaults of member banks could be counted as part of their vault cash reserve. This provision would permit the member banks to substitute Federal Reserve notes for gold and gold certificates, thereby releasing the gold to the Reserve banks and increasing the free gold of the Reserve banks, that is, the surplus of gold holdings over the amounts that the Reserve banks were required to hold as reserves against notes and deposits. The Board explained, somewhat euphemistically, that the proposed amendments were "designed to provide means of controlling an overextension of loans based on new accretions to our gold stock and to provide for the mobilization and concentration of the gold holdings of the United States so that the flow of gold back to Europe, or to South America, or to the Orient, may be arranged without forcing any violent contraction of loans or causing undue disturbance to legitimate business."[4]

The Board's suggestions were not acted upon at once, but the decision to enter the war was persuasive with the Congress that the Federal Reserve System's powers should be increased and the changes requested were enacted by an amendment to the Federal Reserve Act approved June 21, 1917.

At the same time, Congress also generously made substantial reductions in the reserve percentages required to be held by member banks. The old National Bank Act, it will be recalled, had required a reserve against deposits and circulation of 25 per cent for reserve city banks and 15 per cent for other banks. The Federal Reserve Act had reduced this percentage to 18 per cent for Central Reserve city banks, 15 per cent for Reserve city banks, and 12 per cent for so-called "country banks," and 5 per cent for time deposits for all classes of banks. The new percentages against demand deposits established by the amendment were 13 per cent for Central Reserve city banks, 10 per cent for Reserve city banks and 7 per cent for country banks. To secure the concentration of the gold stocks of the country, the act provided that all reserves must henceforth be held with the Reserve banks, eliminating any requirement as to cash in vault. The immediate result of these amendments was to transfer additional gold to the Reserve banks and thereby to increase the lending power of the Reserve banks.

Along with these steps to increase the "elasticity" of the monetary system, that is, to extend the note issue and credit power of the Federal Reserve System, the Congress allowed the gold reserve to count as part of the reserve against note issues. (The Federal Reserve Act had somewhat anomalously provided that note issues should be covered by the deposit of collateral to the extent of 100 per cent of the notes issued, which meant in effect 140 per cent coverage, including the gold reserve.)

Fortified with all these new powers, the Federal Reserve System was like Alexander, bequeathed an army, looking for worlds to conquer. The System had been constructed on the theory that circulation and bank credit should expand in accordance with the needs of business as reflected in the demand from the business world, acting through the banks, for increased accommodation. But no demand was forthcoming. At the end of 1914, the Federal Reserve banks, with gold and cash of $268 million to meet the needs of business, had discounted less than $10 million of bills and issued only $10.6 million of notes. During 1915, the banking statistics reflect the evident desire and determination of the Federal Reserve authorities to test their powers. Despite an increase of money in circulation through gold and gold certificates of $250 million, silver and silver certificates of nearly $40 million, and U. S. notes of $36 million, the Federal Reserve managed to put into circulation $168 million of Federal Reserve notes. Part of this increase in total circulation may have been issued to offset national bank notes that were retired from circulation to the extent of $225 million; nevertheless, total money in circulation increased during the year by 10 per cent—a not inconsiderable increase.[5]

The Federal Reserve now began the operation of what has since developed into its most significant and powerful mechanism for the control of the amount of banking credit in circulation. This is what is known as open market purchases. Since the commercial banks showed a reluctance, or indifference, or a lack of any necessity to discount their commercial paper with the Federal Reserve banks, Federal Reserve authorities went into the market and purchased such paper. During 1915 commercial banks had discounted $32 million of bills. The Federal Reserve System itself purchased $16 million of government bonds and $24 million of commercial bills. These purchases were made under Section 14 of the Federal Reserve Act which provided originally that "any Federal Reserve bank may, under rules and regulations prescribed by the Federal Reserve Board, purchase and sell in the open market, at home or abroad, either from or to domestic or foreign banks, firms, corporations, or individuals, cable transfers and bankers acceptances and bills of exchange of the kinds and maturities by this Act made eligible for rediscount, with or without the endorsement of the member banks." Section 14(b) of the act also authorized the Federal Reserve banks to buy and sell bonds and notes of the United States as well as certain categories of securities of states and their subsidiary governmental entities.

The process is officially explained by the Federal Reserve System in the following language:

> The process through which open market operations by the Federal Reserve are reflected in the volume of member bank reserves, loans and investments, and deposits merits simplified description. If the Federal Reserve decides to buy, say, 25 million dollars of Government securities, it places an order with a dealer in such securities and he buys the securities in the open market, or sells the securities from his own portfolio. In payment the dealer receives a Federal Reserve bank check. The dealer deposits the check with a member bank, which in turn deposits it in its reserve account with a Federal Reserve bank. The dealer then draws checks on these funds to pay the seller of the securities or to retire loans which he had contracted in order to carry the securities in his portfolio. The result is that the Reserve bank has added 25 million dollars to its holdings of United States Government securities, and the same amount has been added to the reserve accounts of some member banks.
>
> These banks are now in a position to expand their loans and investments and deposits. In so doing the banks will lose funds to other banks, which in turn may expand their loans and investments and deposits in accordance with the pattern of banking developments illustrated in Chapter II. Thus, while the open market transaction of this example has increased initially the reserve positions of a limited number of member banks, the ordinary course of banking operations will diffuse these funds throughout the banking system. The reserves, the loans and investments, and the deposits of the banking system as a whole will be increased—the loans and investments and the deposits by several times the amount of the added reserves.[6]

Thus, by not waiting for the member banks to use their rediscount privilege, but by going into the open market and buying bonds or commercial paper, the Reserve banks force additional credit, or lending power, into the commercial banking system, by the mechanism just described. To reduce the amount of bank credit in the country the Federal Reserve simply reverses the process.

The pinch met by the Federal Reserve authorities in 1916 was that this mechanism could put bank credit into the economy but not circulating notes. This was because under the law as it then stood, Reserve banks could not issue circulating notes against commercial paper bought in the market. Notes could be issued only against rediscounts.*

Actually, because of the increasing use of the bank check as a medium of transfers instead of paper money (circulating notes), this limitation did not greatly constrict the monetary authorities; nevertheless, since the ultimate of liquidity is cash and as some creditors might prefer cash to a deposit credit, it seemed necessary to make the issue power co-extensive with the credit power of the system. To cure this difficulty, Congress was persuaded in 1916 to amend the Federal Reserve Act to permit bills bought in the open market to be used as security (collateral) for Federal Reserve notes. This permitted the Reserve banks to monetize this type of paper by delivering it to Federal Reserve agents and obtaining notes.

Later, in 1917, the act was again amended to permit the use of member bank promissory notes as collateral. It was not until 1932, however, that the Reserve banks were authorized to use government bonds directly as collateral for notes.

After having obtained these various new authorities, the Federal Reserve System was now in a position to do a handsome job of financing the needs of the war.

When war became apparent, it was recognized that an extensive program of Treasury financing would be necessary, and considerable apprehension was felt among the Reserve authorities as to the extent to which the System would be employed to provide these funds by way of the inflationary process of monetizing public debt instead of by taxation. They soon learned. Secretary of the Treasury McAdoo notified the Reserve he desired to float an issue of $50 million certificates of indebtedness at 2 per cent—a rate so low that they would have to be taken up by the Reserve banks themselves through direct purchase. The proposal created consternation in the banking world, but not enough to modify the program other than to raise the rate to 2 1/2 per cent on subsequent issues. The Reserve banks in consequence took over the entire issue.

There was some evidence that McAdoo intended to finance the war by this means of short term issues to be sold to the banks, much as Secretary Chase had done during the Civil War. Fortunately this extremity was avoided, but the Reserve authorities soon recognized that they would have to provide the main financing, indirectly, by lending on the security

---

*Notes could be issued only against application for notes by a Federal Reserve bank and "the collateral security thus offered shall be notes and bills accepted for rediscount under the provisions of Section 13 of this Act." Section 16.

of government bonds. The main concession obtained by the Reserve from the Treasury was that the Reserve banks should act as fiscal agents for the government, as was originally contemplated by the Act but which had until now been resisted by the Treasury. The effect of this transfer of function was to give the Reserve banks control of the large cash funds previously held by the sub-treasuries.

In order to assure success of the various "Liberty" loan issues, the Federal Reserve set a rediscount rate for customers' notes secured by government bonds that would make it easy for patriotic citizens to subscribe for the bonds, and then pay for them by borrowing against them at exactly the same rate as the bonds yielded. The first Liberty loan carried a 3 1/2 per cent coupon, and the rediscount rate was 3 1/2 per cent. As the Board frankly stated, in its 1917 Report:

> It was necessary, in order to facilitate the operations of the Treasury, that discount rates at the Federal Reserve banks be maintained on a basis in harmony with the low interest rates borne by the Government loans. . . . It was fortunate that this policy could be carried out without infringing too greatly on the resources of the Federal Reserve banks, for it is obvious that any advance in rates paid by the Government on its obligations was necessarily gradual, moving up from 3 per cent, the rate paid on certificates issued in May, to 3 1/2 per cent and later to 4 per cent, the rate carried by the second Liberty loan issue. . . . As the rates advanced it became feasible for the Federal Reserve banks to raise their rates.[7]

It is worth a look at the effect upon the monetary system as a whole of this subservience of the Federal Reserve to the Treasury. Between April, 1917, and the end of 1918, Federal Reserve note circulation increased from $399 million to $2,629 million and deposit credit increased from $804 million to $1,804 million. During this period the amount of gold coin and gold certificates in circulation was reduced from $1,673 million to $618 million, with most of this gold going into the coffers of the Reserve banks to provide a base for increased credit and circulation. Deposits and note issue became the basis, of course, for an expansion of commercial bank credit and this is reflected in the rise in loans and investment of all banks from $24.6 billion (as of June 30, 1916) to $36.6 billion as of June 30, 1919, an increase of nearly 50 per cent. Banks were encouraged to invest directly in U. S. government obligations—principally the various Liberty loans—and the holdings of government bonds increased from $1.6 billion on June 20, 1917 to $5.8 billion on June 30, 1919.

The expansion of Federal Reserve credit had been mainly through the increase in rediscounts on behalf of members, with total bills discounted rising from $28 million at the end of 1916 to $2,215 million at the end of 1919. Bills bought in the open market increased from $128,956,000 at the end of 1916 to $574,104,000 at the end of 1919 and U.S. government securities acquired increased from $55 million to $300 million.

The significance of these statistics may be read in this: that while the banking system itself was not reluctant to utilize the resources of the Federal Reserve System to increase its banking power, even this lavish recourse to the Federal Reserve banks did not seem to be enough, for the Federal Reserve authorities continued to pump credit and circulation into the economy by means of purchases of bills in the open market and U. S. government securities.

All this credit expansion, it may be argued, was merely the response to the enormous drain upon the economy to provide the materials of war both for our own needs and those of our European allies and to keep pace with the steadily rising price level occasioned by the demand for goods and services of all kinds. But this is only part of the story. The availability of free credit stimulated a boom which was becoming beyond the powers of the System to control. This is seen in the continued expansion of bank credit even after the close of hostilities. Thus, by the end of 1920 total reserves of the Federal Reserve System had increased to $2,250 million; bills discounted had risen from $2,215 million to $2,687 million, offset, however, by a decline in bills bought from $574 million to $260 million and a decline of $13 million in holdings of U. S. government securities.

Toward the end of 1920 a new crisis occurred, similar to that of 1907, yet marked by differences, which led the country into new theories regarding the function of money and monetary control.

15.

When to Reef Sail

DURING THE FINAL DAYS of debate in Congress on the Federal Reserve Act, it will be recalled, the distinguished Senator from New York, Elihu Root, rose to make one of the most brilliant, devastating, and significant attacks on the bill that had been heard in the Senate. Speaking on December 13, 1914, Root had declared that the bill was inflationary and dangerous.

"It provides," he had said, "an expansive currency, but not an elastic one. It provides a currency which may be increased, always increased, but not a currency for which the bill contains any provision compelling reduction."

He had gone on to survey the historical experience of inflation in Europe:

> I can see in this bill itself, in the discharge of our duty, no influence interposed by us against the occurrence of one of those periods of false and delusive prosperity which inevitably end in ruin and suffering. For, Mr. President, the most direful results of the awakening of people from such a dream are not to be found in the banking houses—no, not even in the business houses. They are to be found among the millions who have lost the means of earning their daily bread. They are to be found in the dislocation and paralyzing of the great machinery which gives the value to the product of the toiler by transporting it from the place where it is produced, and is worthless there because there is no one to use it, to a place where it can be used and by finding some one to use it who will pay for it.[1]

With remarkable prescience, Senator Root foretold exactly what would happen six and a half years later: "You cannot contest the operation of these laws," he had declared.

> As against the working of that law, your raising the rate of interest, or your attempting to sell government securities, will be just as effective as Mrs. Partington's mop against the Atlantic Ocean, because you do not bring into operation your forces until the damage is done. When confidence is lost, you can raise the rate of interest to the roof, but you do not bring the money until you restore confidence. . . .
>
> My objection is that the bill permits a vast inflation of our currency, and that inflation can be accomplished just as readily and just as certainly by loans of the government paper upon good security as upon bad security; that is to say, upon security that is good until the time comes when, through the process of inflation, we reach a situation in which no security is good.[2]

The Senator's analysis was an admirable blueprint for the post-war collapse. After the Armistice merchant shipping that had been concentrated on the shortest Atlantic crossings now scattered throughout the world seeking cargo. Wool that had been piling up in Australian warehouses for want of means to get it to market, now clogged the London and Boston docks.

Meantime, prices were continuing to rise, to the mounting concern of everyone, from housewives trying to fill the market baskets with the lagging wages of their spouses, to industrialists faced with the profit squeeze of narrowing margins between costs and sales, to the authorities of the Federal Reserve Board, anxious over the "overstrained situation resulting from excessively high prices and wages."

While high prices of necessaries were obviously chargeable to inefficiency and underproduction to a large degree, the Board reported in its summary of business conditions for April, it advanced the belief "that the already high costs of production were aggravated by the added expense of obtaining capital,"—that is, the high interest rates prevailing.

Actually, of more concern to the authorities was the continually increasing demands for goods, which by their very urgency increased dislocations in industry. A railroad strike for higher wages, combined with a shortage of freight cars, had reduced coal mining in Eastern mines to 30 per cent of normal, and in Southwestern mines to about two-thirds of normal, the Federal Reserve Board reported, while sporadic strikes in the manufacturing industries, notably textiles, interrupted production and aggravated unrest. It reported also an acute shortage of labor on farms.

Wages, the Board found, apparently were falling behind advances in prices and the cost of living.

In the light of all these factors the Board prognosticated no general reduction of prices, though it suggested somewhat Delphicly that changes in prices that had already taken place might be the basis for a more far-reaching alteration in the essential price structure.

Meantime, as a measure to discourage excessive use of Federal Reserve credit to finance expansion the Board obtained from Congress an amendment to the Federal Reserve Act (April 13, 1920) to permit Reserve banks to vary or graduate the discount rate charged member banks, based upon the total amount of their borrowing from the Reserve. (Section XIV, 5)

"In this way," explained Governor Harding, "it would be possible to reduce excessive borrowings of member banks and induce them to hold their own large borrowers in check without raising the basic rate. The Federal Reserve banks would thus be provided with an effective method of dealing with credit expansion, more nearly at the source than is now practicable, and without the unnecessary hardship to banks and borrowers who are conducting their affairs within the bounds of moderation."

He went on to say that "the expansion of credit set in motion by the war must be checked. Credit must be brought under more effective control and its flow once more regulated and governed with careful regard to the economic welfare of the country and the needs of its producing industries."[3]

At this juncture Senator Owen, champion of easy money, launched an attack upon the Federal Reserve's high rediscount rate, charging the Board with responsibility for a $3 billion depreciation in the $26 billion of government bonds outstanding.

"I do not think it wise, I do not think it just, I do not think it decent or ethical," he declared, "for the government agencies to pursue a policy which causes a loss of $3 billion to their patriotic bondholders."

The Federal Reserve Board, in its review of April business, revealed its mounting concern over the price situation. It said:

> The existence of the Federal Reserve System does not relieve a single banker from his individual responsibility to do his share in checking further expansion by exercising a stricter control of the credit he creates; for, except in its limited open market purchases of bankers' acceptances, the Federal Reserve System does not act directly on the volume of credit, but acts only indirectly, through the banks, on whom the primary responsibility rests.
>
> Clearly, the present is not an appropriate time to extend business merely for the sake of increased volume of profits. This applies not only to producers

and distributors, but to bankers as well, for the present opportunities to take on new borrowing accounts and to reloan borrowed money at a profit are tempting to many. Nor is it a time for public or private improvements not absolutely necessary for health and efficiency.

With a shortage of goods and labor, the necessity of conserving both is as great as it was during the war, and requires an even higher degree of self-restraint on the part of bankers, producers, distributors and consumers, since government control no longer exists. Accordingly, the more clearly the banker keeps in mind the conservation of labor and goods for necessary purposes as the object of his control the more clear will be his course in exercising such control.

On May 11 the *Chicago Tribune* reported that Secretary of the Treasury David Houston and the Federal Reserve Board were convening a conference of leading bankers to consider "how to halt the orgy of spending on luxuries and other non-essentials":

> The principal suggestion to be discussed will be . . . how to curtail the advance of credit for the production of non-essentials in an effort to stem the wave of extravagance, on the theory that people will stop spending where there are no luxuries to buy and capital will be forced into the production of necessaries when denied the more profitable field of non-essentials.

The despatch went on to state that "farmers are unable to procure nails, wire and other articles of iron because of the prodigious demand for steel in the automobile industry"—the automobile industry then assumed to be a luxury, and the cry reminiscent of the later complaint of John Kenneth Galbraith against automobiles with fins, and his ultimatum that automobile styles should be government regulated. The author of the despatch (Arthur Sears Henning) went on, however, to point out the difficulties of regulating credit with such ends in view:

> There are numerous difficulties to be faced by the conference, however, in dealing with the curtailment of the production of luxuries and increasing production of essentials.
>
> The impression prevails that such action as may be taken along this line must necessarily be of a general nature. Beyond blanket power to restrict loans, the Federal Reserve Board has no specific authority by law to define essential industries and non-essential industries.
>
> There will also be a discussion of the present rediscount rates, but beyond a modification of those now in effect general increases are not anticipated.
>
> Officials here believe the results of the application of graduated rediscount rates in the Kansas City district have been successful in restraining unnecessary use of credit.

In the midst of these deliberations, on May 20, 1920, wool quotations suddenly plunged from 65 cents a pound to 20 cents a pound, and the absence of buyers forced a closing of the wool exchange. Wheat quotations, also affected by Australian and Argentine supplies coming into the market, felt the shock in August. From an average price of $2.46 a bushel in June, and $2.43 in July, quotations dropped to $2.16 in August and to $1.46 by the end of the year. By the end of 1921 wheat was selling for less than a dollar a bushel, or about where it sold before the war.

Meantime, the entire list was tumbling. From 1913, just before the inauguration of the Federal Reserve System, to 1920, the index of wholesale prices[4] had more than doubled, from 100 to 225.3. Between 1920 and 1921 the index dropped from a high of 247 in May of 1920 to 141 in July of 1921. Available statistics show no greater and sharper drop in U. S. price history.[5]

How responsible was the Federal Reserve for this price debacle?

Beginning in 1918 it had moved to reduce the demand for credit by raising the rediscount rate. The New York Federal Reserve bank—the dominant Reserve bank of the System—raised the rediscount rate on April 6, 1918, from 3 1/2 per cent to 4 per cent, and again, on November 3, 1919, to 4 3/4 per cent. On January 23, 1920, it raised the rate to 6 per cent and again, on June 1, to 7 per cent—the highest rate in the history of the Federal Reserve System until the oil and inflation crises after 1973. The customer loan rate in New York City banks rose in sympathy from 5 1/2 per cent at the beginning of 1919 to nearly 6 3/4 per cent toward the end of 1920—also the highest rate in Federal Reserve history.[6]

These measures, as Senator Root had predicted, were ineffectual in curtailing the amount of bank credit and money in circulation. Total Reserve credit outstanding (the sum of bills discounted for member banks, and the Reserve banks' own purchases of bills and securities) rose from $2.4 billion just before the Armistice to $3.2 billion by the end of 1919 and $3.3 billion just before the May break in prices. Most of this increase was due to member banks rediscounting paper with their Reserve banks, but oddly, in view of the official policy, Reserve bank purchases of bills and securities also continued to increase, adding to the available credit in the banking system. Total Reserve credit continued to increase until October, 1920, flowing in an opposite direction to that of prices, and it was not until November that the movement was reversed, and Federal Reserve credit began to drop in response to business contraction.

Partly the continued increase in Reserve credit in 1920, after prices began to break, was due to the attempt to shore up prices by injection of purchasing power into the economy. This is a device which we shall examine in more detail in relation to the depression following the Great Crash of 1929. In short, the Federal Reserve was using credit much as the country woman used butter on boiled eggs—it was good to soften them when they were too hard, and to harden them when they were too soft. When business activity was rising, credit flowed into the economy to assist business to expand; when business activity was falling, credit was injected to restrain the fall.

Thus, on June 17, 1920, at the suggestion of the Governor of the Federal Reserve Board, W. P. G. Harding, a conference of Western bankers and sheep ranchers convened in Chicago to discuss means of raising $100 million to aid wool growers—and their creditors. Boston bankers, with their portfolios full of doubtful wool paper, were in no position to assist further, and there seemed to be some idea that Chicago might take over the burden of financing distressed holders of wool, and in the process shift the wool trade center to that city. It was announced a few days later that accommodation would be available through rediscounting wool drafts with the Federal Reserve banks, the only requirement being a bill of lading from a railroad company showing that the wool was being shipped. No eventual buyer was required to endorse this paper. The grower simply drew upon his bank, and the bank need only accept the draft. Naturally, the draft would cover only such portion of the value of the wool as the bank considered realizable under forced sale, and such value would be based upon the deflated prices of wool then prevailing. The operation helped the grower to realize some cash on his crop, but it did not raise the market value of the crop. There still remained the painful gap between what the rancher got for his wool, and what he was obligated to pay out in interest on his mortgaged ranch and livestock that had been bought on a basis of much higher wool prices.

The unanswered question that continued under debate among economists is whether the collapse of 1920 was due to economic or monetary causes, whether it was simply a return to "normalcy," a readjustment of livelihood activities to the more ordinary requirements of peace, or a plunge into an economic abyss from the push of artificial manipulation of credit. Again, did the rise in intrest rates precede or follow the rise in rediscount rates, and did the rise in interest rates project or simply reflect the maladjustments of business? The difficlties in reaching any conclu-

FEDERAL RESERVE AND MARKET RATES OF INTEREST
PER CENT PER ANNUM

Date	Rediscount rate New York Federal Reserve Bank	Market rate*
1917		
Jan.	4	3.98
Feb.	4	4.47
March	3 1/2 (21)	4.50
April	3 1/2	4.63
May	3 1/2	5.28
June	3 1/2	5.28
July	3 1/2	5.25
Aug.	3 1/2	5.19
Sept.	3 1/2	5.44
Oct.	3 1/2	5.63
Nov.	3 1/2	5.69
Dec.	4 (5)	5.75
1918		
Jan.	4	5.83
Feb.	4	5.88
March	4	6.
April	4	6.08
May	4	6.13
June	4	6.03
July	4	6.10
Aug.	4	6.22
Sept.	4	6.
Oct.	4	6.
Nov.	4	6.
Dec.	4	6.
1919		
Jan.	4	5.25
Feb.	4	5.13
March	4	5.50
April	4	5.38
May	4	5.25
June	4	5.38
July	4	5.38

Date	Rediscount rate New York Federal Reserve Bank	Market rate*
Aug.	4	5.38
Sept.	4	5.38
Oct.	4	5.25
Nov.	4 3/4 (4)	5.25
Dec.	4 3/4	5.88
1920		
Jan.	6 (23)	6.
Feb.	6	6.38
March	6	6.88
April	6	6.88
May	6	7.38
June	7 (4)	7.88
July	7	8.13
Aug.	7	8.13
Sept.	7	8.13
Oct.	7	8.13
Nov.	7	8.13
Dec.	7	8.
1921		
Jan.	7	7.88
Feb.	7	7.63
March	7	7.63
April	6 (15)	7.63
May	6	6.88
June	6	6.75
July	5 1/2 (21)	6.38
Aug.	5 1/2	6.13
Sept.	5 (23)	6.
Oct.	5	5.88
Nov.	4 1/2 (4)	5.50
Dec.	4 1/2	5.13

*Prime commercial paper, 4–6 months, New York City. Figures in parentheses indicate day new rate became effective.

Source: Federal Reserve Board. *Banking and Monetary Statistics.* 1941.

sion are illustrated in the accompanying chart of the rediscount rates and prime commercial paper rates in New York City for the years 1917 through 1921.

The Federal Reserve authorities managed to take an optimistic view of the fall in prices and reported at the end of September that "business conditions are now definitely on the road to stability of as great and confirmed a nature as the disturbed position of the world at large permits," and added: "Continuance of the process of readjustment in business and industry has been an outstanding feature of the month. This has been accompanied by price reductions and by the resumption of work in branches of industry where hesitation as to the future outlook has led to suspicion." The Board went on to comment on the change in the labor situation: "A notable change appears to have taken place in the efficiency of labor—twenty-one out of thirty-one of the largest corporations in the country reporting improvement, while none report any decrease. Improved railroad operation has resulted in much better marketing of goods. . . . Stock market conditions have partially recovered. . . ."

Meantime, the Board came under attack by Senator Owen, leader of the easy money and fiat currency wing of the Congress. In a letter to Governor Harding on October 22 he charged the Board with responsibility for what he termed the "psychological effect of the policy of deflation" which he asserted originated with New York bankers. The Board, he went on to assert, had by its action destabilized the credit of the United States, assisted in producing industrial unrest and lack of confidence, which had checked production and brought commodity prices below the point at which legitimate supply and demand would fix them.

Senator Owen's letter continued:

> The need for the alleged policy of deflation rests on the premise that the entire country is suffering from inflation, which is fundamentally untrue. Legitimate borrowing and lending for legitimate purposes is not inflation.
>
> We have the greatest crop in the history of the country. The productive and machine power of America and its capacity for organization is greater than ever before in its history. The tremendous demand for credits is justified by these conditions and the credits ought to be extended by the Reserve banks and by the member banks.
>
> The banks are exercising, naturally and properly, a discrimination against the speculator and the profiteer, but the man who produces and the man who distributes is entitled to credit against the value of the commodities which he handles.

You have the power under the Reserve Act to suspend the reserve requirements.

Without suspending the reserve requirements as to the reserve note you
could issue additional reserve notes equal to the amount outstanding without
violating the statute. In other words, you could increase the credits of the
Reserve banks and the member banks three billions immediately, not only
without harm, but with the beneficent effect of immediately restoring the
confidence of the country which has been impaired by the terrible policy of
so-called deflation.

Out of the 1920 debacle and the controversy that it generated began
to emerge the issue of the central function of monetary policy, and the
direction of public policy. The issue was fairly stated in an editorial in the
Times commenting upon the debate between Owen and Harding and
their respective parties:

> The first duty of banks is to keep themselves liquid. In excess of patriotism
> the banks financed the Treasury rather than trade, and thus got into the
> frozen condition from which they are retrieving themselves in the interest of
> all concerned. It is the duty of business to finance the banks as well as of the
> banks to finance business. The reciprocal discharge of all obligations is the
> duty of all.
>
> It is not the duty of the banks to sustain the price of anything. During the
> war there grew up the idea that banks should limit their loans to essential
> credits. That meant that war industries should be supported for the same
> reason that the banks financed the Treasury. Senator Owen now thinks that
> the banks should extend themselves in the interest of "legitimate produc-
> tion" and "legitimate distribution." But who shall decide what is legitimate?
> Governor Harding long ago declared, with general approval, that it was not
> the duty of Washington bankers to decide that for the country. Senator
> Owen's appeal should be to the member banks. But how shall they decide
> upon the degrees of legitimacy of the loans which they make? Solvent cus-
> tomers should be enabled to meet their obligations and required to do so.
> The customers owe to one another what they owe to the bank—liquidation
> of obligations at maturity in whatever kind of production or distribution they
> may be engaged. Banking gets into deep water when it attempts anything
> more than receipt of deposits and making of loans. In that aspect it is one
> of the simplest of businesses, but Senator Owen would have it assume the
> function of a financial Providence. Governor Harding's way is less sympa-
> thetic, but sounder.[7]

16.

The Wounds of War

THE WAR did to the Federal Reserve what battle did to men; it revealed the institution's frailties and imperfections; it changed its character, and wounded it in vital parts. We have surveyed generally the main drift of the economic consequences of the monetary policies pursued during the war; we may now take a closer look at some of the changes in the structure and operations of the System. These changes were not all generated by the war; their origins are to be traced to the misconceptions of the framers of the act as to the realities of the business world which the new banking system was designed to serve; the war was the incubator that hastened their exposure.

Probably no better assessment of these changes is offered than that by H. Parker Willis, who, next to Paul Warburg, was the most influential technician in fashioning the System, and the profoundest authority on its operation. Willis had been a professor of finance in various institutions, and at the time the Democrats came into control of Congress in 1910 was dean of the College of Political Sciences of George Washington University in Washington, D. C. He was appointed expert to the House Ways and Means Committee and later an expert on the House Banking and Currency Committee, to draft the Federal Farm Loan Act. When Wilson was elected in 1912, Carter Glass employed Willis to assist in drafting the banking bill that eventually became the Federal Reserve Act. Later Willis became the secretary of the newly organized Federal Reserve Board and subsequently its director of research, a position he held until 1922.

In 1920, in a lecture in the Blackstone Legal Training Lectures, and again in 1922, at the time of his retirement as the Board's director of research, in an article in the *Political Science Quarterly*,[1] Willis made an appraisal of the new banking system.

The first notable defect of the System of which he makes mention was that of the ineffectuality of the rediscount rate. It had been Paul Warburg's theory, as we have noted, that changes in the System's rediscount rate would be the principal moderating influence upon the general interest rate structure of the economy, since the central bank's lending rate was in effect the ultimate, or marginal, cost of money to which all other rates would be related. This was the famous theory first popularized by Walter Bagehot, in his *Lombard Street*, a classic first published in 1873, that had already gone through thirteen editions by 1913 when Federal Reserve legislation was being debated. Bagehot had demonstrated to the delight and fascination of bankers how a central bank, by manipulating its lending rate, could stimulate or retard the state of business, the movement of merchandise in trade and of gold in and out of the country, all mainly by making the price of money cheaper or more costly, and conversely the price of goods more costly or cheaper. It is an ingenious theory, supported by a vast amount of data from British experience, in which central banking authorities still put faith and on which hang most of their operations to this day, despite the testimony of Willis and the tragic experience of the 1929 stock market crash, as well as numerous later evidences to the contrary.

"The outstanding fact," Willis wrote, "is that there has been no time when the System could be said to be really the leader of the market, or be able to make its discount rate 'effective' for any considerable period."

During the first two years of the System's operations, Willis explained, the banks of the country were too well provided with funds and too little inclined to resort to the Reserve banks for accommodation to permit the discount rates of the latter to be of serious importance. This was due in part to the expansion of the note issue at the outbreak of the war, under the emergency note provision of the Aldrich-Vreeland Act. It was also due to the lowering of the cash reserve requirements for national banks which the Federal Reserve Act authorized. The effect of this "release of reserves," Willis pointed out, was to place in the hands of the banks a very large lending power which they were able to use in expanding their operations. The banks were not slow to take advantage of this power and did increase their lending, and with this broader power of operation it was not necessary for them to do any rediscounting. Some of this slack was taken up shortly before the United States entered the war, and some observers thought that for a few months, early in 1917, the System was able to exercise an influence upon the money market by its discount policy—but this period, Willis declared, was not for long.

With the coming of war, a fundamental question in the financial world was the rate at which the government could borrow. Despite the great propaganda campaign to buy "Liberty" bonds, as they were called, and the patriotic appeal of the propaganda, it was recognized that the discount rate would govern the price at which the bonds could be sold, for buyers promptly used them as bank collateral to put themselves in funds again, a transaction that really meant that the banks were indirectly lending to the government. It was considered essential by the authorities that the rediscount rate correspond with the coupon rate of the war bonds.

The first Liberty loan, as we have already noted, was sold with a 3 1/2 per cent coupon, which paralleled the 3 1/2 per cent rate on notes secured by such bonds. As subsequent issues came on the market, the difficulty of placing them increased and a higher coupon rate was necessary. The higher coupon rates were matched by a corresponding advance in the discount rate.

It was not until the war was over, and had been succeeded by a period of inflation which had brought the country close to disaster, Willis reported, that the discount rate again began to play much part in the control and direction of credit. But he went on to say, "Deflation which set in as a result of a world-wide revolution in demand and prices largely threw the System out of alignment with the commercial credit market, and once more rendered its rates relatively ineffective."

"Today," he continued, speaking of conditions in 1922, "they have practically no relation to, or effect upon, current short-time commercial rates. Reviewing the whole experience and concentrating attention upon the two periods of a few months each, during which the Federal Reserve discount rate was a real factor in current finances, the conclusion to be drawn must be very adverse to the success of the System as a leader of the market or as a moulder of credit."

Confirmation of the appraisal made by H. Parker Willis is found also in the views of Adolph C. Miller, a member of the Federal Reserve Board, who wrote in the *American Economic Review* for June, 1921, as follows:

> From that time [the beginning of the war] forth to the beginning of the year 1920, the discount policy of the Federal Reserve System was shaped not in accordance with money market conditions—not with the idea of using Reserve bank rates as an instrument of effective control of the money market

—but with the primary purpose of assisting the Treasury in the flotation of its great bond issues and its short term certificate issues. In brief, the discount policy of the Federal Reserve System was treated as an element of the Treasury's loan policy, the Federal Reserve System virtually ceasing to exercise, for the time being, its normal function of regulating credit.[2]

Although the war was over in 1918, in a fighting sense, it was not over in a financial sense. The Treasury still had enormous obligations to meet, which were eventually covered by a Victory loan. The main support in the market again was the Federal Reserve. Throughout 1919 discount rates were maintained at artificially low levels.

"The device of an artificial discount rate," said Miller, "provided too comfortable an expedient alike to the Treasury and to the banks of the country, which were still burdened with commitments made under the 'borrow and buy' Liberty Loan slogan, to be easily relinquished. Thus was the Federal Reserve System controlled in the matter of its discount policy at the very time when the interest of the country at large required that it should be free of control in order that it itself might control."[3]

In 1920, the Reserve finally undertook to develop a policy of control by means of discount rates. The consequence, whether because the Reserve's action was too late, or inherently ineffectual, was the debacle we have already described.

Following the business revival that began in 1921, accompanied by a new upward movement in prices, the Reserve took another look at its functions in regard to the discount rate.

The Federal Reserve Board's annual report for 1923, its tenth, reviewed its ten years' history, beginning with a discussion of the responsibility of the System to fix discount rates, as the act stipulated, "with a view to accommodating commerce and industry."

Discussions, the Board pointed out, were usually addressed to the question of the relationship that should exist and be maintained between Federal Reserve bank rates and the rates in the open market. The view most widely held was that the Federal Reserve bank rate "should move in sympathy with general money rates, rising as they rise and falling when they fall."

The Board went on to say, however, that a development of this theory was that the Federal Reserve banks should assume leadership in the money market. It is at this point that the departure in policy appears.

The Board was careful to point out, by a series of tables, that the wide variety of conditions geographically and as to the quality and character of notes made impossible any 1 to 1 correspondence between the official rediscount rate and the open market rate.

"Indeed," the Board concluded, "the observations of the Federal Reserve Board and the experiences of the Federal Reserve banks make it certain that the Federal Reserve banks and the Federal Reserve Board can not adequately discharge their function of fixing rates with a view of accommodating commerce and business by the simple expedient of any fixed rate or mechanical principle."[4]

The year 1922 marks, in a way, a turning point in Federal Reserve policy. Henceforth the Reserve began quietly to abandon reliance upon the discount rate as a modifier of the economic climate and to put its faith and money into open market transactions in which, instead of relying upon the ebb and flow of commerce to bring expansion or contraction of bank credit, it attempted to influence that ebb and flow by forcing credit into the economy—or conversely, withdrawing it—by going into the market and either bidding for paper or offering it for sale.

Closely connected with the failure of the Federal Reserve to develop as a financial leader during these earlier years, through the use of the discount rate, was the withering of the acceptance as a financial instrument. The trade acceptance—that is, the draft drawn by a seller of goods upon the buyer, and accepted by him—simply did not fit the American way of doing business and it never developed to any degree. In its place it was hoped that the banker's acceptance would prove more popular, and considerable effort was devoted to promoting this form of paper, and the Federal Reserve banks, in their eagerness, went to numerous questionable practices, including favoritism and straining their authority. The banker's acceptance differed from a trade acceptance in that the acceptor was a bank rather than the buyer of the goods. It was objectionable in the eyes of many authorities on the subject, principally for the reason that it permitted a weak creditor, or a creditor using funds for purposes that were not for business or commercial purposes, to obtain the funds through the credit of a bank; and encouraged banks, by the temptations of profit, to lend their credit beyond their capacity.

Despite these objections the Federal Reserve continued to exert its influence to the expansion of bankers' acceptances, but balked when a private New York bank applied for a ruling that would have served, practically speaking, to permit it to issue a line of credit to the French government for the purchase of munitions, with the privilege of refinancing itself at the New York Federal Reserve bank. It was the Treasury, and

Treasury influence, that was exerted to obtain the ruling. Under pressure from the Treasury to assist war financing in every way, the Reserve acceded and went on to tolerate various excesses and misuses until the acceptance as an instrument lost most of its meaning. Thus, contrary to the theory that the acceptance was good because it not only carried responsible guarantees but also indicated on its face the exact purpose for which the credit was being used, the acceptance was no longer related to any specific transaction, nor did it have a termination date, and it might or might not relate to a commercial transaction, and in fact might not represent goods in existence. Despite all these defects as commercial paper, it enjoyed a preferential rate with the Federal Reserve simply because it bore the name of a bank rather than an individual or a corporation.[5]

In 1922, a committee of bank examiners filed with the Comptroller a scathing report, listing the abuses that had come to their attention. The effect of this report was decisive. From an estimated maximum of around $1 billion in acceptances outstanding at the height of their use, the volume dropped to around $400 million in 1923. Much of this drop, of course, was due to the business recession.

Subsequently, during the boom just preceding the stock market crash of 1929 the volume of bankers' acceptances rose to around $1 1/2 billion, but thereafter declined to less than $150 million at the end of 1941 just before the U. S. became involved in World War II.

After 1937 the Federal Reserve practically ceased to buy or rediscount such paper, but following World War II the use of bankers' acceptances revived. The average amount outstanding during 1962, for instance, was around $2 1/2 billion—a figure still insignificant in comparison to total bank credit outstanding—but the maximum held by the Federal Reserve banks never exceeded $100 million until toward the end of 1962.

The expansion of acceptance banking that occurred thereafter will be discussed further on in relation to the disappearance of silver coinage, the suspension of gold convertibility and the uncontrollable inflation that began in the 1960s and accelerated through the 1970s. Here we may note that the failure of the acceptance to obtain status during the formative years of the System led the Reserve authorities to seek some other mechanism by which to exercise the latent powers conferred upon them. This they found in the market for short-term government bonds—the official bill market.

The promotion of the banker's acceptance in a generally indifferent market was the first major step in substituting finance in the abstract for finance in the concrete. Backing for the note issue would no longer consist of physical things, particularly goods in the course of production or trade, along with gold, but it would consist increasingly of evidences of debt, of uncertain character and duration, and a declining amount of gold. At first this debt was that of the commercial banker, in the form of the banker's acceptance, whose assets did not consist of physical goods (beyond the bank premises, and the small change in his cash till) but of other evidences of debt. As we have noted, the original character of the banker's acceptance as an instrument representing a further guarantee upon an obligation derived from goods in trade, and having an early maturity corresponding to the time required to deliver or dispose of the goods in the market, had given way to that of an instrument representing an obligation secured by goods in warehouse and not actually in trade, and having an indefinite, or a continually renewed maturity.

The next step was to substitute, for the banker's acceptance, the short-term obligations of the Federal government, which represented often the unliquidated balance of past fiscal deficits, the cost of wars long fought and forgotten, and other consumption activities of the state. This development will be followed in more detail as our story proceeds.

The third major change in central bank theory which the customs of commerce, the independence of trade, and the exigencies of politics forced upon the Federal Reserve System, was in relation to the price level —the notion that somehow the movement of prices should be controlled by the state.

The operations of the Federal Reserve System, as originally constituted, were to be directed to a money and credit supply that served "to accommodate commerce and business."

It was in the 1923 Annual Report of the Board that official recognition was first given to the theory that Federal Reserve policy should be directed not to "accommodating commerce and business" but really to the maintenance of a stable price structure. The Report stated: "Particular prominence has been given in discussions of new proposals [for guides to credit and currency administration] to the suggestion frequently made that the credit issuing from the Federal Reserve banks should be regulated with immediate reference to the price level, particularly in such manner as to avoid fluctuations of general prices."[6]

Adolph C. Miller, the Board member whose opinions we have already cited, raised the curtain on the issue in his *American Economic Review* article which we have already quoted. He said:

> As an abstract proposition, the proposal to substitute a price indicator for the reserve ratio as a guide to discount policy has much economic merit. The rigors of the recent price readjustment process through which the United States, in common with the rest of the commercial world, has been passing, have emphasized the value of price stability. Price disturbances not originating from inevitable natural causes are bad and costly alike to producer and consumer. . . .
>
> . . . As a theoretical proposition, therefore, it is entirely conceivable that the discount policy of the Federal Reserve System might be governed by indications of impending price changes, with a view of mitigating their cyclical fluctuations. While such an undertaking would raise some new and difficult problems of credit administration, no doubt in time the technique of a plan of credit regulation based on price indices could be worked out and made administratively practicable if public sentiment demanded. But there is now no warrant in the statute under which the Federal Reserve banks are organized for undertaking to regulate their credit operations on any such basis. . . .

It is noteworthy of these early managers of the Federal Reserve that they uniformly resisted the idea that price regulation was a central bank function. The 1923 Report discussed the theory of price regulation at some length and concluded:

> Entirely apart from the difficult administrative problems that would arise in connection with the adoption of the price index as a guide and entirely apart from the serious political difficulties which could attend a system of credit administration based on prices, there is no reason for believing that the results attained would be as satisfactory as can be reached by other means economically valid and administratively practicable. . . . Price fluctuations proceed from a great variety of causes, most of which lie outside the range of influence of the credit systems. No credit system could undertake to propose the function of regulating credit by reference to prices without failing in the endeavor.
>
> The price situation and the credit situation are no doubt frequently involved in one another, but the entire relationship of prices and credit is too complex to admit of any simple statement, still less of a formula of invariable application.

The Board then proceeded to analyze in detail some of the difficulties in establishing any cause and effect relationship and to analyze the task of administering credit with a view to "accommodating commerce and business."

Nevertheless, despite its reservations, it was not long before monetary policy had made a complete turn. No longer was the question to be one of "elastic money" but a stable price level, and in the morass of price statistics the Federal Reserve has been mired ever since.

17.

Wading in the Big Pond

THE FEDERAL RESERVE SYSTEM had been designed, as we have noted, to serve the domestic currency needs of this country. At the time, the people of the United States regarded themselves an insular power and aloof from the main currents of international—or at least European—politics.* World War I ended all that. Despite popular rejection at the polls of President Wilson's policy of European involvement, including membership in the League of Nations, the circumstances of trade and finance combined with the ferment of a nascent megalomania to persuade the American public that their government was the bellwether among the nations and that it had world responsibilities to meet. It was not exactly the sense of "the white man's burden"—the cliché that had succeeded in almost exhausting British national vitality within the course of three hundred years, as it had exhausted the Roman and that of other peoples of history; but it was dangerously close to it.

Thus it came about that although the U. S. continued to remain aloof politically from European affairs for another two decades, it became more and more implicated economically. The instrument of this involvement was the Federal Reserve System.

For this reason we must now turn to some of the events abroad during the years we have just covered. World War I had left Europe more exhausted than the U. S. How much of this exhaustion was the dislocations and confusions caused by war-time inflation, and how much was due

*This, despite the fact that for a hundred years the United States had held a major trading position in the Pacific, and assumed to exercise a fiat in Latin America.

to the physical destruction by bombs and gunfire are interesting questions that have never been answered; we may only note the almost miraculous recovery that occurred in Germany after currency stability was restored in 1924 (and again in 1949).

In Great Britain, however, where cities and soil escaped relatively unmarred by bombs and shell fire, a perilous weakness had fallen upon the livelihood system that was not disclosed immediately, and which in fact has hardly yet been cured. The nature of this malaise was revealed when the government attempted to restore the gold monetary system.

We may look for a moment at what had happened to the British pound sterling. The outbreak of war in 1914 had affected business in Great Britain very much as it had here; that is, after a momentary panic forcing the Exchange to close, trade revived, and gold began to return to the banks. Meantime, by what was expected to be a temporary measure to meet demands for cash, the Bank of England was authorized* to increase the fiduciary (that is, unsecured) note circulation by the issue of legal tender £1 and 10s. currency notes. The practical effect of this measure was to abolish the historic gold currency system for a fiat money system. Unlike the German and French systems, adopted in the Federal Reserve System, that allowed currency to be issued against commercial paper, since 1844 the British system allowed currency to be issued only against gold, except for a statutorily limited fiduciary issue. Peel's Act had originally fixed this maximum at £14 million; from time to time the limit had been raised by Parliament, but the principle of an arbitrary and fixed maximum had never been abandoned before 1914. By the Currency and Bank Notes Act of 1914, all limits were removed.

Actually, there was little need for this break with tradition, for during the early years of the war there was a surfeit of circulating notes, for business men in England, as elsewhere, had discovered the advantages of payments by check, and the great demand in trade was not for notes but for bank credit. To meet this demand, that is, to increase the deposit-creating power of the joint stock banks, the Bank of England began to buy bills in the market, exchanging for them its deposit credits. This served to build up the reserves of the commercial banks, and an enormous increase in bank credit was achieved by allowing the Bank reserve, which traditionally had been kept at 40 or 50 per cent of deposit liabilities, to go as low as 20 per cent, and later to 8 per cent.[1]

Subsequently, instead of commercial bills in its portfolio, the Bank

---

*By the Currency and Bank Notes Act, 1914, passed Aug. 6, 1914.

acquired Ways and Means Advances,* Treasury bills, and even long-term government bonds—an intersting but unfortunate parallel with Federal Reserve practice in these same years.

"Thus," says Feavearyear, the English monetary authority, "the original inflation was continued, and the reserves of the other banks remained high. This lending power being proportionally increased, they soon found means of using it, particularly when the large war loans came to be floated."[2]

Feavearyear points out that there was no definite legal abandonment of the gold standard while the war was in progress, but the increase in bank credit, and eventually of the note issue also, meant that the effectiveness of the link with gold was destroyed slowly and insidiously. By 1916 a premium on gold began to appear, and an act was passed forbidding the melting down or defacing of gold coin. While the war lasted there was no specific prohibition on the export of gold. This was a facade maintained only by assistance of the United States. When this country entered the war it began extending large credits to its allies† by which they were able to maintain the stability of their foreign exchange. The dollar-sterling rate was pegged at $4.76 7/16, or slightly less than par, until March, 1919, after which the pound began to drop steadily, falling to a low of $3.195 in February, 1920.

After U. S. financial assistance ceased, the British currency was not the only currency to sink under the weight of excessive war-time issues. The French franc dropped in the international exchange to around a third of its pre-war value, and the German mark, which at the time that Paul Warburg was preaching the benefits of the German system of commercial acceptances and flexible note issue was even stronger than the pound sterling, had depreciated by the end of 1923 to a rate of 42 billion for one cent.

By the end of 1921, there was general talk of an international economic conference to solve the post-war problems of war-bred dislocations: it always seems easier to reform the world around a horseshoe table than in the market place and in the fields. Samuel Gompers, head of the American Federation of Labor, with world prestige in the labor movement, was among the first to broach the idea: it was advanced also by the

---

*Temporary borrowings authorized in the first instance by the House of Commons Ways and Means Committee.

†Totalling $9,647,419,494.84 by November 15, 1919.

General Commission on the Limitation of Armaments; speakers at a Foreign Policy Association luncheon dallied with it; Senator France introduced a joint resolution authorizing and directing the President to convene such a conference. But President Harding had been elected on a platform of repudiation of the League of Nations, and announced that Europe would have to take the initiative. Aristide Briand, Premier of France, seized the leadership and issued an invitation to a conference of British, American, Italian, Japanese, and Belgian government representatives to meet at the Hotel Crillon in Paris.

Immediately, a host of other countries begged to be invited. It was decided to open the doors to all, until the leaders of Soviet Russia indicated their willingness, even eagerness, to attend. Lenin was then introducing his New Economic Policy (NEP) which allowed a modicum of private enterprise. But he was fearful of going to Paris, and the locus was moved to Genoa. At the same time the list of questions to be taken up expanded like a catalog of human sins. The prospective presence of the Russians alarmed the French, particularly when the Soviet war minister and second-in-command, Leon Trotsky, announced from Moscow that the conference would accomplish a revision of the Versailles Treaty. When the Siberian Republic of Pir-Amur vented a protest against the participation of U. S. delegates, it seemed that Babel was ready to reassemble.

The conference eventually came to pass, convening early in April, 1922, along with seven hundred representatives of the press.

What the conference accomplished mainly was to prove that Europe was not yet ready for an international system, despite the League of Nations—or perhaps that the institutions of Europe were not yet refashioned to the needs of an international system. The issue of the conference soon began to turn upon European-Soviet relations, and to hang upon the demand of Belgium for integral restitution of foreign-owned private property in Russia. France supported the Belgian claim, Great Britain less warmly; meantime, the Germans on April 16 signed a separate treaty with the Russians at Rapallo, in which the principal objects of the Genoa conference were achieved, at least as between these parties, in their mutual renunciation of reparation claims and resumption of normal consular and diplomatic relations. The denouement threw the conference into confusion, and awakened fears of a German-Soviet entente that would threaten the peace of Europe. Under the cirumstances, no general economic arrangements were possible, and the conference quietly dissolved.

France now hardened its reparations demands on Germany, and in

1923, when delivery schedules were not met, sent troops into the Ruhr to enforce its claims. The results were as expected: a sullen resentment paralyzed activity and the German economy stagnated and collapsed. The final debacle was the German inflation which reduced the value of money to practically zero.

It was at this juncture that the United States quietly abandoned its post-war mood and policy of isolation and undertook again to intervene in European affairs. President Coolidge announced on December 15 his agreement to a commission to examine German finances and to propose a solution to the reparations impasse, and the appointment of Charles G. Dawes as the principal U. S. member. From this investigation came the Dawes Plan to stabilize the German currency and to revise downward the reparations payments. The Plan was to be financed initially by an international loan of which the principal amount ($110 million out of $200 million) would be subscribed in the U. S.*

In this fragile condition of the European economy, the British government, under the influence of Winston Churchill, then Chancellor of the Exchequer, concluded to restore the pound sterling to its former parity —as a necessity for British prestige and British international finance. U. S. cooperation would be needed, and this was forthcoming. The Federal Reserve System was the agency. In favor of the action was the relative strength of the pound in the international exchanges. Since 1921 it had held at no greater than 15 per cent discount from parity. It was reasoned by British monetary authorities that with some assistance from the U. S. the restoration could be managed. Not everyone was of this opinion, however; indeed, some able economists argued for a devaluation of the pound, and others frankly proposed the abandonment of a metallic standard altogether and the establishment of a managed currency.

The proponents of restoration were aided by prevalent speculation which anticipated the result, and began to bid the pound up, a process which, of course, also promoted their own ends. By the end of 1924 sterling was selling at $4.70 in terms of dollars, and to within 1 1/2 per cent of par early in 1925. This was decisive. On April 28, Winston Churchill announced a return to the gold standard, and authorized the

*This, strictly, was not the first post-war resumption of international activity. In 1921 Harding had convened an international conference on naval disarmament, by which substantial reduction of the world's principal navies was achieved, and about the same time the U. S., as its contribution to the economic rehabilitation of Europe, agreed to a major revision of the war loan repayments.

Bank of England to deliver gold for export against the receipt of any form of legal tender money.

The return was formalized by the passage of the Gold Standard Act of 1925 (May 13), but it was not to the gold standard as historically known in England. While the Act declared that both Bank of England notes and the war-time Currency notes were legal tender, they were no longer convertible into gold coin. The ancient right of all persons to bring gold to the Mint and have it coined was abolished, and this privilege was restricted to the Bank of England. Holders of notes could, however, obtain gold on presentation of their notes, but only in quantities of 400 oz.—the weight of the standard gold bar. The utility of this provision was practically limited to foreign trade.

To support the pound against possibility of heavy unloading of sterling by speculators who now no longer had interest in it, the government arranged for a $300 million credit with the Federal Reserve Bank of New York. Fortunately, this credit was not required.

The significance of this arrangement lies in a related field—the growth of the gold exchange standard. The ability of the U. S. economy to support, almost unimpaired, the gold convertibility of the dollar throughout the war, led to the general acceptability abroad of dollar bank balances as the equivalent of gold. It now became customary—and indeed authorized in many instances by the respective banking and currency laws —for European central banks to treat as the equivalent of gold in their reserves any holdings of convertible bank balances abroad—particularly in London or New York.

Actually the beginnings of the gold exchange standard may be traced to the great shift from silver to the gold standard that took place in the 1870s. Various European banks of issue, faced with insufficient gold reserves for the purpose, began to hold small amounts of foreign exchange in their reserves, to be used to stabilize the external value of their moneys. In 1893, when Great Britain put its Indian dominions on the gold standard, it did so by carrying a substantial part of the Indian reserves in sterling exchange, and the Indian expedient was then adopted by all the colonial powers.[3] It was, however, the resolutions of endorsement of the gold exchange standard by the Genoa Conference that led to its abuse in a fantastic pyramiding of credit.

The way the gold exchange standard corrupted the monetary systems of the world can be illustrated by an example drawn from actual happenings in the money markets during the years 1924–1929:

An Austrian corporation, for instance, obtains a long-term loan in New York, the net proceeds of which are $1 million, credited to the borrower as a deposit in a New York bank. The corporation, which needs schillings, sells these dollars to a Viennese bank. The latter in turn transfers the deposit credit to the Austrian national bank. Because this dollar deposit was then readily convertible into gold, the national bank could treat this deposit as part of its prime reserve. Thus, it was able to increase its notes in circulation or extend credit by about $3 million or about 21 million schillings, assuming a reserve ratio of 33 1/3 per cent (the legal requirement at the time). As these notes or deposits were in turn reserves for the commercial banks of Austria, commercial credit of three or four times this amount could be created.

The loan to the Austrian corporation of $1 million resulted in an equal increase in deposits on the books of the New York bank with which the proceeds of the loan were deposited. Against this deposit the New York bank had to maintain a reserve with the Federal Reserve bank of 13 per cent, or $130,000. The latter in turn was required to maintain a reserve of 35 per cent against its deposits, or $45,500. Thus, under the gold exchange standard system, as it functioned during these years, against an actual gold reserve of less than $50,000 in the Federal Reserve Bank of New York, a central bank abroad operating on the gold exchange standard was able to increase its notes in circulation or demand deposits by about $3 million upon which, in turn, the commercial banks could build a deposit credit structure of $10 million to $12 million.[4]

The subsequent efflorescence of this system into the Eurodollar market, a phenomenon which continues to baffle understanding or control, will be treated later. Here we may note only the advantage of the gold exchange standard to the newer sovereignties that arose out of the ruins of Eastern Europe. American "money doctors"—the most famous of whom was Prof. E. W. Kemmerer of Princeton—were now being invited to assist impoverished governments to reform their monetary systems in accordance with the new dispensation. And so throughout the world, in primitive countries in remote regions of the globe, that hardly knew the meaning of stable government, among peoples to whom banks were practically unknown, the authorities were encouraged to establish the complex institutions of managed money and credit, and for the good silver coinage to which the people were accustomed, to substitute flimsy paper currency of doubtful value and continually depreciating worth.

The effect of the expansion of the gold exchange standard—defended by its advocates as "economizing the use of gold"—was a tremendous pyramiding of credit that was eventually to lead to a new debacle of international proportions, more destructive in some respects of the moral and physical fabric of society than war.

Here in short was the lever by which the modern Archimedes of credit was to upset the whole world in the fateful crash of 1929.

18.

༺ঌঌ৵৵৵৵৵৵৵৵৵৵৵৵৵৵৵৵৵৵৵ঌ

The Lapping Waves of Crisis

THE YEAR 1926 ended with an extraordinary spectacle on the floor of the New York Stock Exchange. During the final hour, a bull rally was going as floor traders sought to fill orders that poured in from a confident public; but their shouts were drowned by the blare of a band, and their finger wagging was hidden in a shower of confetti. Trading came to a standstill as the band played, balloons floated in the air, and stock brokers danced on a floor littered with ticker tape and confetti. Members with more agile feet entertained the packed galleries with exhibitions of the Black Bottom, the current ball room rage. Just before three o'clock the band moved from the gallery to the trading floor and the final gong sounded in the midst of songs and revelry.

There seemed ample reason for rejoicing. It had been a prosperous year—probably the most prosperous in the nation's history. Prices of goods were stable, the public debt was steadily diminishing, gold was flowing to these shores, factories were humming, jobs were plentiful, profits were good, and investors were reaping the rewards of their shrewdness and thrift.

Such a year would not return soon, and when business did again revive, following the worst stock market panic in history, and after an exhausting war, the profits of business were no longer its own, nor its decisions. There would be an immense public debt and interest to pay; there would be an enormous defense cost to meet; taxes on corporate enterprise would now drain over half the profits, and corporate managers, in addition to the internal revenue auditor looking over their shoulders, would find their affairs under the continual scrutiny of dozens of other bureau-

135

cratic and regulatory agencies. Under the system of forced savings instituted under the Keynesian Theory, that individuals should be relieved
of concern for old age in order to be encouraged to spend all they earned,
social security taxes alone were destined to take more from the wage
earner than formerly his total income tax bill.

Whether the post-war prosperity reached its climax in 1926 or 1927
depends upon which series of statistics is used to measure prosperity;
those who gained their livelihood in the stock market were swimming in
profits until toward the middle of 1929; the year 1929 was to record more
income tax payers with incomes in excess of $1 million (513) than in any
year of the next thirty-six.* Nevertheless, by 1926, signs were beginning
to indicate that the bloom was off the boom, and that a tiredness was
overtaking the economy. Chief of these was the divergence that had
appeared in the two main branches of the economy—production and
financing, and their parallels, raw materials prices and prices of securities.
We can give only fragmentary indications, and their value as direction
pointers is highly relative. Still, they possess some historical interest.
Thus, production of steel ingots and castings, the primary substance of
industrial civilization, had climbed steadily, with only one pause, from
19.8 million tons in 1921 to surpass in 1925 the wartime peak of 45
million tons and to reach 48.3 million tons in 1926. Here there was a
pause and a sharp fall off in 1927 to 44.9 million tons, though followed
by a recovery to 51.5 million tons in 1928 and 56.4 million tons in 1929
—a figure not again to be reached until World War II. Meantime there
had been an actual decline going on in new investment in blast furnace
capacity, that had reached a wartime peak of 53.7 million tons, and had
steadily increased to 59 million tons in 1925, but that thereafter began
to fall off and did not again pass the 59 million ton figure until 1942.
Investment in residential construction, and consumer purchases of new
automobiles and other "durable" goods, had also begun to fall off, reflecting an exhaustion of individual purchasing power. Construction of
urban dwellings reached a peak in 1925, and began to drop sharply, to
less than half by 1929.† Production of motor vehicles dropped from $2.5
billion value in 1926 to $1.97 billion in 1927, but recovered to reach
$2.57 billion in 1929.

---

*In 1965, 646 taxpayers reported adjusted gross income in excess of $1 million. Between
1967 and 1976, the number hovered between 800 and 1,300.
†The David M. Blank index dropped from 208.1 in 1925 to 100 in 1929 (1929=100).

The movement of wholesale prices also reflected an incipient lassitude in business. The index—using the Bureau of Labor Statistics data for 1947–49 as a base of 100—had recovered from the unprecedented 1920 break, and had risen from 62.8 in 1922 to 67.3 in 1925. At that point it "peaked" as the statisticians say, and then began a slow but certain decline that accelerated after the stock market crash, and eventually reached a low of 42.1 in 1932.

Meantime, the security markets either ignored, or could not interpret these signs, for security prices, fortified by ample credit, moved spectacularly upward, with the index of 500 stocks (1941–43 = 10) climbing from 8.41 in 1922 to 12.59 in 1926 to 26.02 in 1929, from which height it dropped to 6.93 in 1932. The meaning of these figures will be grasped when they are translated into the billions of dollars which they reflected in quoted prices for stocks and in the balance sheets of corporate and individual investors.[1]

The fact—recognized then as now—was that an unwholesome amount of the country's liquid resources were being drawn into speculative channels. Early in the decade there was a great boom in Florida real estate, but figures are lacking to trace its influence statistically. That frenzy collapsed in 1926, but the significance of the collapse was ignored by the stock market. The volume of stock sales in the New York Stock Exchange increased from 259 million in 1922 to 451 million in 1926, and more than doubled in the next two years with over 1,125 million shares traded in 1929.

These happenings, let us remark, did not go unnoticed by the authorities of the Federal Reserve System; but whether they misinterpreted their significance, or appropriately reasoned that it was neither their function nor responsibility to intervene and to attempt to direct the course of credit, may well be argued. In 1927 the authorities began to take notice of a similar scissors movement in credit. The calm, impersonal, judicial view which they took of this development is reflected in the language of the Board's report for 1927, which we quote:

> In consequence of a somewhat smaller volume of production and employment in 1927 the demand for bank credit to finance trade and industry was no larger than the year before. There was nevertheless a rapid growth of member bank credit, total loans and investments of all member banks increasing by $2,783 million, and that of reporting member banks in leading cities by $1,673 million, or 8.4 per cent. This compares with 2.1 per cent in 1926 and 5.2 per cent in 1925. That the growth of Reserve bank credit has not been due to demand for loans for industry or trade is indicated by fact

that all other loans, which comprise loans for agricultural and industrial purposes as well as commercial loans, actually decreased during the year.

The Report went on to comment that loans on securities meantime had increased 15.8 per cent, and that "the decrease in other loans would have been larger but for the real estate loans, which increased $276 million, while commercial loans proper decreased $230 million."

During 1927, the Federal Reserve, to counter the business decline that had begun, had adopted a moderate "easy money" policy, made effective through authorizing reductions in the discount rate and increasing the System's open market purchase of securities. The discount rate was reduced in August from 4 per cent to 3 1/2 per cent; open market purchase of securities rose from $210 million at the end of June to $392 million at year end, but this was less significant than it appears, for ordinarily the end of June figures ran substantially less than end of year figures.

Early in 1928, the Board concluded that business no longer required the stimulus of easy money, and "determined to exercise its influence toward firmer money conditions."[2] The Reserve banks therefore sold securities in the first six months in approximately the same amount as they had purchased earlier to offset the gold outflow of the previous year.

Actually, the actions of the Reserve authorities to modify the diversion of credit to the security markets remained, in accordance with their stated policy, tentative and modest until early in 1929. On February 7 of that year, the Board addressed the member banks by letter, stating:

> During the last year or more the functioning of the Federal Reserve System has encountered interference by reason of the excessive amount of the country's credit absorbed in speculative security loans. The volume is still growing. . . . The matter is one that concerns every section of the country and every business interest. . . .
>
> The Federal Reserve Board neither assumes the right nor has it any disposition to set itself up as an arbiter of security speculation or values. It is, however, its business to see to it that the Federal Reserve banks function as effectively as conditions will permit. . . . The extraordinary absorption of funds in speculative security loans . . . deserves particular attention. . . . A member bank is not within its reasonable claims for rediscount facilities when it borrows for purpose of making or maintaining speculative loans.[3]

For a less formal and more intimate statement of the theory and convictions upon which Federal Reserve policy moved, we have an illuminating article written by Owen D. Young for *Review of Reviews* for September, 1928. Mr. Young was at this time chairman of the board of General

Electric Company and of the Radio Corporation of America, two of the largest business enterprises of the country, and was also deputy chairman of the Federal Reserve Bank of New York. Explaining the Board's action in 1927 in reducing the rediscount rate from 4 to 3 1/2 per cent, he wrote:

In the summer of 1927, the European exchanges were weak, just at the time that our fall crop movement was coming on. The export of our agricultural surplus was the most important factor of our domestic economic problem. It was obvious that the buying power of Europe for our agricultural products, and to some extent for our manufactured products, would be greatly curtailed if the foreign currencies were at an abnormal discount.
. . .

In August, 1927, the rediscount rate of the Federal Reserve Bank of New York, and of the other banks generally throughout the System, was 4 per cent. Had not this foreign situation existed, it would probably have remained at 4 per cent, but the administrators of the Federal Reserve System concluded to make the rediscount rate 3 1/2 per cent in order that so far as the rate could influence the money market, money in New York might be cheap as compared with the rates in London, Paris, Berlin, Amsterdam, and other financial centers.

This disparity would tend to strengthen the foreign exchanges and increase the buying power of Europeans for our cotton, wheat, and other food supplies, and at the same time provide cheap domestic money for the movement of the crops. It was most important, not only in the interest of our farmers, but in the economic interest of the whole country that our surplus should be exported, rather than be left to depress the domestic price.

That action, which I believe was wisely taken, had the desired effect; and the recent improvement in our agricultural situation as well as the continued export of our manufactured goods has been aided, in my judgment, by that action of the Federal Reserve System. . . . It was also apparent that our domestic business was slowing down, and that as a result we would, in the normal course, have increased unemployment in the winter. Insofar as the Federal Reserve System could stimulate business with a low discount rate it was clearly wise both from the standpoint of our exports and our domestic consumption.

Mr. Young went on to observe that the policy misfired, that business, already financed, did not make use of this credit, and it was instead largely absorbed in the stock market.

"During the late autumn of 1927," he continued,

the question of whether the rate should be restored to 4 per cent was frequently discussed, but that was not done until February 3, 1928.

It may be that the Federal Reserve System could have—without danger to our export situation and our domestic business situation—and therefore should have, advanced the rate to 4 per cent earlier than it did. But it was wise, I am sure, to have resolved the doubt in favor of our export and domestic business situation even if, as a collateral consequence, too much credit was going into the stock market.

The European exchanges being strong, and the European countries being in need of more gold to ballast their currencies, it was quite natural that a gold flow should start out of this country. Looked at in a large way, that was to be desired, because it would reduce the temptation to uncontrolled inflation. Since November, 1927, something like $500,000,000 in gold has been exported. One would have thought that speculators and financial people generally would have given immediate attention to this movement and realized that it would increase proportionately the rediscounts at the Federal Reserve banks. As a matter of fact, no attention was paid to it. Brokers' loans rapidly increased in the face of it, and credit became still further expanded.

The Federal Reserve System thereupon began to sell securities from its portfolio to the market, which would have the effect of tightening money rates. As a result of the gold exports and these sales, the banks borrowed additional sums from the Federal Reserve banks, and in order to discourage borrowing the rate was advanced in New York to 4 1/2 per cent on May 17, 1928.

As a result of all of these factors, rates for call money on the Stock Exchange went up, and as might be expected, in a highly speculative atmosphere they fluctuated widely and abruptly. The result was that although the member banks endeavored to call their loans and reduce the amount of credit in the stock market, private individuals and large corporations withdrew their surplus funds from deposit with the banks, and put them directly on call. This had the effect of taking control of the money market, to some degree, out of the hands of the banks and out of the Federal Reserve System.

The banks are now borrowing over a billion dollars from the Federal Reserve. This amount is double the borrowing of the same banks from the System a year ago, largely because of gold exports and Federal Reserve sales of securities. The banks are trying to pay off some of these loans, because they quite properly believe that Reserve credit should be used only to meet seasonal and other temporary needs. If the banks are to pay off the Federal Reserve they must seek funds to that purpose by restricting their loans both at home and abroad.

Following this narration of Reserve actions, Mr. Young went on to a spirited defense and explanation of Federal Reserve policy and philosophy, as it was then understood:

"Now," he declared,

I would not have any one think from what I have said that the Federal Reserve System has its eye on the stock market. That is the last thing that enters into its consideration. The System has its eye on the business interests of the

United States. It desires to contribute to stability in the purchasing power of our money, and to provide proper credits for business at reasonable rates without wide fluctuations.

When, however, it became apparent that Federal Reserve credit, created primarily for business and made cheap to aid business, is being principally used for speculative purposes, then it becomes the duty of the Federal Reserve System to limit that credit to our commercial needs. It is not its purpose to control prices on the Stock Exchange but it is true that as a consequence of adjusting credit to commercial needs, prices on the Stock Exchange may be affected.

There are some who believe that when the Federal Reserve System knew that its member banks were permitting credit in large amounts to go into the stock market, it should have refused the credit. Also, it has been suggested that if the Federal Reserve System will not undertake the responsibility, then a law should be passed penalizing, through taxation, the use of credit for speculative purposes which Congress might from time to time think undesirable.

I have grave doubts about the wisdom of such action. It is a tremendous power to pass over to a few men in a central bank to determine in specific instances the purposes for which their credit shall be used. . . .

As to Congress using the limitless power of taxation in the assignment of credit, that seems to me to be fraught with much greater danger than the evils which it is designed to cure.

A central bank, as I see it, should be influenced in its action only by the economic conditions of the country as a whole. It cannot determine the size of the pot of credit, nor can it determine the price; but it can, in some measure, influence both; and that influence should be exercised in the light of economic conditions as a whole.

Whether the pot of credit should be used for one thing or another should, in my judgment, be left to competitive economic forces uncontrolled by political interference either directly by law or indirectly through a quasi-governmental institution, such as the Federal Reserve System.

Then, too, it must be remembered that call money on the Stock Exchange is now being supplied in substantial measure by others than the member banks of the Federal Reserve System. Large corporations and wealthy individuals are withdrawing their money from deposit and putting it on call. I suspect even that individuals are borrowing at their banks and putting the money on call, scalping the margins.

All this shows that if we take the member banks out of the call loan market by arbitrary controls, it will not be long before the banks and the Federal Reserve System will have no direct control of the call market whatever. Their influence right now is relatively small. The large New York banks have called a very large percentage of their loans, but the vacuum created by their call has in many instances been filled by their own depositors withdrawing deposits, which again has forced the banks, even against their wills, into the Federal Reserve bank. This development of companies and individuals, and even mutual savings banks, putting money direct into the market is a new one, which is outside the control of the Federal Reserve System.

I think the creation of the Federal Reserve System was a great piece of constructive legislation, and I believe that by and large its administration has been wisely handled in the interest of all the people of the United States. . . .

Owen D. Young's analysis is significant not only as a reflection of the views of the men who were at the time dominant in the determination of monetary policy, but as a revelation of the awareness, on the part of the business community, of the extent and nature of the security speculation then gripping the country, and of its potential for disaster.

As Mr. Young conceded, however, the Federal Reserve was as powerless before this phenomenon as a lone cowhand to stem a stampede of maddened cattle. Too much money was awash in the economy, and it was flowing in to the stock market through a hundred channels other than the banks.

Despite this brave appraisal of the importance of the Federal Reserve System and sage defense of its restricted policy, the fact remained that the Federal Reserve was the ultimate source of this flood of credit.

The Federal Reserve, indeed, was no more than the sorcerer's apprentice, whose witless meddling in his master's absence conjured his disaster.

Before tracing the final movements of the tragedy of 1929, let us look again at the changes in the monetary system introduced by the Federal Reserve Act, and how they provided the leverage for the greatest credit boom in modern times.

19.

The Fulcrum and the Lever

T HE REVIEW OF THE DEBATE leading to the passage of the
Federal Reserve Act, which we have presented in earlier chapters,
has made clear that it was the "liberal" or Bryan wing of the Democratic
Party that carried its way in the formation of the new system. The one
thing it demanded was a mechanism for making money and credit more
plentiful. It was the "flexible currency" provision of the act that obtained
the endorsement of the commercial and banking community. To the
naive or conservative element this meant a release mechanism, a safety
valve, for times of emergency, and for emergency use only; for those
more sophisticated it meant cheaper and more plentiful money, and the
prospect of credit-debt expansion on a scale vaster than ever. To the
bankers, it offered the employment of a larger proportion of total assets
in the market, hence with greater profit on bank capital; to the commercial community, it provided easier credit, with money more freely available, if not at lower rates at least for a wider and more speculative range
of ventures.

A realistic appreciation of these factors was written at the time by the
noted journalist C. W. Barron, whom we quote:

> The "motif" underlying the Federal Reserve Act is not that which is nomi-
> nated in the bond. "An elastic currency" could have been had by an enact-
> ment of twenty lines. The 'means of rediscounting commercial paper' are
> already at hand and such discounts exist to the extent of at least 100 millions
> in the national banking system. It is not "to establish a more effective supervi-
> sion of banking in the United States," for that could be accomplished by
> increasing the appropriation and enlarging the salaries of the examiners, so

that men with larger experience and breadth of vision would perform more effective supervision.

The purpose of the act most largely in its inception was "for other purposes," and these "purposes" can never be wisely or effectively carried out; if persisted in they spell disaster to the country. The hidden purpose or "motif" which inaugurated this legislation, however in effect it may work out under wise administration, is to cheapen money.

The whole primary discussion of this bank act was to make money easier, to cheapen it to the farmer and producer and manufacturer and merchant. Senators and representatives both proclaimed within and without Washington that what they were seeking was a financial system that would give us an average rate approaching that of the Bank of France, where interest over a series of years averages between 3 and 4 per cent. They frankly said they hoped for something under the 4 per cent rate.[1]

The credit leverage provided by the Federal Reserve System, paradoxically enough, was found not so much in the reserve requirements imposed upon the Reserve banks—around which so much of the Congressional debate revolved, as in the reserve requirements for member banks.

At the time of the creation of the System, much emphasis had been placed on the note issue functions of the Reserve banks (the banks being permitted, in effect, to issue legal tender notes against a combined security of gold and certain types of commercial instruments of debt, provided the gold proportion of the reserve constituted at least 40 per cent of the total). Because of the growth of check-money and the expansion of deposit credit, however, the real leverage in the money system occurred in the banking reserve requirements of the System. The opportunity offered for bank credit inflation will be understood by setting forth the various reserve requirements, and the manner in which they were manipulated:

(1) The Federal Reserve System lowered the reserve requirements against deposits. The national banking system had classified banks according to the size of the city in which they were located, as central reserve city banks, reserve city banks, and country banks. For central reserve city banks a reserve of 25 per cent of total net deposits was required to be held in cash in the bank's own vaults; for reserve city banks a reserve of 25 per cent of total net deposits, of which one-half might be held on deposit with designated correspondent banks; and for country banks, a reserve of 15 per cent of total net deposits, of which three-fifths might be held on deposit with designated correspondent banks.

The Federal Reserve Act classified deposits into two categories, demand and time, with separate reserve requirements for each category.

For demand deposits the Act reduced the reserve requirements to 18 per cent for central reserve city banks, of which six-eighteenths (6 per cent of total net demand deposits) were to be held in the bank's own vault, seven-eighteenths to be held on deposit with the Federal Reserve Bank for its district, and five-eighteenths optional, either in the bank's own vault or on deposit with the Federal Reserve bank. Reserve city banks were required to maintain against demand deposits a reserve of 15 per cent, of which five-fifteenths (5 per cent of total net demand deposits) should be held in vault, six-fifteenths on deposit with the Federal Reserve bank, and four-fifteenths optional. Country banks were required to maintain reserves of 12 per cent against demand deposits, of which four-twelfths (4 per cent of total net demand deposits) should be held in vault, five-twelfths on deposit with the Federal Reserve bank, and three-twelfths optional. For time deposits the reserve was only 5 per cent for all classes of banks.

(2) By the Act of June 21, 1917, as an aid in floating government war loans, the reserve requirements were further relaxed, the proportionate reserves being reduced to 13 per cent, 10 per cent and 7 per cent, according to the classification of the bank, with 3 per cent for time deposits for all classes. The amendment provided that all reserve cash should be held on deposit with the Federal Reserve banks.

Since till, or vault, cash could no longer be counted as reserves, the effect of the amendment was to encourage the banks to maintain even smaller amounts of vault cash, in order to expand their operations to the maximum, and to rely on the nearby Reserve bank for accommodation to meet sudden cash withdrawals. For instance, between June, 1917, before the new reserve requirements went into effect, and June 30, 1930, net demand plus time deposits of member banks of the Federal Reserve System increased from $12 billion to $32 billion, but holdings of vault cash at the same time decreased from about $800 million to less than $500 million. By making progressive economies in their use of vault cash at a time of rapid increase in their deposit liabilities, member banks were able to reduce their vault cash to less than 3 per cent of their net demand plus time deposits by 1919, to less than 2 per cent by 1924, and to less than 1.5 per cent by 1930. In New York City, for instance, member bank holdings of vault cash in June, 1930, averaged only three-fourths of 1 per cent of their net demand plus time deposits and less than 1 per cent of their net demand deposits alone. The practical effect of the 1917 amendment was, it was found, to reduce reserves against net demand deposits from 18 per cent to 14 per cent for central reserve city banks and from

15 per cent to 12 per cent for reserve city banks, with no change for country banks.[2]

(3) During the decade ending 1930, at a time when the banking power of the country was being strengthened inordinately by large accretions of gold from abroad, the banking system further diluted its reserves by a process of wholesale reclassification of demand deposits into time deposits in order to take advantage of the lower reserve requirements. A special investigation conducted in May, 1931, by the Federal Reserve System revealed that out of $13 billion of time deposits held by member banks at that time, $3 billion consisted of individual accounts with balances in excess of $25,000. Even though accounts of this size may consist of inactive deposits with a low turnover, the Committee on Member Bank Reserves concluded that they were not the typical small savings accounts for the accommodation of which the low reserve against time deposits was primarily instituted. In 1914, when national banks were required to maintain the same reserve against all of their deposits, they held only about $1.2 billion in time deposits. Following the lowering of the reserve requirements against these deposits, time deposits increased steadily and amounted to about $8.7 billion at national banks alone in 1930. During the same period, time deposits of non-national commercial banks, including both state member and non-member banks, increased from about $2.8 billion to $10.2 billion and savings deposits of mutual and stock savings banks from $4.8 billion to $10.5 billion. The increase in time or savings deposits for national banks was over 600 per cent, for non-national commercial banks over 250 per cent, and for savings banks 120 per cent.

"With only a 3 per cent reserve required against time depsoits," the Committee found, "there is an inducement for member banks to persuade or permit commercial customers to classify a large part of their working accounts as time deposits and then to permit a very rapid turnover on that small part of these accounts that remain in the demand-deposit classification."

As a result of these various provisions and subterfuges, the Committee reported, between 1914 and 1931, the period covered by its survey, total net deposits of member banks increased from $7.5 billion to $32 billion or more than 300 per cent in less than two decades. Some of this increase reflected the accession of state banks to membership in the Federal Reserve System, but the greater part reflected the expansion of member bank credit. While war financing and the huge inflow of gold which followed the war constituted the immediate driving force back of much of this expansion, it was facilitated by a progressive reduction in effective member bank requirements for reserves. Thus member banks actually held (in 1931) about $2.9 billion of reserves against $32 billion of net deposits. These reserves were both the legal reserves which they held with the Federal Reserve banks and cash which they held in their vaults. If the vault cash requirements of national banks prior to 1914 had been retained in the Federal Reserve Act, member banks would have been required to hold about $4.4 billion instead of $2.9 billion. This means that, in the aggregate, total reserve requirements were about 34 per cent less in proportion to their deposits than they were before the Federal Reserve Act was passed. "It is clear, consequently," said the Committee, "that the largest expansion of member bank credit since 1914 has been facilitated by a progressive diminution in reserve requirements as well as by large imports of gold."

(4) As the reserves held by member banks against their deposit liabilities are concentrated in the Federal Reserve banks, so these reserves in turn constitute deposits with the Federal Reserve banks. Against these deposits, which are the prime reserves of the commercial banks, the Federal Reserve banks were required to hold gold to the extent of only 35 per cent. In other words, just as commercial banks were enabled to expand their liabilities on the basis of small amounts of cash, so the Federal Reserve banks were enabled to expand their liabilities upon small amounts of gold. This was achieved by permitting member banks to strengthen their reserves with the Federal Reserve banks by borrowing upon the security of government bonds and by the discounting of their commercial paper. If a bank wished to expand its operations, and had not the cash for the minimum reserve requirements it could, in effect, create a fictitious reserve by borrowing the credit of the Federal Reserve bank. The only limit was the legal restriction upon the Federal Reserve bank against permitting its gold reserve to drop below the 35 per cent minimum ratio to its deposit liabilities. Thus, if the average reserves held by the commercial banks against their deposits were taken as 10 per cent, and the gold reserves held by the System against these reserves at 35 per cent, the actual gold held against the commercial deposits of the System could be reduced to as low as 3.5 per cent.

(5) The final mechanism by which deposits could be inflated was that of "open market operations" by the Federal Reserve banks themselves.

Theoretically designed to enable the central banks to regulate the volume of bank credit, and hence to check, as well as encourage, expansion, it proved more effective as a spur than as a restraint to expansion. Under the Federal Reserve Act, a Federal Reserve bank was authorized to invest not only in rediscounts and advances to member banks, but in a defined category of commercial obligations.* These items could be purchased and sold "in the open market, at home or abroad, either from or to domestic or foreign banks, firms, corporations, or individuals."[3] Such dealings in the money market directly with the public were called "open market operations."

A purchase of investments on the open market is paid for by the Federal Reserve bank either in Federal Reserve notes or by check drawn on itself, depending on whether the bank wishes to increase the actual quantity of money in circulation, or the banking power of the System. If paid in notes, the money passes directly into circulation; if paid by check, the recipient of the check deposits it with his commercial bank, which in turn presents it to the Federal Reserve bank for credit. This credit thus becomes a deposit to the account of the member bank, and as such deposits constitute banking reserves for the member bank, the lending power of the member bank is thereby multiplied. Conversely, of course, the effect of selling portfolio holdings by the Federal Reserve banks is to reduce reserve credit outstanding, and to restrict the lending operations of member banks.

In 1924, with the object of creating money conditions in the international markets favorable to the efforts of Great Britain and a number of lesser European countries to return to the gold standard, the Federal Reserve System embarked on its famous "easy credit" policy, by reducing the rate at which it lent to member banks (the rediscount rate) and by forcing Reserve bank credit into the banking system by heavy open market operations. As a result, between the end of 1923 and the end of 1927, $548 million of Federal Reserve credit had been forced into the banking system by purchases of bills and securities. This amount must be multiplied many times to appreciate its effect on the credit power of the banking system.

During the early years of this policy, the effect of this leverage was nullified to some extent by the more cautious policy of the commercial

---

*United States government securities, and certain types of agricultural credit obligations, municipal warrants, trade acceptances and bankers' bills.

banks themselves, which took occasion to reduce their own borrowings at the Reserve banks from $857 million to $314 million during the year 1924. They soon began to get the idea, however, and encouraged by the reduction of the rediscount rate from 4.5 per cent to 3 per cent (in New York), they began again to borrow to increase their reserves, and their own lending power. By the end of 1927 they were again in debt by the amount of $609 million.

When the central bank authorities became alarmed in 1928 over the results of their easy credit policy, and attempted to halt the further expansion of credit, it was too late. As rapidly as the Reserve banks drew credit out of the banking system by the process of selling bills and securities, it was siphoned back in by the banks increasing their own borrowing. By the end of July, 1929, the Reserve banks had reduced the volume of their open market purchases to $222 million, but meantime member banks had increased their borrowings to $1,076 million, and when the Reserve authorities began to shake their fingers in warning, the head of the largest American bank replied by thumbing his nose and announcing that his institution would continue to support the security markets, and had $25 million to lend.

The actual degree to which the gold reserves of the Federal Reserve System were thinned out behind the deposit liabilities at any one time cannot be precisely stated as the gold holdings of the System support both deposit and note liabilities. On December 31, 1928, when the speculative frenzy was approaching a climax, the gold holdings of the System amounted to only $2,584,232,000 against note liabilities of $1,838,194,000 and total net deposit liabilities of member banks of $33,397 million. As the Federal Reserve Act required, as a minimum metallic reserve against notes issued, gold in amount equivalent to 40 per cent of note liabilities, or $735,277,000 at this date, the remaining gold holdings represented a reserve of only slightly over 5.5 per cent of the total commercial deposit liabilities of the System. Actually, of the gold held by the Reserve banks, $1,307,437,000 had been deposited as security against notes issued, so that the remaining gold held by the Federal Reserve banks ($1,276,795,000) constituted a reserve of only 3.9 per cent against the total deposits of member banks.

Not all the gold reserves of the country were concentrated in the Federal Reserve banks, nor, on the other hand, did the Federal Reserve System comprise the total banking power of the country. The greater number of banks were outside the System. At the end of 1928 the total adjusted* deposit liabilities (demand and time) of all banks and trust companies, and currency outside banks, amounted to $55,638 million and the total monetary gold of the country amounted to $3,854 million, representing a reserve of 6.9 per cent.[4]

---

*To exclude inter-bank deposits, items in process of collection, and U. S. government deposits.

20.

⟿⟿⟿⟿⟿⟿⟿⟿⟿⟿⟿⟿⟿⟿

The Gushing Fountain

MEANTIME, along with the relaxation of banking discipline permitted by reserve requirements, an extraordinary change had been going on in the direction in which credit was flowing. We have already noted the vast increase in security speculation. Some further details are in order.

Between June 30, 1921, and June 30, 1929, total loans and investments of member banks increased from $24,121 million to $35,711 million. At the same time, ordinary commercial loans, which traditionally should form the major portion of the assets of deposit banks, fell from one-half to one-third the total. It is a remarkable fact that these loans were actually less in the boom year of 1929 than in the depression year of 1921 in spite of a rise of nearly 80 per cent in industrial production. These loans stood at $12,844 million on June 30, 1921, and at $12,804 million on June 30, 1929.

During these eight years, the more speculative and less liquid loans on securities and urban real estate together rose nearly $8 billion, representing almost three-fourths of the total increase in loans and investments during the period. Diversion of credit into these markets had the two-fold consequence of financing a prolonged and colossal speculation and of loading the banks with the kinds of assets which are particularly difficult to liquidate under conditions of declining prices. From 1922 to 1929, the ratio of loans on securities to total loans and investments of reporting member banks advanced from 25 per cent to somewhat more than 43 per cent; while from 1924 to 1929, the prices of industrial common stocks more than tripled, as we have noted above. On September 30, 1929, New

York banks and trust companies alone had over $7 billion loaned to New York Stock Exchange brokers to finance security speculation.

In addition to the bank credit that flowed into the security markets through stock collateral loans, vast amounts of bank credit were used indirectly, through the investment banking system, in the flotation of new issues. During the five years ending 1924, the average annual volume of new capital issues, exclusive of refunding issues and United States government issues, was $4,280 million. During the next five years the average annual volume mounted to $7,730 million and in 1929 over $10 billion of new capital was subscribed. The total amount of new money made available to corporations, states and municipal bodies, and to foreign governments and corporations, either by way of shares or loans, was in excess of $38 billion in these five years. All these loans and security flotations were sustained and assisted by the use of bank credit.

Not only did the commercial banks assist the process of security speculation by financing the investment banker and the pseudo-investor, but they purchased large blocks of bonds outright. The prospects of high yields and large profits from the turnover of investments filled the portfolios of banks with many high coupon bonds of foreign governments and corporations and with second, third and fourth grade bonds of American companies and municipalities. Between 1921 and 1929, member banks' holdings of securities, aside from United States government securities, increased from $3,507 million to $5,921 million. The result was to convert many a bank from the status of a commercial credit institution to that of an investment company. The unsoundness of this process became apparent later when banks had to liquidate these holdings on a falling market. It was a policy of borrowing at short term (using deposits which are payable on demand) and lending at long term (for bond holdings, despite the fact that they are marketable, are loans at long term) which the banks would never have tolerated on the part of their commercial customers.

A second outlet during the nineteen twenties for the excessive credit created by the banking system was in financing urban real estate. We have already commented upon the Florida land boom. This was not an isolated phenomenon. During the decade 1920–1930, the movement to the cities had accelerated: the population of the sixty-three metropolitan zones (cities of 100,000 or more, plus adjacent counties) rose from 46,491,000 to 59,118,000, or from 44 per cent of total population to 48 per cent.

Seventy-four per cent of the increase in total population during the decade occurred in the metropolitan areas.

A building boom had followed, with the Federal Reserve Board index of building contracts awarded, 1923–1925 taken as 100, rising from 63 in 1920 to 122 in 1925, and 135 in 1928. A characteristic of this activity was that it was concentrated largely in skyscraper offices and expensive apartment house developments, whose notes were more readily marketable, rather than in the modest single family accommodations. The result was that when the era had passed the slums still existed, like rats' nests around the whitened skeletons of downtown mastodons.

The part played by the Federal Reserve System in this unbalanced real estate activity may be noted. Until 1927, national banks were limited in their real estate loans to amounts no greater than 25 per cent of their paid-in capital and unimpaired surplus or one-third of their time deposits; nor could they make loans on improved real estate for more than one year. In 1927, in response to demand for liberalization of these requirements, the MacFadden Act was passed permitting the making of real estate loans to 25 per cent of paid-in capital and unimpaired surplus or one-half of time deposits. In addition, banks could now extend loans to a maximum of five years.

By 1929, member bank loans against real estate, other than farm land, amounted to $2,760 million, against $875 million in 1921, but the growth of bank credit on real estate is not fully indicated by these figures. There is reason to believe that a considerable and increasing proportion of the "commercial" loans made by banks in this period were directly or indirectly loans on real estate. The tremendous urban developments, begun and completed in this decade, and the continued rise in the assessed valuation of real property, coupled with the large real estate holdings of banks disclosed during the resulting depression afforded convincing evidence to the President's Research Committee on Social Trends "of the magnitude of speculative enterprise in real estate and of the important role which banking credit played in its unfolding."[1]

Two other important groups of borrowers appeared at the sylvan pool of credit during this decade, ready to draw off purchasing power as rapidly as it was replenished from the copious springs of the banking system. From the end of World War I down to the end of 1929, over $9 billion was lent abroad, the movement reaching its peak in the four years 1925–1928, when nearly $4.8 billion in foreign government and corporation issues were floated in the New York market. This money was provided, through investment banking channels, by private investors, but the movement was stimulated greatly by the assistance of the commercial banks. While much of this money was invested more wisely than is generally regarded, it is true that sums were provided for all sorts of unwise purposes, from financing reparations payments (in Germany) to building battleships (in Chile) and removing a mountain (in Rio de Janeiro). By 1931, a nominal amount of $2,383 million invested in South America had suffered a market depreciation of over 80 per cent; $1,793 million of European government loans had declined 43 per cent,[2] and by March, 1934, approximately $2,930 million foreign loans were in default.[3]

At home, consumers were discovering the ease of going into debt for automobiles, radios, furniture and groceries. What is now regarded as one of the stronger categories of assets in a bank portfolio, that is to say, consumers' paper, was then a new, undigested, and relatively speculative form of obligation. After the enactment of the Federal Reserve System, the use of consumer credit grew at an astounding rate. In 1910, of total retail sales of $20 billion, approximately 10 per cent are estimated to have been made on credit. By 1929, half the $60 billion of retail sales in that year were credit transactions, and of the $30 billion worth of goods sold on credit in that year, some $7 billion were sold on instalments.[4] Sales made on open account were financed by the store itself, generally by resources supplied by the commercial banks; sales made on instalments were financed through instalment finance companies which in turn discounted a large part of their paper at the banks.

Thus, so effective had been the smiting of the rock that by 1929 the United States was overwhelmed by a flood of credit. It had covered the land. It was pouring into every nook and cranny of the national economy. Flimsy structures of business—the speculative and trading element—it carried away on the crest of the wave, while those of a more substantial and conservative sort it either submerged or destroyed by undermining their foundations.

PART III

Debacle of an Idea

21.

The Crumbling of the Dikes

O N AUGUST 2, 1927, Calvin Coolidge, then vacationing in the Black Hills of South Dakota, issued a cryptic twelve word message: "I do not plan to be a candidate for re-election in 1928." Its effect in the stock market was such as the assassination of Julius Caesar may have had in the trading precincts of the Roman forum: there followed, as the *New York Times* reported, "a pell-mell scramble to sell stocks and opening prices were from 2 to 15 1/4 points lower than the previous day's close."

The market flutter was short lived as banks, institutions, investors rushed in for bargains, and the *Times* took comfort in the "demonstration of the market's inherent strength."

Actually, the market was showing signs of instability that foreshadowed the later collapse. The market had behind it a long period of advances, which were mainly perpendicular during the preceding month. The short interest, which usually cushioned a fall, had been driven out. A week later the tenuous condition of the market became evident when a pool* in Manhattan Supply Co. collapsed—presumably because their credit ran out, this in turn because they could no longer find buyers at still higher prices—and the quotations plummeted 60 points. This was to halve the value of the stock, and the loss of so much paper value ruined a good many investors.

The Manhattan Supply blowup had not been the first. The year before had seen similar bubbles pricked—Devoe & Raynolds, and the Founda-

---

*Meaning a more or less loosely organized group of traders, speculators, or investors.

tion Company—but a few days later the announcement of the receiver-ship of A. L. Fuller Company which was involved in Manhattan Supply touched off a mass of selling which carried with it market leaders like U. S. Steel and General Motors.

Again recovery set in, and William C. Durant, one of the more pictur-esque and spectacular figures of the era, announced that in his opinion the country was "drifting [sic] into a so-called bull market unprecedented in magnitude, which will extend over a period of many years to come—good securities will sell higher than ever before in the history of this country." He went on to say that "money is so plentiful that it is almost a drug on the market, with a prospect that in the very near future the present rate for time money will be considerably reduced."[1]

By September, the stock market was again wildly bullish. In one day Commercial Solvents rose 16 points, General Motors was being bid higher and higher; another stock shot up 19 points. On September 15 the *Times* reported, "Paying no attention to anything but a further fractional lowering of Stock Exchange money rates, yesterday's stock market re-peated many of the extravagancies which have distinguished recent trad-ing. . . . With what even Wall Street for a moment described as a tinge of recklessness, several selected stocks were driven up 7, 8, and 10 points apiece, with advances of 30 to 50 points numerous elsewhere. . . ."

Serious questions were now beginning to trouble the press regarding the speculative nature of the market, but the consensus was that it was all justified by sound prosperity and basic values. The *New York Times* fairly reflected current sentiment when it argued:

> The extravagant rise of the New York stock market, in the Civil War paper-inflation days, is too remote to be recalled; but many people will recall that in 1923, by the *Frankfurther Zeitung's* compilations, the combined stock exchange prices of active German shares rose from 376,685 in January to 22,987,500 in October. That was a fairly respectable achievement in the way of inflation; but it had to be considered, even on the Berlin Bourse, in relation to other markets. The German index number of commodity prices, for instance, based on 100 for 1913, had risen from 43,223 in September, 1922, to 36,200,000 in September, 1923. This, like the rise on the stock exchange, was attributed, not to "credit inflation" but to the fact that the currency's gold value had depreciated at such a rate that, whereas 4 1/2 German marks would once have bought a dollar, the price got to ten billion marks in the Autumn of 1923 and to eight trillion shortly afterward.
>
> The Durants of Berlin in 1922 and 1923 were entirely warranted in prophesying a "bull market of unprecedented magnitude," which was never

to stop rising so long as that type of inflation lasted. But there is not the least analogy between the conditions of that market and conditions now prevalent at New York. Not only is our present Reserve note circulation $25 million less than a year ago and not only, despite our gold importations, has the twelve-months' increase in the total stock of money been only 1 1/2 per cent, but even the so-called "purchasing power of the dollar in pre-war cents" has been rising. . . . Neither "currency inflation" nor "credit inflation" was reflected in general prices.[2]

The market recovered, as it had done repeatedly, but a month later, on September 3, a new storm of selling "out of a clear sky" broke on the Exchange, which in one hour—described as "one of the most hectic hours in the history of the Exchange"—"wiped out thousands of small speculators who up to now had been riding along comfortably on their paper profits."

Roger Babson, the noted market analyst and statistician whose words were accepted as oracular, now came out with a prediction that stocks were due for a collapse not unlike the collapse of the Florida real estate boom. In his opinion, from 60 to 80 points would be shorn from the averages. His reasoning is of interest. He pointed out that while forty leading stocks of the year before, which stood at an average of 190, had maintained this position and had shown gains of some 42 per cent, the number of stocks declining had steadily increased. "There are today about 1,200 stocks listed on the New York Stock Exchange," the statistician said. "If we subtract from this list the forty leaders, we find that about one-half of the remaining stocks have declined during the past year. This means that a great many people have lost money as well as made money. In fact, 614 stocks listed on the New York Stock Exchange are today selling at less than on January 1."[3]

Babson's views were promptly challenged by Professor Irving Fisher, the Yale savant, who announced from New Haven the same day, "Stock prices are not too high and Wall Street will not experience anything in the nature of a crash."

As so often when the experts disagree, the public took its own view, which was recklessly confident, and within a couple of days the market was again boiling, and prices soaring. On September 6 over five million shares traded on a rising market.

The *Times* found wry humor in the influence exerted by assertions of sober economists that "would have been described in the unregenerate past as 'tips on the market.'"

Meantime, little noticed events abroad had been adding their burden to the overweighted, top-heavy credit structures. In April of 1928 a leading Wall Street house, overestimating the enthusiasm of the market, had offered an issue of Danish government bonds at an unprecedented rate of slightly less than 4 per cent. The market refused to absorb the offering and the issue went "sour," with the underwriters compelled to take over the bonds themselves. That marked an end of the bull market in foreign lending, and the repercussions were to be felt a year later in the domestic securities market. Foreign enterprises, finding the fountain drying up, began to curtail their commitments, and Europe began to experience business recession.

At the same time the European banking and monetary structure had become as overstrained as in the United States. There was, to use a phrase, a shortage of liquidity. Despite new gold supplies from the mines at the rate of some $400 million a year, a gold famine prevailed. Gold represented a smaller and smaller percentage of central bank reserves. By the beginning of 1929 the four principal commercial countries—the United States, France, the United Kingdom, and Germany—had increased their gold holdings by 2.4 times over pre-war, but the credit structure had increased even faster, with a steady decline in the reserve ratio. In 1929 the ratio of gold to total reported bank deposits in these countries stood as follows: United Kingdom, 11.3 per cent; France, 7.4 per cent; United States, 6.9 per cent; Germany 3.1 per cent.

In August, 1929, the English promoter Clarence Hatry found himself unable to get further credit, and his empire suddenly collapsed. The disclosure of his defalcations and his arrest on September 20 sent a shudder through the market; investors with suspicions aroused began to sell to realize cash, and American securities held in England began to be offered on the New York Stock Exchange.

Public apprehension mounted. The *Times* commented that, in the words of one customer's man, the brokers are "run ragged" for quotations, and "many of the downtown firms had been obliged to double or triple their switchboard facilities in recent months."

On September 21, Charles E. Mitchell, the exuberant chairman of the National City Bank—which had been the bellwether in leading the commercial banks into the securities flotation business—issued a statement on the eve of sailing for Europe that "there is nothing to worry about in the credit situation."

Meantime, call money went to 10 per cent, and on the twenty-sixth the *Times* reported that "more gullible than usual, Wall Street reveled yesterday in alarmist rumors, whispered stories that this or that firm was 'in trouble,' that pools had collapsed; that banking interests were going to the rescue of or abandoning large operators." It added that "careful enquiry established that all of the stories were baseless."

On the same day the Bank of England raised its discount rate from 5 1/2 per cent to 6 1/2 per cent.

The collapse came as with a dynamited office building or a struck vessel, or a bull in the arena that has received the blade, with a slow settling, with a hurt surprise, and disbelief. This phase, we can now observe in retrospect, began early in October, as day after day reported more declines than rises in the market. October 5 was marked by some "hysterical selling," followed by a week-end recovery, but the following days were of increasing weakness.

On Saturday in the short session of October 19, stocks were driven down in heavy selling which registered losses of from 5 to 20 points, and the rumor spread that the noted speculator, Jesse Livermore, was heading a powerful short interest that was hammering stocks down. The following week was one of combined breaks and declines, marked by a recovery on Wednesday and on Thursday the twenty-fourth a climax with an unprecedented 12,894,650 shares traded and the papers reported the event in four column headlines. Again the House of Morgan became the donjon where the leading bankers gathered and from which communiques issued that basic conditions were "sound" and that the break was "technical."

But Morgan the Elder was no longer on the scene, and the word from J. P. Morgan, Jr. lacked some of the authority of the old man. While Wall Street gave the banking leaders credit for arresting the decline—which was indeed stemmed by banking support—the public had lost hope of ever rising prices and brokers were busy shoring up impaired margins by issue notices for more collateral.

President Hoover—the "engineer in the White House," who had come to office as an oracle of business after eight years as Secretary of Commerce—now issued a reassuring statement that failed to reassure.

On Monday, October 28, the Exchange was overwhelmed with a week-end pileup of orders to sell. Trading volume reached 9,212,800, but this was not the end. Tuesday, October 29, was to go down as the blackest in Wall Street history, with a crash the memory of which has faded; nevertheless, the effects of which after over fifty years still mark the face of business and color the temper of politics and government. On that day the market disintegrated under a volume of 16,410,030 shares, with leading stocks down 25 to 45 points, and with the collateral tragedy of bankruptcies and suicides.

Frantic efforts were made by the business community to restore confidence. U. S. Steel promptly announced a $1 extra dividend and American Can raised its dividend rate from $3 to $4; banks reduced margin requirements to 25 per cent; John D. Rockefeller announced that he was buying stocks; the Bank of England reduced its rediscount rate from 6 1/2 per cent to 6 per cent, followed by a reduction of the New York rate from 6 to 5 per cent; and the press reported that sentiment in Wall Street was more cheerful. But despair did not evaporate, stocks continued to weaken with another big break on November 12, with 6 1/2 million shares traded in a 3 hour session and a still more disastrous break on the thirteenth when 7,761,450 shares were traded. By the end of the year $40 billion had been shorn from paper values of securities; and the effects were beginning to spread throughout the business world and abroad.

22.

The New Thermopylae

THE EFFORTS OF THE HOOVER ADMINISTRATION to arrest the spreading business and social disintegration that followed the stock market collapse may be likened to the stand of the Spartans at Thermopylae. Though the issue was never clear-cut, the failure of these efforts marked in a sense the rout of individualism in American life, and the acceptance of the theories of statism, authoritarianism, government planning, group responsibility.

The significance of the event needs a word, for in fact the issue has never been clearly drawn—or clearly understood—in American politics. The Revolutionary War was fought against the encroachments of authoritarian government into what was conceived to be the proper domain of the individual or the community. Yet in the drafting of the Constitution, and in its early interpretation, the influence of those who believed in strong central government was pronounced, and those in opposition, like Jefferson, who put their faith in individual and community decisions, were frequently of mixed mind in the face of particular situations.

Advocates of the individualistic view, under the label of "laissez faire," have too often been brought to confusion by their faith in the infallible goodness of humankind, and the certainty that the sum of individual actions will result in a general good.

The nature of the cleavage is to be found elsewhere. It lies in the moral responsibility of man. Primitive peoples, as the researches of Lévy-Bruhl[1] show, live predominantly in a state of fear of surrounding natural forces, born perhaps of ignorance. Against these forces their defense must be a group defense, which leads to a group responsibility. That is, in pagan, polytheistic societies, all objects of nature have each their presiding spirit, and any offense to one of these objects by a member of the group (as for instance moving a stone from its place, or breaking the twig of a certain tree) may result in a vengeance taken upon the group, that is, upon the tribe or the clan. Hence the importance of taboo, the breaking of which by any member of the group may lead to condign punishment to propitiate the wrath of the offended spirit. A consequence of this fear, leading to group responsibility, is the limited freedom found in such primitive groups—such that freedom can hardly be said to exist.

Vestiges of this system of beliefs and social governance are found in Old Testament history and teachings. Because Dinah, the sister of Jacob's sons, was defiled by Shechem, the son of Hamor, the prince of the country, as the tribe of Israel encamped before Shalem, the sons of Jacob connived and slew all the males of Shechem and spoiled the city.[2] It was also an Old Testament teaching until Prophetic times, that the sins of the fathers were visited upon the children until the seventh generation. The notion of individual rather than group responsibility does not begin to emerge until Jeremiah, who proclaimed: "In those days they shall say no more, The fathers have eaten a sour grape, and the children's teeth are set on edge. But every one shall die for his own iniquity: every man that eateth the sour grape, his teeth shall be set on edge."[3]

The idea of individuality, along with individual responsibility, found its fullness in the teaching of Our Lord, who declared: "Are not five sparrows sold for two farthings, and not one of them is forgotten before God? . . . Fear not therefore: ye are of more value than many sparrows."[4]

The Old Testament had removed one source of fear, by bringing all subsidiary spirits (nature gods) under the sovereignty of one deity, who was, while a god of vengeance, also capable of mercy. The Christian Dispensation emphasized the mercy of God, and raised mankind from the status of creatures of God (from "slaves" or "servants" to that of "children").[5] The teaching finds its fullest expression in the words of Jesus, "I am come that they might have life, and that they might have it more abundantly."[6] and in Paul's rejoicing in "the glorious liberty of the children of God."[7]

The progress of economic philosophy, however, was to accept the freedom of mankind without the responsibilities which freedom entailed, and in "laissez faire" doctrine teach that the economic system would function best under the natural impulses of man—which were assumed to be good—and without authoritarian interference. Such philosophy ignored the meaning of "original sin" and was therefore defective, and its defects resulted in its ultimate rejection for a return to the pre-Christian and pre-Judaic view of the necessity of authoritarian controls.

This digression into what may be termed theology rather than economics has been necessary to present the dilemma in which President Hoover found himself in his efforts to restore order following the 1929 collapse.

Hoover was dedicated to individualism, though it is not apparent how defined and explicit his convictions were. He was also subject to the political and intellectual currents of his times, and these were already running strongly against individual solutions and in favor of increased governmental and authoritarian intervention. While Secretary of Commerce, Hoover had directed studies to be made to the extent to which the recurrent business cycle could be slowed or modified by counter-cyclical public work expenditures—hardly anticipating either the extent of the future depression or the magnitude of the adopted remedy.

On November 15, 1929, Hoover announced a conference of leaders of business, industry, and finance, on ways to spur business under private initiative, by expanding construction and maintaining employment and wage rates. He thus indicated where responsible leadership should lie, but at the same time he announced that the government at all levels would assist with building projects.

A preliminary conference of Eastern railway presidents issued a statement that they were "unanimous in their determination to cooperate in the maintenance of employment and business progress. . . . The railways would proceed with full programs of construction, and betterments."

Among those attending the November 21 conference were such figures as Henry Ford and Alfred P. Sloan, Jr., heads of the automobile industry; Walter Teagle of Standard Oil, representing the petroleum industry; Owen D. Young of General Electric and the electrical utility industry; Walter Gifford, head of the Bell Telephone System; E. G. Grace and Myron Taylor, of the steel industry, and Julius H. Barnes, representing the U. S. Chamber of Commerce. The press statement that followed was reassuring: construction work would be expanded; the Bell system would spend in 1930 more than the $600 million spent in 1929; other utilities would do likewise. While the automobile representatives were less optimistic, Grace and Taylor promised for the steel industry that plant replacements would be made. Most significant was the commitment of these representatives in regard to wages—cautious, and non-committal: "The President was authorized by the employers who were present . . . to state on their individual behalf that they will not initiate any movement for wage reduction."

Subsequently, the President met with a group of labor leaders headed by William Green, president of the American Federation of Labor, with a resultant statement to the effect that as employers had agreed not to initiate wage reductions labor would not seek wage increases. Henry Ford spectacularly announced that not only was he not reducing wages, but he was raising them.

These conferences were followed by a wire from the President to the governors and mayors urging their cooperation in a program of public works expansion. At the same time he announced a $2 billion program of federal public works.

The editorial of the *New York Times* on these conferences is a fair summary of the Hoover approach:

> It is certainly an experiment "noble in motive" which President Hoover has been trying this week. He is attempting to change the mental attitude of a whole people. By methods which he has made familiar before, and which are now apparently effective, he has sought to bring about a shift in mass psychology. . . . It is a sort of mental transformation which President Hoover is endeavoring to produce. For boom and apprehension he would substitute confidence and hope, founded upon the stable elements in our business and industrial fabric. . . . The best of it all is that in all the outgivings by the Washington Administration, a note of caution has been sounded along with the optimism.[8]

But as the depression spread, with bankruptcies and falling prices, and unemployed men and bread lines, the cry went up as before the Prophet Samuel in ancient Israel, "Make us a king to judge us like all the nations,"[9] and the Administration was impelled more and more into authoritarian programs.

For some years, of course, an increasingly influential school of intellectuals had been urging the virtues of state planning, and authoritarian controls, and Hoover himself, as we have noted, had accepted the idea of public works expenditures as a counterbalance to cyclical dips. Now, leaders of the business world, long champions of "private enterprise," individual effort and "laissez faire," began to urge the importance of state intervention. Among these was William Randolph Hearst, who in 1931 threw the tremendous influence of his newspaper empire in favor of a $5 1/2 billion dollar public works program. The "progressive" Republican Senator Robert M. La Follette, Jr. of Wisconsin introduced a bill to provide $3,750 million for loans to state and other public bodies for public works, and early in 1932 Democratic Senator Robert F. Wagner

(N. Y.), offered a bill providing $750 million as an emergency measure to "prevent starvation and distress in the present crisis."

Hoover resisted all these efforts to involve the federal government, holding that the principal service the federal government could perform was to balance the budget. This position he held to, and it remained the core of the Administration's policy until toward the end of 1931. However, the Administration did support certain actions in what had long been accepted as the proper field of government policy. The Federal Reserve attempted to stimulate business by a further lowering of the discount rate from 5 to 4 1/2 per cent and by the open market purchase of $500 million of securities. In December, 1929, Congress authorized, at Administration request, a reduction of 1 per cent in the income tax, and to cope with falling farm prices the Federal Farm Board advanced $500 million to marketing cooperatives.

Meanwhile, the domestic problem was complicated by the economic deterioration abroad, and when the Credit-Anstalt of Austria failed, there began a general crumbling of credit. In June, 1931, Hoover took the initiative in obtaining a one-year moratorium on German reparation payments but on September 21 the over-valued pound sterling became no longer supportable, and England went off the gold standard. Sweden, Norway, Denmark, Finland, Australia, India and Egypt followed in October.

Hoover now responded to the pressure for more decisive government intervention, but again pretty much on his own terms and in line with his views of the limited functions of government. He announced on October 6, 1931, that he would recommend the creation of an agency similar to the War Finance Corporation with "available funds sufficient for any legitimate call in support of credit."

On January 22, 1932, Congress authorized the Reconstruction Finance Corporation with a limited life of two years (that stretched out for a quarter century and longer) with a revolving lending fund of $2 billion. It could lend to bank and other credit institutions and to railroads, but not to new enterprises.

At the same time, Hoover opposed measures that brought the government in contact with the problems of individuals. He resisted the demand for immediate payment of the veterans' bonus, which was not due for another fifteen years, and vetoed a bill to lend them half the sums due. He opposed direct unemployment relief, holding this was a state and local responsibility. In July, 1932, however, Hoover did agree to the Emergency Relief and Construction Act which authorized $300 million in loans to states and territories for relief and work relief, and $1 1/2 billion for loans or contracts for various kinds of works projects. The funds were made available through the Reconstruction Finance Corporation and could be lent to states and subdivisions, to regulated housing corporations for slum clearance and for housing low-income groups, and to private corporations for a wide variety of construction projects devoted to public use. The act also authorized some $322 million for emergency construction of certain authorized public works. Finally, it amended Section 13 of the Federal Reserve Act to permit Federal Reserve banks in emergency directly to discount certain classes of eligible paper that formerly came to them through member banks.

By the middle of 1931, the voluntary movement to hold wage levels had broken down, and in September the U. S. Steel Corporation began wage cuts, a policy which soon became general. In harmony with his philosophy, Hoover opposed the rising demand for government unemployment insurance schemes.

At the same time that Hoover, at the cost of his political career, opposed the spreading demand for government intervention, he approved an amendment to the Federal Reserve Act that laid the foundation for the greatest invasion of government into the economy in American history. Probably he could no longer withstand the rising demand for inflationary measures, particularly in the House of Representatives, which came under Democratic Party control in the 1930 elections.

The existing Federal Reserve statute, as we have noted earlier, required Federal Reserve notes to be backed by 40 per cent gold and 60 per cent eligible short-term commercial paper. This was in accordance with the theory that the circulation should respond to the ebb and flow of commercial transactions requiring cash.

It was now asserted that the note issue power was being restricted by reason of the scarcity of eligible paper. Meantime, federal revenues had fallen drastically, from $4,177 million in 1930 to less than half that in 1932, and there was an urgent need for cash to meet the federal deficit, which amounted to $2.8 billion for the fiscal year 1931 (ending June 30).

The Administration-sponsored Glass-Steagall Act of February 27, 1932, allowed government bonds as a substitute collateral for commercial paper in the note reserve. The act also loosened the eligibility requirement for discount by allowing the Federal Reserve banks to make advances to member banks on their promissory notes secured by any assets satisfactory to the Federal Reserve bank. While this act was a temporary measure, limited to one year, its effects persisted, for it broke the shell of accepted central banking theory that the note issue should be based upon commercial paper. Like many "temporary" and emergency measures, it was repeatedly extended, and eventually made a permanent part of the Federal Reserve System.*

In May, the House passed the Goldsborough Price Stabilization Bill, which would have directed the Federal Reserve authorities to use their power over money and credit to restore and to maintain the pre-depression price level. However, the bill met opposition in the Senate both from Republicans and from conservative Democrats like Carter Glass, now a Senator, and to forestall it, an amendment to the Home Loan Bank bill, known as the Borah-Glass National Bank Note Expansion Amendment, was offered as a substitute. This made eligible as security for national bank notes for a period of 3 years all U. S. Government bonds bearing interest of 3 3/8 per cent or less—totalling then about $3 billion. This permitted, on the basis of the bank capital outstanding, an expansion of about $920 million in the currency.

At the November, 1932, election, the electorate gave a vote of no-confidence in the Hoover Administration and the Hoover policy; and shortly thereafter, by runs on the banks throughout the country, signalled an equal distrust of the incoming administration. Franklin D. Roosevelt stepped forward in the Capitol plaza to take the oath of office in a land in which every bank and credit institution in the country was in default and no check was cashable, no promissory note valid, no government bond or paper redeemable.

Roosevelt, however, held in his hand the power to reopen the banks, to make money again almost as freely available as water. He had the power, through the Federal Reserve System, to manipulate and manage the money system.

Individualism, as a system of philosophy, was about to disappear from American life under the influence of a new exponent of statism—the English economist John Maynard Keynes.

---

*It was extended for another year before Hoover left office, subsequently for another year with authority to the President to extend it for an additional two years, and became permanent in the Act of June 12, 1945.

23.

⟋⟍⟋⟍⟋⟍⟋⟍⟋⟍⟋⟍⟋⟍⟋⟍⟋⟍⟋⟍⟋⟍⟋⟍

The Keynesian Influence

JOHN MAYNARD KEYNES was not the father of the trend toward government intervention in the economy that has been traced in the preceding pages, but he was its heritor and its most persuasive exponent of the twentieth century to date. Moreover, he provided the movement with such an array of documentation—particularly mathematical, so awe-inspiring to amateurs—and such formidable, if devious, logic, along with a variety of technical formulae for its execution, that he is generally accepted as its apostle. John Maynard Keynes indeed is a phenomenon of this century whose counterpart, in more ways than one, is John Law of the eighteenth, the execution of whose elegant proposals to convert the wealth of France into *livres* bankrupted that fertile kingdom and brought on the French Revolution.

John Maynard Keynes—later to become Lord Keynes—was at once a mathematician, a philosopher, a master of the complicated phrase, as well as an administrator and executive, who in addition to his writings in economics found time to head a large insurance company, help govern the Bank of England, edit a leading economic journal, and to sponsor ballet and drama. Educated as a mathematician, he had entered the Indian Civil Service, and soon won recognition as an economist for his book *Indian Currency and Finance.* This work, published in 1913, foreshadowed his philosophic tendencies and influence.

The government of India, in imposing a gold standard upon a people accustomed to a circulating medium of silver had been in continual difficulties in maintaining a stable exchange rate, and had developed the practice of keeping part of its monetary reserves in London in sterling.

This practice, which he described as the gold exchange standard, Keynes defended with eloquence: "So long as gold is available for payments of international indebtedness," he wrote, "it is a matter of comparative indifference whether it actually forms the national currency."[1]

Keynes returned from India to become a lecturer at King's College, Cambridge. During World War I he was attached to the British Treasury and was its official representative at the Paris Peace Conference up to June 7, 1919. He also sat as deputy for the Chancellor of the Exchequer on the Supreme Economic Council. Frustrated at what he regarded as the fruitlessness of the negotiations and persuaded of the hopelessness of abating the harshness of the peace terms being imposed, he resigned and wrote a book called *The Economic Consequences of the Peace.* His book was widely read, and its impact was profound. It was almost as influential as the course of events in the subsequent modification of the war settlements.

In fact, Keynes in this and later writings was to prove what he himself was to write, somewhat ironically, regarding the influence of economists:

> The ideas of economists and political philosophers, both when they are right and when they are wrong, are more powerful than is commonly understood. Indeed this world is ruled by little else. Practical men, who believe themselves to be quite exempt from any intellectual influences, are usually the slaves of some defunct economist. Madmen in authority, who hear voices in the air, are distilling this frenzy from some academic scribbler of a few years back. I am sure that the power of vested interests is vastly exaggerated compared with the gradual encroachment of ideas.[2]

The influence attained by Keynes is not easy to explain except by the profound respect—almost idolatry—paid to economics and its high priests in an age that worshipped the standard of living above all other reality, and in the United States gave the position of privy council to the Chief Magistrate exclusively to the profession of economics.* What put Keynes above his competitors was partly his capacity for irony and scorn, of which we have just given an example, and his willingness to use it to reduce to ashes all other theories but his own. At the same time he had skill to dress his own ambiguities with such density of verbiage, such mystifying abstruseness, and such mathematical dogmatism as was exceeded only by Karl Marx. All of which served, just as it served the necromancers and astrologers of Babylon, to compel a submissive awe among his readers and listeners. Like Marx, also, Keynes had an infinite

---

*The President's Council of Economic Advisers.

assurance in the immaculateness of his theorems, and they promised in the capitalistic order what Marx promised for the socialistic. Both offered a new world of arrangements that was perfectly explained in accordance with mathematical logic. Actually, while Keynes professed to hold a traditional view, and to uphold the capitalistic order that then seemed in such dire need of defenders, the effect of his theories was to lead mankind down the path of statism, of centralized, bureaucratic planning, and absorption of all energies and all decisions in the governmental apparatus as Marx himself had done.

Space does not here permit an extended discussion of Keynesian economics—a subject on which already libraries exist—beyond the outline of certain features as they bear upon the course of monetary development in this country, that is to say, Federal Reserve policy and practice.

Keynes' economic theories had their beginning in a concern for the unemployment that plagued Great Britain following World War I. A million persons were chronically out of work. He thought a major cause of this condition was the premature attempt to return to the gold standard, which we have discussed in an earlier chapter. In a treatise, *The Economic Consequences of Mr. Churchill,*[3] he argued that raising the international value of the pound sterling to its pre-war parity had made sterling exchange some 12 per cent more expensive to foreign buyers, which meant that British goods for export cost foreign purchasers that much more than formerly. This lessened the demand for British goods and threw out of employment men engaged in making such products. Stated in conventional terms, sterling was over-valued to the detriment of the export trade.

The classical solution to this dilemma would be to reduce production costs accordingly—which meant mainly wage rates, since other costs, such as interest and depreciation, are relatively fixed. Such a reduction in the wage level, Keynes argued, might bring more jobs, but the total wage bill would not be affected (since a larger number of workers would be working at lower individual wages) and hence the total purchasing power of the community would remain at a depressed level. This would tend to throw more men out of work, for the reason that not all wages received go to buy goods that require men's labor, but some part is saved. While some part of the saved portion will be invested in building new factories, houses or other enterprises that give jobs, and hence is returned to the stream of trade, a residue is not invested, but kept in the till or sock.

Out of this theoretical statement of how affairs go, Keynes developed several key propositions of which only two need concern us here.

The first is the Keynes' theory of unemployment, which, to be brief, he traced to lack of adequate investment in new products or productive enterprise. Keynes' significance in current politics arises from the remedy he proposed: monetary control and manipulation. Particularly after World War II, when the fear of economic dislocations following demobilization led to an obsession with "full employment" schemes, Keynes became the prophet of the new order.

Actually, for all that is made of the "Keynesian revolution," Keynes was pretty much in the main stream of economic thought as it flowed out of the fountains of Adam Smith. That stream of thought had always been mechanistic in its treatment of economic phenomena. Adam Smith's *Wealth of Nations* had appeared in the same decade—we might say the same year (1776)—that produced Isaac Watts' steam engine and the Declaration of Independence. It was Watts' achievement, rather than the political ideas fermenting in the New World, that created the profounder impression on Adam Smith. The immaculate working of Boyle's law of gases, that had made the steam engine possible, was too fascinating not to influence a thinker grappling with the mysteries of human behavior in the livelihood activities of mankind. Could not equally universal and immutable laws of human behavior be discovered? Smith thought so: he posited several of them. The law of supply and demand is the most famous, along with the laws of rent and interest.

Keynes' immediate predecessors had already developed the basic framework of Keynes' principal proposition. His contribution lay in the modifications he gave to it, and even more in its applications. Actually, a dispassionate review of the literature leads one to conclude that Keynes was much more a synthesist than a philosopher or a seer. The vogue for his theories is certainly not due to his exposition. The clarity of *The Economic Consequences of the Peace* degenerates to a murky fen of abstractions in *The General Theory of Employment, Interest and Money.*

Other economists—like Schumpeter, Spiethoff, and Robertson, for example—had reasoned that the principal cause of the business cycle was investment fluctuations, and that the balance between savings and investment determines the interest rate. Although Keynes modified this theory of interest determination by his "liquidity-preference" postulate, the substance of his view was not significantly different. It was that the business cycle was caused by variations between the rate of investment and the rate of savings, and that fluctuations in prices are a result of discrepancies between savings and investment.

The dilemma of the day, as it appeared to Keynes and his school, was that when people save they have less money to spend on the products of the factories, and thus they restrict the employment opportunities. This can be overcome by investing in new factories or enterprises the amounts withdrawn by savings. The gap appears in the phenomenon—as it seemed to Keynes—that savings and investment are not the same: some savings are immobilized and do not return to the stream of purchasing power through the investment process. This could be true only when savings could be held in the form of coinage rather than instruments of debt—a remote possibility, the more remote as the so-called money stock consisted more and more of central bank notes and bank deposits.

What made Keynes' theory of significance to central banking—and to this account of the Federal Reserve System—was his solution to the dilemma. This was that governments directly, or through their central banks, should fill in the gap by creating purchasing power. A corollary of this theory was that the public should, indeed, be discouraged from saving in order to use its funds to buy the goods produced by the investments made through the government's manipulation of money. This is the way full employment would be achieved, the way everybody would be supplied with everything, and everyone made happy.

Keynes lived in a world of mathematical symbols: human beings were to him little more than integers in a statistic, or the functional element of an equation. From this viewpoint the errors of his synthesis are more evident, and the structure is seen to be no more than a house of cards. What is less evident is the ease with which this apostle of the mathematical man found such following, particularly in the U. S. where his views made their initial impact upon Franklin D. Roosevelt and governed the great experiment in economic manipulation by government that was the New Deal, and have since become well nigh settled public policy.

The simplest observation, for instance, should be sufficient to demolish the cornerstone of the Keynesian system—that employment is governed by the rate of investment. One need only walk down any street, observe two shops of identical frontage, side by side, selling the same merchandise, and note that one is doing more business and requiring more sales people than the other; that is to say, creating more employment with the same investment. An even simpler demonstration is that of doubling the shift in a factory; here employment has been doubled with no increase in investment.

The fact is, as is apparent to anyone who is willing to look behind the facade of economic theory, the chief factor in employment is human beings and their intelligence and morale. A well-managed enterprise can produce many times the amount of goods as an inefficiently managed one, and employees with good morale are more productive than employees with poor morale.

Some day, we may hope, economists will abandon their efforts to explain and to control the subject matter of their discipline by mathematical formulae and their corollary, laws and regulations, and instead consider it in the light of a moral reality within which human beings act and react.

We may note briefly one further fallacy of Keynes' theory of employment. In today's technology, investment is not made to create employment, rather to create unemployment. That, at least, is the immediate and direct purpose of the huge investment now going on in various processes of automation to replace men with machines, which means of course throwing men out of work. This was also a characteristic of the period in which Keynes was writing—a characteristic which brought forth a school of thinkers, the "technocrats," who proposed to solve this problem not by monetary means but with the slide rule and the steam shovel.

The first task in the examination of any system of philosophy is to analyze its basic propositions. These rest, in every case, upon certain terms or concepts which require definition. This is peculiarly the case where a theorist like Keynes treats concepts as solid, palpable quantities or integers, which can be dealt with in mathematical formulae and equations, and from which can be derived immaculate, unchangeable corollaries. This has, of course, been the perennial failing of economists since Adam Smith. Keynes himself is caustically derisive of the vagueness and ambiguity of economic terminology.

Thus, speaking of capital formation, capital consumption, and capital equipment, he says, "I have, however, been unable to discover a reference to any passage where the meaning of these terms is clearly explained."[4]

Again with reference to the term "marginal efficiency of capital," so common in economic literature, he complains, "But it is not easy by searching the literature of economics to find a clear statement of what economists have usually intended by these terms."[5]

Of the classical theory of the rate of interest, he says again, "Yet, I find it difficult to state it precisely or to discover an explicit account of it in the leading treatises of the modern classical school."[6]

There are others, but the foregoing suffice. Yet for one set of ambiguities Keynes substitutes another, even fuzzier and more abstruse. Thus, his fundamental proposition is that "employment can only increase *pari passu* [step by step] with investment."[7] Yet he presents only the vaguest idea as to what investment is. Investment is considered somehow to be the part of savings spent on capital goods. As he states it, investment represents the "net addition to all kinds of capital equipment, after allowing for those changes in the value of old capital equipment which are taken into account in reckoning net income."[8] His definition includes "fixed capital" and "working" or "liquid" capital.

Now this definition may be meaningful to an accountant drawing up the balance sheet and profit and loss statement of a corporation, in which he makes a subjective assessment of the loss of value of the plant and equipment due to wear and obsolescence, and deducts that value from operating income; but as a statement of an economic principle, on which to hang a whole system of corollaries, and on which a great and powerful nation may base its fiscal policy, it is sheer superficiality if not fatuity.

In Keynesian economics, when a plant manager buys a high powered vacuum sweeper to rid the factory floors of dust and debris that impede efficiency or reduce an accident hazard, that is capital investment; when a housewife buys a one horsepower vacuum sweeper to keep her floor clean, that is consumption expenditure. Why this distinction? Both serve the same utilitarian purpose; both affect the stream of economic activity in the same degree; both have the same economic effects.

What are these economic effects? Contrary to the Keynesian theories which we have quoted above, the investment in both cases tends not to increase employment but to create unemployment. Thus the vacuum sweeper in the factory releases the toil of workmen who formerly at the end of the day were compelled to go about with brooms to clean up the litter. Undoubtedly, the introduction of the machine sweeper allowed the factory manager to dispense with a certain amount of hired labor. Likewise, the vacuum sweeper in the hands of the housewife relieves her of a certain amount of labor and to that degree makes her unemployed. Simple observation discloses that vacuum sweepers, refrigerators, and the various household appliances of the modern world have been main factors in freeing women from household work and permitting them to enter the "labor market," where they add to the number in the statistical compilations of the employed—or unemployed.

Thus, the observed fact is quite contrary to the Keynesian thesis that employment increases *pari passu*—step by step—with investment: actually employment initially tends to decrease *pari passu* with investment. The secular decline in manufacturing employment, along with a tremendous rise in manufacturing output, is so plain in the statistics that the influence of Keynesianism becomes all the more extraordinary. Since these forces were obvious even when Keynes was writing, it is still more remarkable that he should have proclaimed such a theory, and that intelligent men should have accepted it.

The fact, which the late Franklin W. Ryan, the profound student of interest with reference to consumer, or household credit, was the first to point out, is that there is no economic distinction between consumption and investment. The family, as Ryan made clear, is the greatest productive enterprise in society, and it is a mistake to draw distinctions between capital investment and consumer spending, or between consumption and investment.[9]

It is true that Keynes admits to some awareness of this problem, as when he concedes that a problem exists as to whether to regard the purchase of a motor car as a consumer purchase, and the purchase of a house as an investment purchase;[10] but he mostly avoids the issue by resting on the term "entrepreneur" and defining capital goods as the sales made by one entrepreneur to another. Without bothering to define "entrepreneur" in his mathematical glossary, he simply inserts a new equation $(\Sigma A - A,)$ as the amount of consumer expenditure. There are other superficialities in Keynes' reasoning that disclose his ignorance of, if not contempt for, human nature, or the motions of the human spirit as a factor in economic phenomena. We have space to mention only one more. This is the meaning of labor in Keynesian economics. Conceding that "our precision will be a mock precision if we try to use such partly vague and non-quantitative concepts as the basis of a quantitative analysis,"[11] he proceeds to build his system on two concepts, money and labor, as the common denominators to which he believes he can reduce all economic phenomena.*

Labor he defines as follows: "The quantity of employment can be sufficiently defined by taking an hour's employment of ordinary labor as one unit and weighing an hour's employment of special labor in proportion to its remuneration."[12]

The weakness of this concept, apart from the absurdity of trying to devise the weights for "special labor," lies in its misunderstanding of the

---

*"In dealing with the theory of employment I propose to make use of only two fundamental units of quantity, namely, quantities of money value and quantities of employment." (*Op. cit.* p. 41.)

true key to economic production, or output, which has nothing to do with monetary demand and everything to do with human morale—by which is meant the skill and intelligence of management, the skill and intelligence of workmen, together with their common understanding of their task, its importance, and their own importance and significance as human beings. It is well known that where plant morale is good, productivity can be increased with little reference to added capital investment. Some of the best equipped factories have the lowest output.

Until the 1930s Keynes was regarded in Great Britain as an orthodox economist of brilliant if eccentric tendencies, but he never was admitted to the inner circle of policy advisers. His star began to shine when the world grew dark with the credit crisis of 1932. In 1929 he had championed Lloyd George's proposal for public spending to stimulate employment, and in a visit to this country he had met and expounded his views to Franklin D. Roosevelt. They found fertile soil here. An administration that was then grasping at any flotsam that would hold the economy afloat after the 1932 debacle seized upon his theories as the framework of the New Deal. To these developments, as they turned upon Federal Reserve policy, we may now give our attention.

24.

〜〜〜〜〜〜〜〜〜〜〜〜〜〜〜

The Not So New New Deal

T HE AFTERMATH OF THE STOCK MARKET CRASH had been an increase in bank failures. From 498 in 1928 the number had risen to 659 in 1929 and to 1,380 in 1930. The larger, more conservative institutions were now being dragged down by the defaults of customers and correspondent banks. In 1931, 2,293 banks suspended. By 1932, however, the number had begun to fall off, with only 1,453 closing in that year—a significant substantiation of the Hoover thesis that the depression had run its course by the time of the elections. Meantime, the effect of the British suspension of the gold standard in 1931 was a withdrawal of $700 million gold from the U. S. within six weeks, with consequent further impairment of bank reserves. It was in the Far West where the crack opened. In October, 1932, Leuchtenberg has noted, the Governor of Nevada declared the first of the state "bank holidays," which permitted the banks to close their doors and suspend payments without going into actual insolvency.[1] On Valentine's Day, 1933, the banks of Michigan— where the depression in the automobile industry had been most disastrous—were closed by similar action. The movement now spread, and by March 3, the eve of Roosevelt's inauguration, the banks of twenty-three states were closed, and on the morning following, Governor Lehman of New York issued a proclamation closing the banks in that state, an action that was immediately followed by the remaining states. Throughout the United States it was impossible to cash a check, and since some 90 per cent of all payments were made by check rather than cash, the consequence was that business was at a standstill.

With the country in practical paralysis, and in a condition of near panic,

179

Congress was prepared to grant dictatorial powers to the incoming administration and the wonder is at the modesty of the *carte blanche* which it requested. While Roosevelt was an experimenter and innovator, his philosophical—or perhaps more correctly, his sentimental—attachments were to the old order—the capitalistic system, the tradition of wealth and aristocracy of the Dutch patroons, of whom he was descended. Franklin Roosevelt was at this stage certainly far less radical, that is, less inclined toward state intervention than the earlier Theodore. Still he was inclined to gather power into his hands on the same theory as many predecessors in history—in order that he might return it to the people: he restricted their liberty in order to enlarge their freedom. In this respect he stood, of course, in the tradition of the Caesars and Augusti of Rome.

The National Recovery Administration, with its attempt to organize labor and business in quasi-autonomous groups operating under "codes of fair competition" that were to be self-enforcing and self-administered, was a recall of the medieval guild system; and the mass of new regulatory laws and agencies were a reversion to the state interventionism of Elizabethan England.

From our viewpoint, the most interesting throw-back was the New Deal solution to the money crisis, which had its origin in the reforms of Solon in Athens of the sixth century B.C.

That story has been told elsewhere:[2] here we can repeat only the highlights.

Solon, a war hero, and universally popular, had won election as archon in the midst of mankind's first monetary crisis. Coinage was relatively new at the time, having been introduced into Greece from Lydia probably not more than a century earlier. The existence of a uniform standard of payments—the Greek drachma was noted for its purity and beauty—facilitated trade and promoted the spread of banking and credit. The peasant landowners, particularly, went into debt with the evidence, in the form of engraved stone pillars, standing on the mortgaged land. At the same time, the growth of shipping had brought the cheap wheat of the fertile Egyptian Delta into competition with the hard-won tillage of the stony Greek hills. Falling prices, and mortgage payments to meet, induced an agricultural crisis similar, we may imagine, to the farm strikes of the Hoover era and the later peasant protests in France.

Solon's first action as archon was a decree—the *Seisachthia* or Overthrowing of Pillars—that effectively abrogated the farm mortgage debt in favor of the Greek landowners. To meet the resultant complications—the loss to the city merchants and banker creditors—he authorized the payment of commercial debts in drachmas of reduced weight. The devaluation was approximately 26 per cent.

The devaluation of the drachma—the first debasement of money which history records, but not the last—seems to have been successful, but it is noteworthy that thereafter the municipal officials of Athens in assuming office were required to take an oath not to tamper with the currency and this restraint characterized subsequent Greek monetary experience.

Devaluation of the dollar was not indeed part of the Roosevelt New Deal program. Upon his inauguration, he had issued an Executive Order under the dubious authority of the war-time Trading with the Enemy Act of 1917, by which he forbad the export of gold and trading in gold and proclaimed a national bank holiday. When the Congress was convened by him on March 9, in an atmosphere of war-time crisis, it was generally anticipated that he would call for nationalization of the banking system. The bill which he now submitted for passage did not go so far. Part of this may have been due to the influence of the advisers whom he called in: George Harrison, Governor of the New York Federal Reserve Bank; Arthur Ballantine, Hoover's Under Secretary of the Treasury, whom Roosevelt kept on in the same post; and Ogden Mills, Hoover's Secretary of the Treasury. While the bill validated his executive decree and gave the government the monopoly of gold, it went no further than to authorize the issuance of Federal Reserve bank notes against whatever collateral the banks held—dollar for dollar against government bonds and notes, and 90 per cent of the value of notes, drafts, bills of exchange or bankers' acceptances tendered. Commercial banks were put under the absolute control of the Secretary of the Treasury, so long as the emergency was declared in effect, and the Comptroller of the Currency was authorized to appoint conservators to supervise the operations of individual banks. At the same time, to hasten the reopening of banks by restoring their reserves, the Reconstruction Finance Corporation was directed to purchase the preferred stock of banks at the request of the Secretary of the Treasury.[3]

The passage of the Emergency Banking Act, followed by the President's radio "fireside chat" on the following Sunday evening (the twelfth), assuring the American people that their deposits were now safe, was electric in its effects. By March 15, about half the banks, holding some 90 per cent of the deposits of the country, were reopened, and within three weeks some $1,185 million of currency had been redeposited in the banks. By the end of June, all but 3,871 of the 18,394 banks in being at the beginning of the year had been reopened, but many small communities continued without banking facilities for months longer, and many banks never reopened.

Meantime, the debates on other, not quite so urgent, legislation to resolve the crisis disclosed the strong inflationary mood of the country. The principal problem, of course, was prices, which had plunged downward, to the disaster of those who owned money—though not so steeply nor so far as during the price debacle of 1920.* In the Senate, Burton K. Wheeler advocated, and nearly obtained, passage of a bill restoring free coinage of silver at the ratio of 16 to 1, and in the debate on emergency farm legislation, Senator Elmer Thomas of Oklahoma introduced as an amendment an omnibus inflation authority. Roosevelt opposed the amendment, but following a spirited White House conference with the sponsor and with Senator James F. Byrnes, and to the dismay of his advisers, he agreed to accept the amendment if the amount of the greenback issue were limited, and the other authorities were discretionary rather than mandatory.⁴ Probably a factor in Roosevelt's mind was the almost unlimited discretionary power over the money system which it gave him.

The significance of the Thomas amendment is that it formally took the U. S. off the gold standard. It gave the President authority to reduce the statutory gold and silver content of the dollar by as much as 50 per cent, to accept at 50 cents an ounce up to 400 million ounces of silver in discharge of foreign government debts owing the U. S., and to issue silver certificates to the extent of such silver received. Since the silver was monetized at $1.29 per ounce (unless the silver dollar should also be devaluated as permitted by the Act) this meant multiplying by more than two and a half times the purchasing power of silver acquired. It also gave to the Executive authority practically to direct the Federal Reserve banks to purchase up to $3 billion of government securities, under penalty of direct issue of $3 billion Treasury circulating notes ("greenbacks") under the Civil War Act of 1862. The Thomas amendment met unexpected opposition from conservatives, among them Carter Glass, who had been offered the post of Secretary of the Treasury; but the Roosevelt influence, combined with the crisis mood, was decisive.

Despite the apprehensions of Roosevelt's advisers—Lewis Douglas, the budget director, thought the Thomas amendment marked "the end

*The BLS index of wholesale prices, all commodities, (1926=100) dropped from 95.3 in 1929 to 64.8 in 1932, compared with a drop from 154.4 in 1920 to 97.6 in 1921. (*Historical Statistics of the U. S.*)

of civilization"—Roosevelt was circumspect in his use of the Thomas amendment powers. What seems to have been decisive in bringing him to an about-face, and to the adoption of radical monetary measures, was the writings of a Cornell University economist, Professor George F. Warren, whose specialty was land management rather than money, and Herbert Bayard Swope, who was a journalist. Swope had written a memorandum on the advantages of domestic price lifting and Warren had written a book on gold and prices with Professor Frank A. Pearson, which seemed to demonstrate conclusively that prices moved in accordance with the price of gold. Roosevelt was a country squire by temperament, and he had always shown an especial interest in rural economics, and it was natural that the views of an agricultural economist should obtain his sympathetic attention. Warren held—and Roosevelt was persuaded—that by raising the price of gold, it would be possible to achieve all that legislation and monetary policy had been seeking to achieve, namely a rise in the general price level.

The natural Rooseveltian conservatism of these early days was particularly manifested in his attitude toward the World Monetary and Economic Conference at London, which he "torpedoed"—to adopt the opprobrium of his critics. The conference had been initiated during the Hoover Administration, and its objectives were restoration of international trade mainly through agreement to avoid competitive currency depreciation and return to the gold standard.

Roosevelt at the first had shown considerable enthusiasm for the conference and had sent his Secretary of State to head the American delegation, but it soon became evident that Roosevelt's views did not accord with those of the European delegation or even of his principal negotiators. From the conservative viewpoint, Roosevelt's view seems the sounder. A declaration had been drawn declaring that stability in the international exchanges was of prime importance and a first object of policy, and that there should be a return to the international gold standard—but the schedule should be optional with each country. However, the statement proposed that countries still on the gold standard should maintain the free working of the standard at current gold parities, while countries not on the gold standard should limit exchange speculation, and all central banks should cooperate to achieve these objectives.

Raymond Moley, the President's closest adviser at the time who had been sent to London as Roosevelt's personal liaison officer, cabled his urgent recommendations of approval of the statement. Roosevelt, however, had meantime come under the Warren influence and had become convinced that international stability began with domestic stability and that until economic recovery had been achieved at home, attempts to stabilize foreign exchanges would be fruitless.

In this view he was, of course, on sound ground. Unfortunately, he was persuaded that he could restore domestic prosperity by monetary manipulation to raise prices. He cabled Moley, after some delay, refusing to accept the declaration, and followed it with another that astounded the delegates by its practical repudiation of the American delegation: "The sound internal economic system of a nation is a greater factor in its well being than the price of its currency in changing terms of the currencies of other nations."

He went on to say that "national budgets must be balanced," and that "the U. S. objective would be that of giving currencies a continuing purchasing power which does not vary greatly in terms of the commodities and need of modern civilization."

"Let me be frank," he concluded, "in saying that the United States seeks the kind of dollar which a generation hence will have the same purchasing and debt-paying power as the dollar value we hope to attain in the near future. That objective means more to the good of other nations than a fixed ratio for a month or two in terms of the pound and franc."

It would be uncharitable to the memory of the departed to recall how far short of this pious ideal the efforts of the New Deal fell—largely because it fixed its eye upon the goal rather than the means. Nevertheless, the responsibilities of an historian of money require that the course of this decline be traced in moderate detail.[5]

25.

The New Deal and the Federal Reserve

To the economic historian the phenomenon known as New Deal offers fascinating excursions, but we must confine our attention here to its relations with the Federal Reserve System.

One point may be made clear at once: without the Federal Reserve the New Deal would not have been possible. Monetary management was the core and the motor of the New Deal. The Federal Reserve provided the mechanism by which money was managed. It also was the veil by which these manipulations were concealed and given the illusion of normal fiscal operations in the traditional convention. It permitted the Administration to avoid the naked seizure and exercise of power. By filtering its activities through the monetary fabric, government retained the appearance of functioning within the historic private enterprise system. Thus, government was never compelled to requisition or sequester property for its needs; it could always acquire it by purchase, since its means were unlimited.

We do not say this was by conscious design; rather it was the product of a mixture of economic heresy and morbid fear of depression and unemployment on the part of the public by which they demanded or accepted whatever controls and mechanisms were recommended by the experts.

As we have noted above, the early Roosevelt was attached to traditional monetary and fiscal policy. During the campaign, in several of his speeches, particularly in the Western mining country, in Salt Lake City, Butte, and Seattle, he had attacked Republican charges that Democratic control would mean abandonment of the gold standard, but he was vague as to just what his policy would be beyond maintenance of a "sound" currency, and he did not dispel fears of his radical leanings even among his own party. Carter Glass, as remarked, declined the Secretaryship of the Treasury. Nor were these fears allayed by Roosevelt's inaugural address, in which he seemed to outdo the earlier Roosevelt in condemning the bankers as "money changers in the temple."* Roosevelt's ambivalence came out in his second message to Congress, on March 10, 1933, the day after Congress convened to grant him emergency powers, in which he requested authority to balance the budget by reducing veterans' payments and government salaries by a total of $1/2 billion. The bill was strongly opposed in his own party, with ninety dissenting Democrats in the House, but it carried under the influence of the crisis.

The Emergency Banking Act was followed by the Banking Act of June 16, 1933, which appeared to be directed toward establishing more conservative banking and monetary practices. It was, in major respects, a revision of an earlier bank bill which Glass had introduced in January of the year before. Early in 1931 he had begun drafting reform bank legislation, but his bill, which he had eventually succeeded in getting reported out by the Senate Banking and Currency Committee, proposed such stringent controls on the use of bank credit that it met with a flood of protests, and it was sent back to the Committee. Again reported, the Federal Reserve Board entered a formal protest, and it eventually was lost by removing it from the Senate calendar. The objections of the Board are of interest, since they are an excellent statement of the philosophy of the System at that time. The pertinent paragraphs follow:

> It was the original intention of the Federal Reserve Act to decentralize the banking power of this country by establishing 12 autonomous regional Federal Reserve banks. The Federal Reserve Board itself was originally planned to be largely a supervisory and coordinating body. The proposed act, however, tends to increase radically the power of the Federal Reserve Board at the expense of the individual Federal Reserve banks and to make of the Federal Reserve System in effect a centralized banking institution. In support of this statement attention is called to the following sections:
> Sec. 3 delegates the power of direct action to the Federal Reserve Board which even if practical would result in so embarrassing the operations of

---

*"It seems a pity that he [Roosevelt] let slip the opportunity to utter some assurance of the fundamental soundness and safety of our financial system. . . ." (*New York Times,* March 5, 1933)

member banks as to lead to the elimination of important and necessary activities and to the eventual surrender of individual bank management to the Federal Reserve Board.

Sec. 8 gives power to the Federal Reserve Board to fix the percentage of capital and surplus which any member bank may lend in the form of collateral loans, and it is within the power of the Federal Reserve Board to change this percentage at any time upon 10 days notice.

The power of control of the Federal Reserve Board over actions of the Federal Reserve Open Market Committee, as authorized in Section 10, might possibly tend to slow up open market operations.[1]

At the same time that the bill was under consideration in the Senate, Henry Steagall, chairman of the House Banking and Currency Committee, had been hammering out a bill for the guarantee of bank deposits, but the conservative Glass, whose influence in the Senate was still paramount, refused to accept it, even though it may have meant a compromise acceptance of his own measure.

As the crisis subsided, banking legislation had come again to the fore. The Senate was now under Democratic Party control, and Glass in control of the Banking and Currency Committee.* Glass now undertook a major investigation into banking practices with a vigorous young lawyer, Ferdinand Pecora, as chief counsel. The disclosures—among them that twenty Morgan partners had not paid income tax for two years†—added to the opprobrium which Roosevelt had visited upon banking in his inaugural address, and assured passage of whatever legislation Glass might ask. However, he seems to have modified some of his own conservative views. In any case he now agreed with Steagall's deposit guarantee scheme, and the new bill went through the Senate without a dissenting vote. Except for the deposit guarantee, however, the bill was pretty much a Glass bill, and indeed for some time Administration approval, and Presidential signature, were in doubt.‡

---

*His seniority entitled him to chairmanship, but Roosevelt wanted him to head the Appropriations Committee, rather than Senator Kenneth McKellar, and it was arranged that Senator Duncan Fletcher would head the Banking and Currency Committee but allow Glass to run it as vice-chairman.

†This was hardly extraordinary, in view of the business losses that were being sustained, but the legal devices they employed to establish the amount of their losses struck many as unethical.

‡It is curious that the annual reports of the Secretary of the Treasury for both the fiscal years 1933 and 1934 omit the text, and any discussion of this act, although often going into great detail in regard to monetary legislation and decrees, and giving the text of major legislation. Particularly, a chronology of action relating to gold in the *Report* for 1934 (Exhibit 25) fails to mention this act.

For all Glass's conservatism it was this bill, and the course it set, that provided the leverage for later, more extreme measures of monetary control by the Executive.

The deposit guarantee provision can be disposed of briefly. The merits of the scheme are not easy to appraise, since the country has experienced no credit crisis since its establishment. As constituted, a government controlled institution, the Federal Deposit Insurance Corporation, was created with capital supplied to the extent of $150 million by the Treasury, by member banks to the extent of 1/2 per cent of their deposits, and by Federal Reserve banks to the extent of half their surplus on January 1, 1933. Membership in the insurance scheme was compulsory for members of the Federal Reserve System, and depositors were eventually to be insured as to the first $10,000 of their deposits and to a lesser proportion for deposits beyond $10,000 (75 per cent between $10,000 and $50,000 and 50 per cent beyond $50,000).

In the 44 years through 1978, total assessments amounted to $10.3 billion; it had disbursed in deposit insurance operations some $5.1 billion, with losses on these disbursements of $350 million. At the end of 1978, its assets totalled $9.3 billion, 90 per cent of which was held in U. S. government obligations. The fund represented about 1.3 per cent of insured deposits; of total deposits of $1,025 billion in insured banks, some $722 billion were covered by insurance.

From the foregoing, it is apparent that the fund provided another source of financing government deficits; it also reduced the chances of panic by allaying public apprehension over the security of deposits; but it may be questioned whether its operations have tended to make bank lending more cautious or whether the contrary has resulted. In any case, under conditions of panic, the fund would be inadequate to meet a public clamor for cash, since its own assets are not in cash but in government bonds that somehow would have to be converted into cash, either in the market or, more likely, by purchase by the Federal Reserve and the further printing of irredeemable paper notes.

The principal immediate effect of the deposit guarantee was to bring more banks within the orbit of Federal Reserve influence. So far as the Federal Reserve System was immediately concerned, the Banking Act of 1933 was in the direction of greater authority and more centralized authority over banking. Banks were forbidden to engage in security underwriting and were required to divorce their investment banking affiliates. Banks were now permitted to establish branches and to engage in group banking to the extent that state law permitted. Membership in the System was widened to include savings and industrial banks. New minimum capital requirements were established. Limitations on loans to one borrower were also set, as well as other restrictions on the granting of credit. Federal Reserve banks were given increased control over the use of credit by member banks. Particularly the Reserve banks were required to keep informed of the extent to which member banks were granting loans for purposes of trading in securities, real estate and commodities, and they were now given power to discipline an offending bank by refusing it Reserve accommodation or even formally suspending it.

Among other restrictions on banking operations was the prohibition against acting as agent for non-banking firms in making loans on securities to brokers and security dealers, a device by which banks had circumvented Federal Reserve control over speculative credit in 1928 and 1929.

The act took note of the findings of the Federal Reserve Committee on Member Bank Reserves by prohibiting the payment of interest on demand deposits by member banks and by giving the Board authority to limit the rates of interest paid on various classes of time and savings deposits. It did not incorporate the other important recommendations of the Committee that reserve requirements be made uniform for all banks and based in part upon the velocity of circulation (as measured by the ratio of debits to deposits).

The Board was also given control over international banking relations by subjecting to Board control all negotiations by Reserve banks with foreign central banks and institutions.

Of particular significance was the strengthening of the Open Market Committee. Until now, this influential group had been informal in character, consisting of one representative of each of the twelve Reserve banks. The act now gave statutory authority to the Committee and all open market purchases and sales of securities and paper were subjected to its regulations.

Public sentiment for inflationary remedies and direct monetary management continued to outpace the Administration thinking and during the 73rd Congress numerous bills to this end were introduced. Among them was another bill, by Representative T. Alan Goldsborough, that would have established an independent monetary authority. Roosevelt managed to have this buried on the necessity for further study.* Several

---

*Goldsborough brought his proposals forward again in 1935, in a bill to establish a new Bank of the United States with $4 billion capital. (House Resolution 2998, 74th Congress)

Senate bills would also have abolished the Federal Reserve Board and created a new monetary authority.

Meantime Roosevelt was coming round to the views of George Warren that the quickest way to restore prices was by raising the price of gold, which would cause a similar movement in the prices of all other commodities. Warren calculated and promised that a 75 per cent increase in the price of gold from $20.67 to $36.17 an ounce would restore prices to the 1926 level.[2] He was supported by the influential Committee for the Nation, which was urging a $41.34 price for gold, that is, a 50 cent dollar.

The chronology of the development of the gold policy is of interest. On March 10, the day following the signing of the Emergency Banking Act, Roosevelt had issued an Executive Order prohibiting the export of gold except under license. This had been followed by an Order on April 5, that forbade the private holding of gold and gave the Secretary of the Treasury authority to regulate by license all transactions in gold, both domestic and foreign. On April 20, a further Order terminated the export of gold and took the U. S. off the gold standard. Following the April 20 Order, the dollar began to depreciate abroad; that is, the price of gold began to rise, with the premium going to 23.2 per cent by June 10. At the same time the prices of basic commodities began to move upward, and this was taken as confirmation of the Warren gold-price theory.

On May 12 the Thomas amendment was enacted, which gave the President authority to devalue the dollar by as much as 50 per cent, with corresponding authority to revalue silver.

On June 5, by Public Resolution, all "gold clauses" contained in dollar obligations, excepting currency, were declared to be against public policy; and such obligations, whether or not they contained a "gold clause," were declared to be discharged upon payment, dollar for dollar, in any coin or currency that was legal tender at the time of payment. The Resolution also declared all coins and currency of the United States to be legal tender.

The gold clause abrogation was pushed through the House in three days (from May 26 when the Resolution was introduced to May 29) and a little longer in the Senate. It represented a profound break in U. S. banking practices. Since the Civil War currency depreciation it had been customary in bond indentures to specify payment of principal and interest in gold coin of "the present weight and fineness." It had become federal practice by the Act of February 4, 1910, which provided that "any bonds and certificates of indebtedness of the United States, hereafter issued, shall be payable, principal and interest, in United States gold coin of the present standard of value."

As an estimated amount of $100 billion of public and private obligations bearing the gold clause were outstanding, it was argued that the clause was meaningless since there was not enough gold in the world for the purpose. That the argument equally applied to all the monetary obligations outstanding in relation to the available money stock carried little weight. The constitutionality of the Resolution was subsequently challenged in the courts and in a series of famous "gold clause" cases the abrogation was sustained.

On July 22, Roosevelt sent his message to the London Economic Conference which practically foreshadowed a competitive debasement of currencies, in his declaration that "the United States seeks the kind of a dollar which a generation hence will have the same purchasing and debt-paying power as the dollar we hope to attain in the near future."

On October 22, in a radio address to the country, Roosevelt formally launched his famous experiment in lifting the price level by purchasing gold in accordance with the Warren theory. In his address he reiterated that the definite policy of the Government "has been to restore commodity price levels." He stated that when the price level had been restored, "we shall seek to establish and maintain a dollar which will not change its purchasing and debt-paying power during the succeeding generation." Stating that "it becomes increasingly important to develop and apply the further measures which may be necessary from time to time to control the gold value of our own dollar at home," and that "the United States must take firmly in its own hands the control of the gold value of our dollar," the President announced the establishment of a Government market for gold in the United States. He stated that he was authorizing the Reconstruction Finance Corporation to buy gold newly mined in the United States at prices to be determined from time to time after consultation with the Secretary of the Treasury and the President. "Whenever necessary to the end in view," the President added, "we shall also buy or sell gold in the world market." He continued, "Government credit will be maintained and a sound currency will accompany a rise in the American commodity price level."[3]

The operations of the program were formalized by an Executive Order on October 25 and were carried out by a special committee consisting of Jesse H. Jones, chairman of the Reconstruction Finance Corporation; Dean Acheson, Under Secretary of the Treasury; and Henry Morgenthau,

Jr., then governor of the Farm Credit Administration. Roosevelt, however, took personal charge of the program and he seems to have done so with the enthusiasm of a sports car fan with a new model.

The first offer was set at $31.36, the equivalent of a 66 cent dollar, and the idea was to raise the offer by degrees. The committee met daily at the White House to fix the prices for the day and the amount of the increase seems to have been a matter of caprice. Morgenthau, in his Diary, reports that Roosevelt one morning suggested a 21 cent increase: "It's a lucky number, because it's three times seven."[4]

On January 17, 1934, the price of gold had been advanced to $34.45 plus handling charges, at which price it was held. Roosevelt now concluded that he needed a stronger legislative mandate for his proposed reform of the currency system and in a message to Congress on January 15 he outlined in comprehensive form the objectives of the new monetary policy. Repeating language he had used to the London Economic Conference, he declared his purpose to be that "of arriving eventually at a less variable purchasing power for the dollar." Although extensive hearings had been scheduled by the House Committee on Coinage, Weights and Measures, the leadership pushed the bill through the House by 360 to 40, with only one day of debate.

Roosevelt's gold buying program in many ways marked the divide between his earlier policy of fiscal conservatism and the outright acceptance of managed money, fiscal manipulation and government intervention. It caused the first major shift in his staff of advisers. Dean Acheson resigned as Under Secretary of the Treasury and was replaced by Henry Morgenthau, Jr. on November 17. William H. Woodin pleaded his illness to resign the Secretaryship of the Treasury and was replaced by Morgenthau on January 1. James P. Warburg and O. M. W. Sprague also retired from the scene.

In the hearings on the new gold legislation before the Senate Banking and Currency Committee, the leading testimony from such authorities as Professor E. W. Kemmerer of Princeton, Dr. Benjamin M. Anderson, Jr., economist of the Chase National Bank of New York, and H. Parker Willis, one of the authors of the Federal Reserve Act, was all highly critical; nevertheless, the bill passed and was reported on January 30.

The Gold Reserve Act of 1934 transferred to the United States title to all gold of the Federal Reserve System (by giving in exchange gold certificates); it amended the Act of May 12, 1933 (the Thomas amendment) so as to provide that the weight of the gold dollar should not be fixed in any event at more than 60 per cent of the weight then existing. No gold should thereafter be coined, and no gold coin should thereafter be paid out or delivered by the United States. Gold coin was ordered withdrawn from circulation and formed into bars, and redemption of the currency thereafter should be only in gold bullion bearing a Mint stamp and to the extent permitted by the Secretary of the Treasury by regulations to be issued with approval of the President. Thereafter gold could be acquired, transported, melted or treated, imported, exported, earmarked or held in custody for foreign or domestic account only to the extent permitted by Treasury regulation. The act also created a fund of $2 billion for the purpose of stabilizing the exchange value of the dollar, to be derived from the profit accruing from the devaluation. This profit amounted to $2,811,397,066 by the end of the fiscal year.[5]

On the following day, January 31, Roosevelt issued his Executive Order that fixed the weight of the gold dollar at 15.238 gains of gold, 9/10 fine, representing a reduction of the gold in the dollar to 59.06 per cent of its former content of 25.8 grains, 9/10 fine. The amount of fine gold represented by the dollar was now 13.714 grains instead of 23.22 grains.

At the same time the Secretary of the Treasury issued a statement to the effect that immediately, and until further notice, he would buy imported and domestic gold at $35 an ounce, less Mint and handling charges, and would sell gold for export to foreign central banks whenever the exchange rate with gold standard currencies reached the gold export point, that is, $35 an ounce plus 1/4 per cent handling charge. All gold sales would be made through the Federal Reserve bank of New York as fiscal agent.[6]

The Gold Reserve Act of 1934 gave the President authority to make further changes in the gold content of the dollar (within the tolerance of 50 to 60 per cent of the former content) for a period of two years, and by proclamation of emergency to extend the period for an additional year.

The discretionary authority over the content of the dollar and the stabilization fund was extended for one year by Presidential proclamation in January, 1936, and subsequently by Act of January 23, 1937, until June 30, 1939. Opposition to the extension was largely perfunctory in 1937 but in 1939, when the President again asked for a two-year extension, the opposition was overcome only by the utmost Administration pressure. By 1941, World War II had intervened and the authority finally expired.

In the interval, Roosevelt had reason for disenchantment with the Warren thesis, for by 1939 not only had prices not responded in correspondence with the 69 per cent increase in the price of gold, but the abundance of new money and credit in the economy had not forestalled another severe depression in 1937. The wholesale price index (1947–49 = 100) had risen only from 42.1 for 1932 and 42.8 for 1933 to 56.1 in 1937 and thereafter had fallen off to 50.1 in 1939, the latter index representing an increase of 19 per cent. Moreover, the economy had continued sluggish. The gross national product, defined as the market value of goods and services produced by the nation's economy, increased from $58.5 billion in 1932 to $91.1 billion in 1939, or only to the 1930 level, and still less than the $104.4 billion of 1929. The achievement is somewhat better if stated in constant dollars. In terms of 1929 prices, gross national product increased during the decade from $104.4 billion to $111 billion. This modest increase hardly matched the increase in population (which rose from 121.8 million in 1929 to 130.9 million in 1939), so that gross national product *per capita* declined in the decade from $857 to $695 and in constant (1929) dollars from $857 to $847.[7]

26.

New Bridles for Old

THROUGHOUT THE FIRST YEAR of his administration Roosevelt clung to his policy of a balanced budget and fiscal integrity, but it became increasingly apparent that the condition was stronger than the theory. The condition was the political demand that government powers be used to restore the economy and get more people back to work.

It was at this juncture that there appeared on the scene a figure who was ideally suited to resolve this dilemma and to provide Roosevelt with a less assailable philosophical framework than the Warren thesis had proved to be. This was Marriner S. Eccles, a millionaire banker and capitalist of Ogden, Utah, whose various banks and financial enterprises had managed to stay afloat during the storms that raged during 1931 and 1932.

Eccles asserts in his *Recollections* that he had never read Keynes and was not familiar with his theories; nevertheless his proposals were in the main stream of Keynesian economics—or perhaps in another but parallel branch of the stream fed from the same source.[1] In an address to the Utah State Bankers Convention, in June, 1932, he had diagnosed the depression as due to "our capital accumulation getting out of balance in relation to our consumption ability." The difficulty, he went on to say, was that "we were not sufficiently extravagant as a nation."[2]

Keynes had argued that employment marched with investment. Eccles sensed one of the errors in this thesis—that it rested on the belief that people and banks will not indefinitely hold money in idleness. Government may flood the economy with credit, he saw, but banks will not lend, nor borrowers put their names to loans, for enterprises for which they see no demand. As he stated in an address to the Utah Educational Association in October of 1933, "A bank cannot finance the building of more factories and more rental properties and more homes when half of our productive property is idle for lack of consumption and a large percentage of our business properties are vacant, for the want of paying tenants."[3]

Eccles' solution to this problem was for the government itself to embark on large-scale spending. He declared that "the fundamental economic plans, when they are finally established, will of necessity center on the distribution of purchasing power and in the allocation of income between investment and expenditure. So long as money is used as the means of distribution and of allocation, the fundamental economic plans will be plans for determining the flow of money. These plans will involve public and semipublic expenditures on an expanding scale for cultural and quasi-cultural services. They will involve relief of taxation that rests on the consumer; the reduction of sales taxes, of real estate taxes, of tariffs, and of public service charges. They will involve the establishment of heavy income taxes, especially in the upper income brackets. They will involve heavy taxation of undistributed corporate surplus to force corporation income into dividends and wages. These plans for determining the flow of money are fundamental. Without them or their equivalent, no permanent adjustment can be made."[4]

Eccles' novel views attracted the attention of Rexford Tugwell, one of the Roosevelt "brain trust," then Under Secretary of Agriculture, who invited him to Washington for a conference.

It was a time when the tensions within the New Deal were strong, with Acheson, Sprague and Warburg holding the conservative fort and Warren, Hopkins and Wallace, supported by men like La Follette and Norris in the Senate, urging more vigorous government action. A friend of Eccles, a former governor of Utah, George Dern, was Secretary of War and Eccles' partner, E. G. Bennett, had been appointed a director of the newly created Federal Deposit Insurance Corporation. The liberals were in a dilemma. There were already doubts as to the efficacy of the gold buying policy. As Eccles stated,

"They at least knew that ringing manifestos by themselves did not solve problems. The pressures of human distress to which their work exposed them bore home the painful lesson that the task of removing fear and want from the land could not be accomplished within the framework of a balanced budget. On the other hand, they needed more than the doc-

trine of Christian charity to advance what they wanted to do in the face
of strong political resistance. They needed arguments on how a planned
policy of adequate deficit financing could serve the humanitarian objective with which they were most directly concerned; and second, how the
increased production and employment that the policy would create was
the only way a depression could be ended and the budget balanced."[5]

In his *Recollections,* he went on to say, "I had arrived in Washington at
a time when the search was on for a body of ideas that could bridge the
two worlds. Deficit financing except for war or defense could not by itself
absorb all the unemployed and put them to work, for the government did
not own the means of production; the means were privately owned. If.
however, there was to be deficit financing of some sort, there had to be
an underlying objective that the deficits were to gain. What should it be
and how should it be sought?"[6]

Eccles' arguments and personality made an impression upon his listeners. Tugwell undertook to introduce him to various New Deal powers,
and in February he was appointed special assistant to Morgenthau (who
had meantime become Secretary of the Treasury) to deal with monetary
and credit matters.

Eccles promptly found much to bite into. The elements of the Eccles
philosophy had already been in involuntary practice. The President's
budget balancing program had gone with the wind in his budget message
of January 13, 1934, and the Treasury was faced with the problem of
raising funds. To give employment, a Civilian Conservation Corps for
reforestation work had been authorized March 31 of the year before to
provide work for some 250,000 jobless male citizens between the ages of
18 and 25. In May the Federal Emergency Relief Act appropriated $500
million for relief projects, and at the same time the Agricultural Adjustment Act, to which the Thomas amendment had been an attachment,
established subsidies to farmers. Later in the same month the Tennessee
Valley Authority was created and authorized to construct dams and
power plants, and to develop economic and social well-being in the
Tennessee Valley region. In June the Homeowners Refinancing Act
created the Home Owners Loan Corporation to refinance home mortgage
debts for non-farm owners; it was provided with $200 million capital
stock and authorized to issue $2 billion in bonds. In June also the Public
Works Administration was established for the construction of roads, public buildings and other projects, for which a fund of $3,300 million was
authorized. In October the Commodity Credit Corporation was created
under the Agriculture Adjustment Act with authority to draw upon the

Reconstruction Finance Corporation for funds to extend loans to farmers on their crops. In November the Civil Works Administration was established as an emergency unemployment relief program for the purpose of putting four million jobless persons to work on federal, state and local made-work projects. By the time it terminated in March of 1934 it had spent more than $933 million on 180,000 works projects. In February of 1934 the Civil Works Emergency Relief Act authorized $950 million for use by the Federal Emergency Relief Administration until the end of the fiscal year 1935 for operating the program of civil works and direct relief. Also in the same month the Export-Import Bank was established under powers already granted to encourage the flow of overseas commerce by financing trade with foreign nations.

Having abandoned for the time the idea of a balanced budget, Roosevelt was now ready for the proposals of the more extreme wing of his advisers that the government launch a massive public works spending program. Eccles belonged to this wing along with Harry Hopkins, Federal Relief Administrator; Rexford G. Tugwell, Under Secretary of Agriculture; and Harold Ickes, Secretary of the Interior; but his views were somewhat muffled by the conservative influences in the Treasury, particularly those of Lewis Douglas, Director of the Budget, and Thomas Jefferson Coolidge, who had replaced Acheson as Under Secretary, as well as by Morgenthau's insistence that all Treasury opinion offered to Roosevelt be funneled through himself.

Meantime, in June, Eugene Black resigned as Governor of the Federal Reserve Board, and Morgenthau offered Eccles' name to the President for the post. Eccles was now free to express his views, and in conversation with Roosevelt on November 4 he presented a memorandum which he had prepared on banking reforms with the assistance of Lauchlin Currie, then a member, as Eccles recalls, of the "Freshman Brain Trust" in the Treasury.* This proposal ultimately became the controversial Title II and core of the Banking Act of 1935. The Eccles memorandum began with the statement that "if the monetary mechanism is to be used as an instrument for the promotion of business stability, conscious control and management are essential." Without that control, the memorandum went

*Ibid. p. 166. Currie, a Canadian by birth, subsequently came under suspicion as a member of a Soviet spy ring that included Harry Dexter White, Morgenthau's assistant in monetary matters. He was investigated by the Federal Bureau of Investigation and by the House Committee on Un-American Activities and apparently satisfied the Committee that his associations with known Communists were innocent. Subsequently, he moved to Colombia and renounced his American citizenship.

on to say, experience showed that "the supply of money tends to contract
when the rate of spending declines. Thus during the depression the
supply of money instead of expanding to moderate the effect of decreased rates of spending, contracted, and so intensified the depression.
This is one part of the economy in which automatic adjustments tend to
have an intensifying rather than a moderating effect."[7]

Eccles apparently made such an impression upon the President in his
exposition of his theories that Roosevelt decided at once to appoint him
as Governor of the Federal Reserve Board despite the opposition of
Carter Glass, whose antagonism to Eccles was steadily mounting. On
November 10, Eccles' appointment was announced and on November 16
he was sworn in as a recess appointee; but Glass's opposition succeeded
in deferring Senate confirmation until the following April.

Eccles now through his influence outlined a spending program that
would represent "an addition to private investment and spending and not
a subtraction,"[8] providing the economic arguments while Hopkins and
Ickes supplied those from the well of human sympathies.

The ultimate result, Eccles states, was that the State of the Union
message of January, 1935, was devoted almost exclusively to the proposal
that Congress enact a relief program with an initial appropriation of some
$4.5 billion.[9]

As Governor of the Federal Reserve Board, Eccles now began to reform the internal administration to draw more authority to himself while
waiting action by the Congress on the bank legislation which Roosevelt
had appointed an inter-departmental committee to draft.

His first assault was on the Federal Advisory Council. This was the body
of twelve bankers, elected by the directors of each Federal Reserve bank
to represent and speak for the private banking system. The Council had
issued a public statement calling for a prompt balancing of the budget.
Eccles at his first meeting with the Council demanded that the Council
clear its statements with the Board. The demand aroused opposition but
was accepted. Eccles now moved to abolish the Committee on Legislative
Program and in doing so incurred the hostility of George Harrison,
Governor of the New York Federal Reserve bank. Under the threat of the
Roosevelt influence the Board agreed to its abolition, and Eccles now
became the spokesman for the Board on legislation.

Early in February the Administration presented the draft of new banking legislation on which the interdepartmental banking committee had
been working. It immediately roused the antagonism of Carter Glass,

whose allergy to Roosevelt was only less than his antipathy to Eccles, and both were aggravated by the neglect to consult him on the bill or even to show him an advance copy of the bill.* Although the bill was introduced in the House on February 5, by Congressman Steagall, Glass refused to have anything to do with it, and in the Senate it was sponsored by Senator Duncan U. Fletcher. Glass, as chairman of the subcommittee having jurisdiction, did not schedule hearings until April 19. The House meantime had concluded its hearings on April 8.

The bill, which became the Banking Act of 1935, was presented in three titles. The first dealt with matters relating to deposit insurance and need not detain us here. Title III dealt with technical amendments to the banking laws. Title I and Title III were brought into the bill to serve political strategy. Title I liberalized the insurance assessments to the advantage of participating banks, and Title III extended the grace period for the repayment of loans which banks had made to their executives during the emergency. The core of the bill was Title II, and as it was a reflection of Eccles' views, it is useful here to quote the pertinent passages of his memorandum of November 4:

> First: That the power over open-market operations, which has such great bearing on the supply of reserves and the volume of money and credit, should be taken away from the privately run Federal Reserve banks, acting through their governors; that the power should be vested in an Open Market Committee of the Federal Reserve Board in Washington; that this committee of the Board should have the right to initiate open-market policies and be responsible for their execution and results.
>
> Second: That the separate office of chairman of the board of directors of a Reserve bank should be abolished and its functions merged with those of the governor; that by law the governor should be made the formal as well as the actual head of the Reserve bank; that he should be chosen annually, and the Federal Reserve Board be empowered to approve or reject any nomination of a governor made by Reserve bank directors.
>
> Third: That the explicit definition of 'eligible paper' that could be rediscounted at the Federal Reserve banks should be deleted from the Reserve Act; that with the substitute concept of 'sound assets' as a guide, the power of the Federal Reserve Board in Washington to define 'eligible paper' should be clarified; that, in accordance with the state of the national economy, the Federal Reserve Board should be able from time to time to issue regulatory

---

*Eccles had promised to discuss the draft with Glass, he states, but was unable to do so by reason of the fact that he himself did not receive the draft until it was sent to Congress. (*Op. cit.* pp. 194 ff.) Nevertheless, the bill was completely an Eccles bill.

orders defining the character of sound assets with corresponding orders affecting changes in reserve requirements."[10]

Title II aroused not only the opposition of Glass, but the conservative banking element generally. At one point it was hinted to Eccles that he might obtain his confirmation as Governor of the Federal Reserve Board if he would abandon Title II. Glass, as a strategy, inverted the usual procedure of hearing Administration witnesses first, and on the pretext that James P. Warburg had to make a boat for Europe began by hearing the opposition, beginning with this ex-New Deal adviser.

Warburg opened the attack with the charge that the Federal Reserve had already become the obedient tool of the Administration—even though it was designed by law to be independent—and that the fiscal and monetary policies of the Administration were not being impeded by any obstacles which the proposed measure would remove. He summed up the opposition by stating: "In conclusion, Title II is a proposal (1) to make a centralized system out of a regional reserve system; (2) to bring the system so created under political domination and control, and (3) to remove almost entirely the automatic control inherent in the existing law."[11]

Warburg's views were echoed by a long list of witnesses including representatives of the Economists' National Committee on Monetary Policy, and authorities like Professor E. W. Kemmerer of Princeton; H. Parker Willis; and O. M. W. Sprague, who had only just resigned as adviser to the Treasury.

Owen D. Young, who followed James Warburg on the stand, came to the heart of the proposal in pointing out that it was an attempt to force revolutionary changes in the Federal Reserve System under the pretext of an emergency. He stated:

> I know of no emergency, either expressed or prospective, which requires legislation now. Everything which can be done by the Federal Reserve System to relieve the depression either has been or is now being done. . . . The only justification that I know of for new legislation now of the character proposed is to centralize responsibility so that we can better control another boom. I venture the opinion that we have ample time for study before that power is needed.
>
> My chief objection, Mr. Chairman, to the pending bill—and this is a very basic objection—is that it sets up in fact a central bank and destroys the regional system under which we have operated for so long. . . .
>
> This apprehension is not alleviated but rather increased by the present state of our budgetary unbalance and the necessity of issuing large amounts

of government obligations. There should be no removal of checks on the bank of issue against taking government obligations direct and not through the market. It was the exercise of the very kind of power which led to the currency and credit downfall in Germany and the ultimate destruction of the Reichsbank. I recommend that government financing direct through the central bank, except for unusual temporary advances, be prohibited in any bill.[12]

Eccles' answer to this argument, which he stated in a speech at Scranton on May 5 and when he was finally called to testify on May 10 was that if the country did not approve the government's spending program, the place to curtail that program was through the ballot and not through the Federal Reserve System. So far as the German inflation was concerned, he pointed out that if the German government was prepared to appropriate money it was equally prepared to change the Reichsbank law if necessary.

Glass managed to delay action on the bill by absenting himself from the Senate until a crisis arose over the July 1 deadline by which bankers were expecting relief under Title III. Presidential influence was again brought to bear on July 2 and the bill eventually went to the President in August and was signed August 23.

The bill, as enacted, contained most of what Eccles wanted, except the dilution of the requirements of eligibility for rediscount. In the House, where inflationary sentiment was rampant, a policy statement had been written in redefining the functions of the Federal Reserve System, broadening them to the point of giving it overall economic planning authority. The statement, offered as a new subsection (O) of Section 11, read as follows:

> It shall be the duty of the Federal Reserve Board to exercise such powers as it possesses in such manner as to promote conditions conducive to business stability and to mitigate by its influence unstabilizing fluctuations in the general level of production, trade, prices, and employment, so far as may be possible within the scope of monetary action and credit administration.

Representative Goldsborough offered a further amendment, that lost only by a vote of 128 to 122, extending the Committee's language to charge the Federal Reserve System with the duty of manipulating the money system so as to restore the purchasing power of the dollar to the 1921–1929 level.

In the Senate the policy declaration was deleted. The Senate also rejected the proposal, accepted by the House, repealing the requirement for collateral against Federal Reserve notes other than the 40 per cent gold cover, and making the notes secured by all the assets of the Reserve banks.

The bill that went to the President for signature provided the following:

(1) Reorganization of the Federal Reserve Board. The name of the Board was changed to the Board of Governors of the Federal Reserve System and the membership was reduced from eight to seven, to be appointed by the President. The ex officio memberships of the Secretary of the Treasury and the Comptroller General were abolished. Eccles is authority for the statement that it had originally been intended only to eliminate the ex officio membership of the Secretary of the Treasury and to leave the Comptroller General on the Board but both were excluded when Morgenthau's sensitivity was offended that one of his subordinate officials should be on the Board while he was removed.

The Chairman of the Board was to be designated by the President for a four-year term.

(2) The executive authority of the Federal Reserve banks was transferred from the chairman to the governor and deputy governor and the title of these officers changed to president and first vice president. These officials were appointed by the board of directors for five years but the appointments were subject to the approval of the Board of Governors of the Federal Reserve System.

(3) The Open Market Committee, consisting of the twelve governors of the Federal Reserve banks, was replaced by a new committee composed of seven members of the Board of Governors of the Federal Reserve System and five representatives of the twelve Federal Reserve banks, who were to be selected annually by the boards of directors of the Federal Reserve banks: one by Boston and New York; one by Philadelphia and Cleveland; one by Richmond, Atlanta, and Dallas; one by Chicago and St. Louis; and one by Minneapolis, Kansas City, and San Francisco.

(4) The Board of Governors was now authorized to change the reserve requirements for both demand and time deposits of member banks without the declaration of an emergency. Such changes, however, were to be within the minimum then required by law, and a maximum of not more than twice the amount.

(5) The law made no change in regard to setting discount rates except that Federal Reserve banks should establish these rates with the approval of the Board of Governors every fourteen days, or more often if deemed necessary by the Board.

(6) The law did not go so far as Eccles had desired in permitting any

sound asset to be eligible for rediscount, but it did grant permanent authority to any Federal Reserve bank, under regulations of the Board of Governors of the Federal Reserve System, to make advances on any "satisfactory" as well as eligible paper to a member bank.

(7) The act liberalized the restrictions on real estate loans.

(8) The law further eased the requirements for admission to the Federal Reserve System.

(9) Technical changes relieved the Board of Governors of certain administrative details.

(10) The act prohibited the direct purchase of government securities by the Federal Reserve banks—an authority which the Thomas amendment had implied but not specifically granted. This provision was not among those sponsored by the Administration and Eccles later complained that it only served to add to the cost of purchase the brokers' commissions.[13]

27.

Where Two Tides Meet

THE BANKING ACT OF 1935 practically turned the Federal Reserve System over to Franklin D. Roosevelt and New Deal influences. It did so by abolishing the old Federal Reserve Board and creating a new Board of Governors, to be appointed by the President. Fortunately for those who believed in an independent banking system, Roosevelt was inclined to temporize when it came to political appointments, and Marriner S. Eccles, to whom he had promised the chairmanship, was a man to arouse antagonism rather than to conciliate antagonists. His Mormon father had taken two wives, and Eccles disputed the inheritance with his half-brothers; his own marriage was unsuccessful and resulted in divorce; no sooner had he been appointed head of the Federal Reserve System than he alienated the influential Governor George Harrison of the New York Reserve bank; his confirmation to the post lay in jeopardy by reason of his inability to gain the confidence of the powerful Carter Glass, who not only suspected Eccles' monetary conservatism but even the means by which Eccles had risen to wealth and position. Eccles never quite succeeded in placating the Virginian or gaining his support; in fact, as time passed he rather exacerbated the old man's animosity, as he also awakened the resentment of his patron Morgenthau.

In 1935 banking opinion became alarmed over the prospects of a new stock market boom. There was abundant cash and liquid assets in the banking system, as a result of the government spending program, but a slackness of commercial demand for credit, and funds were being absorbed either by the government or by the stock market, which had been steadily rising since March.

A few statistics will illustrate the condition that was causing concern. The revaluation of gold, along with gold receipts from abroad, had more than doubled the dollar and gold reserves (from $4,036 million at the end of 1933 to $10,072 million at the end of 1935). Much of this gold increment had flowed into the Federal Reserve in the form of gold certificates, where they provided additional banking reserves.* In addition, the Federal Reserve banks had acquired $2,432 million of government bonds by the end of 1934; and although no more were being purchased, these purchases (since they were paid for by checks on the Federal Reserve banks) provided the commercial banks with additional reserves. Rediscounts by the banking system had practically ceased by 1934, falling from the peak of $1,096 million in the middle of 1929 to around $6 million at the end of 1935, while other bill holdings of the Reserve banks also continued to drop. (In 1939 the Reserve banks ceased altogether to buy bills.)

Excess reserves of member banks—that is, commercial bank deposits at Federal Reserve banks, in excess of their required reserves—had been a nominal figure until after the stock market crash and the beginning of the Depression. In June, 1929, total member bank reserves amounted to $2,314 million, of which $42 million were excess. Just before the revaluation of the dollar, in January, 1934, total reserves were $2,764 million of which $1,898 million were required and $866 million were excess. By the end of 1935, however, total reserves had reached $5,716 million, of which $2,733 million were required and $2,983 million were excess.

It was this nearly $3 billion excess reserves that troubled the thinking bankers, since it represented a potential inflation of $18 billion in bank credit.

It is necessary in looking at the meaning of these items to have also at hand the figures for total banking assets. In June, 1929, for instance, the commercial banking system had outstanding total loans and investments of around $49.5 billion, of which $35.7 billion were in the form of loans, and $13.7 billion in investments in securities; but of this $13.7 billion only $4.9 billion were invested in U. S. government securities. By June 1935, however, total loans and investments had fallen off to $34.5 billion, due to the lack of commercial demand. Loans had dropped to $14.9

---

*The gold itself is held by the Treasury, which issued its certificates of deposit. Custody of the gold is with the Mint, except for the amounts held in the Treasury Stabilization Fund. The Mint keeps the gold at the various mints, the New York assay office, but mainly (since 1937) at a large depository at Fort Knox, Kentucky. The gold in the Stabilization Fund is in the custody of the New York Federal Reserve Bank.

billion. In order to earn on the deposits held, the banks invested the difference, totalling $19.7 billion, in securities, of which $12.7 billion were government securities. During approximately the same interval, also, the Federal Reserve banks had increased their holdings of government securities by some $1.9 billion.* In short, government was replacing business as the great user of credit, and the banks had become the principal suppliers of that credit. Of the increase of federal interest bearing debt from the time Roosevelt took office in 1933 until June 1936, totalling $12.4 billion, some $11 billion had been lent by the banks. The banking system was becoming primarily an agency for financing the federal deficit.

At the November 14 meeting of the American Bankers Association, the issue of the government's spending program and its inflationary consequences came to a head. Both Eccles and Glass had been asked to address the convention. Eccles agreed on condition that he be the final speaker, and thus be given the last word. When Glass learned this he sent his regrets. Eccles was still on hold-over appointment, and in fact Roosevelt had not yet announced his appointments to the new Board of Governors. Nevertheless, Eccles boldly defended his policies.

Orval W. Adams, the incoming president of the Association, had called upon the bankers to boycott government bonds as a form of pressure to reduce deficit financing. Eccles answered by recalling how the government had bailed out the banks following the Crash, and declared that orderly economic progress required a degree of government intervention.

"The government," he asserted, "must be the compensatory element in the economy: it must unbalance its budget during deflation and create surpluses in periods of great business activity."[1]

A week later Eccles issued a statement which in effect denied that there was undue speculation in the stock market, or that an inflation existed. His statement was generally interpreted as another Coolidge-like blessing on the stock market rise, and the *New Yorker* quipped: "After its unfortunate experience with pigs [the New Deal pig slaughter program] the government has decided not to shoot the bulls."[2] Roosevelt also mildly warned Eccles of the dangers of too much optimism.

Meantime, the Federal Reserve Advisory Council on November 21 adopted resolutions recommending Federal Reserve action to reduce

---

*Figures for year end holdings of government securities by all commercial banks were not compiled prior to 1936.

excess credit in the economy. The Council, of course, since it was chosen
by banks of the several Reserve districts, did not see eye to eye with the
Eccles expansionist program. It pointed out two alternatives, either to
reduce Federal Reserve credit outstanding by selling off System holdings
of securities, or to raise bank reserve requirements. Under the 1935 Act,
it will be recalled, the Board had authority to raise reserve requirements
by as much as 100 per cent of the minimums set by the 1917 amendments
to the basic act.

The recommendations, supposedly private, did not remain so, and
immediately became a subject of public debate—not so much as to the
desirability of the action as to the choice of means.

It was not the commercial bankers in general, but the powers now in
control of the Federal Reserve System, who stood in opposition to tighter
credit. Among the bankers who supported new credit controls was Win-
throp W. Aldrich, Chairman of the Chase National Bank, New York City's
largest bank. S. Parker Gilbert of J. P. Morgan & Co., however, took an
opposite view, in support of Eccles. The Board of Governors and the
Federal Open Market Committee now issued statements to the effect that
business recovery—which was the principal object of Reserve policy—
had not advanced far enough to warrant such action, and that there was
no evidence of credit overexpansion.

Throughout this controversy, Eccles was still in the position of an
interim appointee, with his status under the new banking act still obscure.
Roosevelt continued to procrastinate in appointing the new Board of
Governors, but to quiet rumors and to forestall opposition he did announce in September his intention to nominate Eccles to the new Board
of Governors and to designate him as chairman. There remained, however, the question of a board membership that would support Eccles'
policies. On this issue, the opposition of Glass was to be expected.

Time was running out. The new Board had to be appointed by February 1, 1936, when the act became effective. Eccles was not above using
what he admits were Machiavellian tactics to hoodwink Glass and to
hamstring his future opposition. He proposed to Roosevelt that Glass be
given the privilege of naming three of the seven members of the new
Board, but only from a list which Roosevelt would pick beforehand (all
of whom would of course be New Dealers). It was like playing with
marked cards, but Glass, whether wittingly or no, accepted, probably
realizing that the Roosevelt tide was running too strong to resist. The
new nominees went to the Senate, and were confirmed without a hearing
and without a record vote.

The conservative opposition to Eccles' management and policies did not fade, however, and a running battle continued over Federal Reserve objective and policies down to the outbreak of World War II.

Eccles seems at last to have recognized that some tightening of credit was indicated. On July 14 the Board responded by raising member bank reserve requirements by 50 per cent, to be effective August 15.

Meantime, the lesson was being learned that the presence of cheap money does not necessarily stimulate investment, Keynesian economists to the contrary. The principal discount rates were at 1 1/3 per cent, and the banks were full of money, with their only outlets government bonds and the stock market. The rate on prime banker acceptances had fallen to the unprecedented low of .15 per cent (compared with 5.03 per cent in 1928) and stock market call money was available at .55 per cent (compared with 6 per cent in 1928). As Eccles noted, "The presence of excess reserves did not of itself result in the creation of new deposits or in a more active use of the existing supply."[3]

On January 30, 1937, a further raise in reserve requirements was imposed, to bring them to the maximum allowable. The raise was to take effect in two steps, on March 1 and on May 1. The new reserve requirements, when effective, would be for demand deposits, respectively 14 per cent for country banks, 20 per cent for reserve city banks, and 26 per cent for central reserve city banks; on time deposits the reserves required would be 6 per cent in all classes of banks.

There was some apprehension of the effect of this action on the prime money market, and there did indeed occur a brief sell-off of "governments," so that Morgenthau became alarmed and threatened to release gold to the System (which would serve to create new reserves and help bolster the market). Eccles relates that he had to go to Roosevelt to call off Morgenthau, and to promise that the Open Market Committee would promptly move to support the government bond market.[4]

The significance of the incident lies in the evidence it offers of the extent to which the once independent Federal Reserve System had become the instrument of federal fiscal policy.

Whether because of Federal Reserve intervention, or, as Eccles argued, from other causes, signs of a new business depression now began to show. Stock prices, which had recovered to a level of 60 per cent of the 1928 index, now tumbled again, falling from an average of 15.47 (1941 −43=100) in 1936 to 11.49 by 1938. (The stock market, barometer of business, was to continue downward until war influences again began to course through the economy in 1942.)

Again, the nostrum for recovery, for which Eccles was the physician and the Federal Reserve the apothecary, was increased federal spending— what Eccles called "compensatory spending." Morgenthau, as the chief fiscal officer, in an address before the American Political Science Academy on November 10, 1937, had come out publicly for a balanced budget. This had been with Roosevelt's approval, for Morgenthau was always careful in clearing his positions with the President. Eccles, by his championship of spending, was able to win over the vacillatory Roosevelt, and thus become practically the fiscal as well as monetary policy framer for the New Deal. In this he had the stout support of Harry Hopkins, reputed author of the saying, "We will spend, spend, spend, and elect, elect, elect."

Following a conference in Warm Springs with the President, in the following April, in which Eccles was joined by three other Roosevelt advisers, Leon Henderson, Aubrey W. Williams, and Beardsley Ruml, Roosevelt was won over, and in his message to Congress on the fourteenth he asked for resumption of large-scale spending.

Eccles' rise to dominant influence in both fiscal and monetary policy was not without bruises. He was, as he states, "rapidly losing the few friends I had and influencing fewer people." Among those now in opposition to him was the powerful junior senator from Virginia, Harry F. Byrd, with whom he engaged in acrimonious debate, first by letters, and later by radio; Senator James F. Byrnes, later to become a Supreme Court justice (1941) and still later (1944) head of the Office of War Mobilization; and not least, Eccles' former chief and patron Henry Morgenthau.

Eccles, it must be recognized, was not in the forefront of his times. An increasingly vocal element in Congress—representing an increasingly vocal element in the electorate—was showing increasing impatience at the failure of monetary policies to restore prosperity and to reduce the rolls of the jobless. Chief among these were Senator Elmer Thomas, father of the Thomas amendment, who succeeded in having reported out of his Senate Committee on Agriculture a bill that would have devalued the dollar by half, and made the Federal Reserve System responsible to restore prices to the 1926 level.[5] Fortunately, the bill was referred to the Committee on Banking and Currency for further consideration and so buried. A bill originally introduced by Congressman Charles G. Binderup of Nebraska proposed to deprive the Federal Reserve System of all independence, by means of government purchase of all the stock, and by creating a new Board as the direct monetary agent of Congress to regulate the value of money and to control the volume of bank deposits.[6] A feature of the bill was that it would require a 100 per cent reserve by banks to be held in lawful money or government securities. The bill authorized the government to finance old-age pensions, public works, and loans to industry through the Federal Reserve banks, without increase of the public debt, until the price level was restored to the 1926 level and full employment had been obtained.

When Binderup was defeated for re-election he organized the Constitutional Money League, and his bill was re-introduced by Congressman Jerry Voorhis of California the following year.[7]

Other monetary bills of similar tenor were introduced by Senator M. M. Logan of Kentucky, who also wanted the Federal Reserve System to be wholly under Congressional control, and monetary policy geared to restoration and maintenance of the price level;[8] by Representative Wright Patman of Texas, and by Representative Usher L. Burdick of North Dakota.

Among the non-political figures in the arena was the Reverend Charles E. Coughlin, a parish priest of Royal Oak, Michigan, who found a nation listening to his radio program when he turned from the salvation of souls to saving the country from the bankers.

What probably saved the country from more radical monetary legislation was the continuing abundance of money, and an enormous receipt of gold from abroad, fleeing from a Europe in fear of Hitler. During the six calendar years, 1934–1939, inclusive, the country gained $10 1/2 billion of gold in addition to $3/4 billion of silver.

Meantime, the policy of spend and spend undoubtedly made many of the electorate happy with the Democratic Administration, and by August, 1939, the face of the world had changed with the German invasion of Poland, and the Federal Reserve System faced a new set of conditions and policies.

28.

The Reversals of War

T HE REVERSAL in German-Russian relations from entente to hostility in 1941 was more world-shaking in its effects than that which
occurred about the same time in the Eccles-Morgenthau relations; but in
our account of the Federal Reserve System the latter is of interest and
significance.

For Eccles, the spender, the involvement in war meant a new fiscal
policy of caution and pay-as-you-go. Morgenthau, the advocate of the
balanced budget, now insisted that the Federal Reserve exercise its powers to the full to provide the financing needed by the government. The
reversal was the less remarkable in the case of Eccles, for he had never
urged budgetary deficits except as "compensatory financing"—the theory Hoover had toyed with, of balancing the cyclical declines in private
business activity with government spending, mainly for public works.

Eccles, at that time, stood close to Roosevelt, so close indeed that he
was able to see Roosevelt's budget message before it was shown to Morgenthau, and more often than not, directed his public statements and
private counsel to matters of fiscal policy, so that many thought of him
as the Administration's chief fiscal adviser. Nevertheless, it was Morgenthau and the Morgenthau policies that were the ultimate victor.[1]

In support of the cautionary attitude on the part of Eccles and the
Reserve authorities was the tremendous increase in the country's gold
reserves resulting from the flight of capital from Europe. During 1939
gold imports had amounted to the enormous sum of $3.4 billion, and at
the year end the country held $17,650 million of gold, or two-thirds of

the world's stock. During 1939 total reserves of member banks had risen by $2.7 billion. This had followed a rise of $1.9 billion in 1938; during the two year period the amount of excess reserves of the banking system had increased from $1 billion to $5 billion, the highest on record. At the end of 1939, nearly half of the $12 billion banking reserves were in excess of the statutory requirements. This gave the commercial banks a credit power and an independence from restraint that would naturally cause Federal Reserve authorities uneasy nights.

It was, however, the commercial banks themselves, through their representatives on the Federal Reserve Advisory Council, that showed the greater concern. On October 8, 1940, the Council made a recommendation to the Board of Governors regarding the financing of the war defense program that was roundly critical of fiscal and monetary policies and that urged the Board to use its influence to the end that future issues of government securities be placed with individuals and corporate investors rather than with banks of deposit, where they would add to the potential credit power of the banking system.[2]

Following this recommendation, the Board, the presidents of the twelve Reserve banks, and the Federal Advisory Council joined in an unprecedented statement in the form of a special report to Congress on monetary and fiscal policy. The report appeared on December 31, 1940.

"While inflation cannot be cured by monetary measures alone," the Report declared,

the present extraordinary situation demands that adequate means be provided to combat the dangers of overexpansion of bank credit due to monetary causes.

The volume of demand deposits and currency is 50 per cent greater than in any other period of our history. Excess reserves are huge and are increasing. They provide the base for more than doubling the existing supply of bank credit. Since the early part of 1934, $14 billion of gold, the principal cause of excess reserves, has flowed into the country. The necessarily large defense program of the government will have still further expansion effects. . . . Interest rates have fallen to unprecedentedly low levels. Some of these are well below the reasonable requirements of an easy money policy. . . .

Specifically, the report recommended that Congress: (a) increase the statutory reserve requirements for demand deposits to 26 per cent for central reserve city banks, 20 per cent for reserve city banks, 14 per cent for country banks, and 6 per cent for time deposits; (b) empower the Open Market Committee to make further increases of reserve requirements sufficient to absorb excess reserves, to the extent of double the percentages mentioned; (c) consolidate the authority of the Open Market Committee by transferring to it the power vested in the Board of Governors to change the reserve requirements within these limits; (d) make reserve requirements applicable to all deposit banks rather than to member banks only; (e) exempt reserves from assessments of the Federal Deposit Insurance Corporation.

The report also recommended repeal of the authority to issue $3 billion greenbacks contained in the Thomas amendment, as well as the termination of the monetization of foreign silver acquired through the silver purchase program. It recommended also the termination of the President's power to devalue the dollar.

The report went on to recommend that new gold accretions be insulated by being held in the Treasury rather than paid out to the Federal Reserve banks (in the form of gold certificates).

Finally, and most significantly, it recommended that government deficits be financed by drawing upon existing deposits rather than by creating additional deposits through bank purchases of government securities; and that the budget be balanced as the national income increased.[3]

The report did not please Morgenthau, particularly as the market for governments sold off just in advance of the report; nor did it please the liberal wing within the Party, which raised the cry that it was a bankers' play for higher interest rates.

At a press conference on January 9, 1941, Morgenthau invited attention to the fact that from the day the report issued, interest rates started to rise and added, "The decline was absolutely not warranted. There is no reason I know of for interest rates to harden at this time unless some such proposal as that of the Federal Reserve Board should be put into effect."[4]

As the feud between the two men sharpened Eccles appealed to Roosevelt for a hearing and for support. Roosevelt as usual temporized and assured Eccles that he was "confident that it is going to work out all right."[5] But things did not work out all right and the Federal Reserve soon found itself again the tool of federal fiscal necessities. Between the end of 1932 and the end of 1939, of the increase in public debt of $20,997 million, $9,453 million, or 45 per cent, had been absorbed by the Federal Reserve banks and the commercial banking system. In order to assist in financing the defense program the System announced on September 1, 1939, that it would make advances on government securities at par at the discount rate. The rate was then 1 per cent in New York City and 1 1/2 per cent elsewhere. At the same time, the Reserve undertook to maintain a market for government bonds through operations of the Open Market Committee.

In this connection there occurred an important change in the System's open market policy—one of the landmarks in tracing the evolution of the Federal Reserve System. Until 1939, the determinant in the System's open market purchases of government securities had been the condition of commercial bank reserves. Government bonds were bought or sold as the necessity arose to increase or diminish the reserves available to the commercial banking system. For some years the amount of the securities held had not changed appreciably from the figure of $2 1/2 billion. In 1939, to meet the possible shocks arising from the outbreak of war again in Europe, the System undertook to buy and sell government bonds in accordance with the need to stabilize the capital market. This marked a fundamental divergence from policy in the past. As the Board's 1940 Report stated, "The System's open market policy involved the use of flexible portfolios for the purpose of maintaining orderly conditions in the government's securities market."[6]

As the prospects for war increased, the Federal Reserve retreated still further from its policy of credit stringency and in April, 1942, directed all Reserve banks to purchase all Treasury bills offered at a discount rate of 3/8 per cent per annum. Congress now gave the Board authority to change reserve requirements of member banks in one class of banks without changing the requirements for other classes of banks (Act of July 7, 1942) and the Board now reduced requirements for central reserve city banks from 26 to 20 per cent. The reduction was made effective in three steps, August 20, September 14, and October 3.

Meantime, Congress had extended for two more years the power of the Reserve banks to use U. S. government obligations as collateral for Federal Reserve notes (Act of June 30, 1941).[7]

Despite some nominal efforts to place government securities with non-bank investors through Savings Bonds, Savings Stamps, and 2 1/2 per cent long-term bonds not eligible to be held by banks for a period of ten years after issue, the commercial banks as a class continued to be the chief buyers of government obligations. At the end of 1941 they held $21.8 billion of the government debt, or some 34 per cent. During 1942 an additional $47.8 billion of debt was incurred, and at the end of 1942 the banks held $41.3 billion, or more than 37 per cent.

Among the legislation of the period affecting the Federal Reserve operations was the Second War Powers Act of March 27, 1942, which authorized the Federal Reserve banks to purchase government securities from the Treasury, not to exceed $5 billion, the power to extend until December 31, 1944.

This authority has been repeatedly renewed, at short term, but so faithfully by Congress that it may be assumed as a permanent feature of Federal Reserve power.*

Like Goths crossing the Danube in the waning years of the Roman Empire, Federal Reserve influence steadily infiltrated and became authority in more and more provinces of the economy long considered the domain of the free market. In 1934, the Securities and Exchange Act had empowered the Federal Reserve to fix margin requirements "for purposes of preventing the excessive use of credit for purchasing and carrying securities." In 1941, under the 1917 Trading with the Enemy Act, Roosevelt gave the Federal Reserve temporary authority to regulate the terms of instalment sales. This authority lapsed, but was renewed in 1947 and, again, as a temporary measure, during the Korean War. Finally, by the Credit Control Act of December 23, 1969, it was made permanent.

The Act of July 7, 1942, which permitted the Board to change the reserve requirements of the various classes of banks also amended subsection (a) of Section 12(a) of the Federal Reserve Act to provide a regrouping of the representation on the Federal Open Market Committee. Because of the importance of the New York Federal Reserve Bank from its location in the principal capital market, and the fact that it acted as agent of the Open Market Committee, the amendment gave it continuous representation on the Committee. The Boston, Philadelphia, and Richmond banks were to be represented by one member; one representative each was allotted to Cleveland and Chicago; to Atlanta, Dallas, and St. Louis; and to Minneapolis, Kansas City and San Francisco.

As the war continued into 1943, the public debt increased by $57 billion, of which $25 billion was taken by the banking system; the commercial banks taking 34 per cent of the increase as against 41 per cent in 1942. Including the Federal Reserve banks the total purchases by the banking system represented 43 per cent of the increase in the debt as against 49 per cent in 1942. During the year, the rate on government securities was maintained at rates corresponding to 3/8 per cent on

---

*Prior to the Banking Act of 1935, there was no question of the authority of the Federal Reserve banks to deal directly with the Treasury. That act restricted such dealings to the open market.

three-months bills, and 2 1/2 per cent on long-term bonds.

Additional legislation during 1943 affecting the banking and monetary system was the Act of April 29, 1943, which extended to June 30, 1945, the Stabilization Fund and the powers relating thereto, originally provided by the Gold Reserve Act of 1934, which otherwise would have expired. The act also extended to June 30, 1945, the power of the Federal Reserve banks to use government obligations as collateral for Federal Reserve notes.

During 1944 war expenditures totaled $91 billion, of which more than two-thirds, or $62 billion, was financed by increases in the public debt and of this amount non-bank investors took 59 per cent, compared with 58 per cent in 1943 and 51 per cent in 1942.

Finally, the Act of June 12, 1945, reduced reserve requirements of the Federal Reserve banks from 40 per cent against notes and 35 per cent against deposits to a uniform 25 per cent and extended indefinitely the authority to use direct obligations of the U. S. as collateral for Federal Reserve notes. At the same time the act terminated the authority of the Federal Reserve banks to issue Federal Reserve banknotes as well as the authority to issue greenbacks under the Thomas amendment.

The war having been brought to a successful conclusion in 1945, we may review briefly the fiscal burden of that enterprise. Between June 30, 1940, and December 31, 1945, the government raised $380 billion, of which $153 billion came from taxes (40 per cent) and $228 billion by borrowing. Of the borrowed dollars, $133 billion, or 60 per cent, came from non-bank investors and $95 billion, or 40 per cent, from the commercial banks.[8] The Federal Reserve System now felt called upon to invite attention to the consequences of borrowing from the banks. It said:

> It is important to understand that borrowing from the banking system, whether by Government or others, creates an equivalent addition to the country's monetary supply. As a consequence (of the war financing) the country's money supply, as measured by demand deposits and currency in circulation, more than tripled, increasing from $40 billion in June, 1940, to $127 billion at the end of 1945.

The Reserve called upon the government to reverse the process. It pointed out that the policy of maintaining a rate of 7/8 per cent for one year certificates made it possible for banks to increase their reserves by selling short-term, low yield government securities to the Reserve banks, and thus "acquire reserves which, on the basis of present reserve requirements, can support a six-fold expansion of member bank credit." It pointed out that outside the banks were some $20 billion of bonds eligible for bank purchase plus $34 billion that would become eligible within the next fifteen years, all with inflationary potential.

It went on to say:

> If the Federal debt occupied the relatively subordinate place in the economy that it held even up to 1940, the problems of debt management would be far simpler. . . . However, the Federal public debt at the end of 1945 had reached $280 billion, or nearly six times what it was five years before. Whereas it was equal to about one-fourth of the entire debt of the country in 1940, by the end of 1945 it was now two-thirds.[9]

The Board now proposed that the policy of maintaining the government market be abandoned, at least so far as the short-term rate was concerned, while it offered to continue to hold the long-term rate at 2 1/2 per cent.

In 1946 the preferential rate of discount of 1/2 per cent on government securities was finally discontinued. Nevertheless, the Treasury continued to hold an iron grip on Federal Reserve policy, and, as Eccles somewhat bitterly commented, "The pattern of war finance had been firmly established by the Treasury; the Federal Reserve merely executed Treasury decisions."[10]

Eccles was a man who had to be riding a white charger; his responsibilities now being confined, as he said, to a routine administrative job, he began to look around for something to challenge. He now (1944) proposed what he had thought of years before, the unification of the various authorities over the monetary-banking system now distributed among the Federal Reserve Board, the Comptroller of the Currency, and the Federal Deposit Insurance Corporation.

Roosevelt, however, did not think this an opportune time, when the country was still at war, to raise issues that would undoubtedly provoke dissention, particularly as there was the doubtful legality of his war powers to execute such an administrative change under the pretext of war necessity. Eccles tried to find support elsewhere for his proposals, particularly from James F. Byrnes, who had been taken from the Supreme Court bench to head the Office of War Mobilization, but the effort bogged down. Eccles' term as Chairman of the Board of Governors was now expiring, and Eccles in frustration asked not to be reappointed; but Roosevelt would not hear to it, and he continued as head of the System for another four years, until 1948.

29.

oⁿⁿⁿⁿⁿⁿⁿⁿⁿⁿⁿⁿⁿⁿⁿⁿⁿⁿⁿⁿ

Doubtful Victory

No HEAD of the Federal Reserve System provided more dynamic leadership, more clear-cut policy conceptions, or more fervent championship of Federal Reserve independence of function than did Marriner S. Eccles during his seventeen years in official capacity, of which fourteen were as the chief executive officer (governor or chairman) and three as a member of the Board of Governors. It was Eccles' boldness, stubbornness, and presumptuousness that finally brought the issue of Federal Reserve-Treasury relations into open feud and what seemed ultimate victory for the Federal Reserve. Nevertheless, the extent of this victory remains doubtful.

Following the close of hostilities, in 1945, as we have noted, Eccles, no longer the champion of spending, became the advocate of fiscal solvency, together with credit controls to prevent what he foresaw as a runaway inflation. Specifically, he urged that the war-time controls of the economy be retained until peace-time production had been restored and that reduction be made in the money supply in the hands of the public. Some success was achieved in the latter. The Treasury managed to obtain budget surpluses from mid-1946 to mid-1948 which resulted in some reduction of government debt held by the banks, but the precipitate removal of war-time controls led prices to move upward in response to the tremendous consumer demand.

A factor in the defeat of the advocates of credit control was the general fear that the country would plunge into a depression as soon as war-time orders and employment eased off; in early 1946 (February 20) Congress enacted the Employment Act of 1946, which declared "the continuing policy and responsibility of the Federal Government to use all practical means . . . to coordinate and utilize all its plans, functions, and resources for the purpose of creating and maintaining . . . conditions under which there will be afforded useful employment opportunities . . . for all able, willing and seeking to work. . . ."

The pressure, which the Federal Reserve could not resist, was on to continue to maintain low interest rates that would encourage private business investment and expansion.

Following Roosevelt's death on April 12, 1945, and the succession of Harry S. Truman to the Presidency, Eccles' influence at the White House began to decline, despite the fact that Truman maintained Eccles in the chairmanship until the end of his term in February, 1948. By the end of the war prices had already moved substantially above pre-war levels, particularly real estate and securities, into which investment, blocked off by price controls of commodities, had moved. Farm land was up some 44 per cent over the 1935–39 level,* urban real estate up from one-third to one-half above prewar,† and stock prices some 75 per cent above the 1942 average.‡

Eccles urged a penalty tax on capital gains and retention of the wartime excess profits tax; but the country was in no mood for restraint, either of prices or of credit, and during the summer and fall of 1945 most of these war time controls were removed. At the same time, to head off the possibility of a depression, the government embarked on a program to stimulate housing through veterans' loans and easier terms of payment under Federal Housing Administration insured loans. In order to broaden the demand for these loans and to maintain the market, the Federal National Mortgage Association, a subsidiary of the Reconstruction Finance Corporation, undertook to purchase large quantities of mortgages. The effect was prompt and decisive. The volume of mortgage financing on homes of one to four family units rose from $18.6 billion in 1945 to around $45.2 billion in 1950. The annual volume of mortgages rose from $4.8 billion to $16 billion.[1]

As Eccles and the Federal Reserve Board attempted to exercise influence in the direction of tighter credit, the difference between the Trea-

---

*From $33 per acre average for U. S. to $47 (*Historical Statistics of the U. S.,* Washington, G. P. O. 1960).

†Median asking price for existing houses, Washington, D. C. rose from $6,416 in 1939 to $10,131 in 1945. (*Ibid.*)

‡Index for common stocks (1941–43=10) moved from 8.67 in 1942 to 15.16 in 1945. (*Ibid.*)

sury and the Federal Reserve became more acute. The fact that Fred Vinson supplanted Henry Morgenthau as Secretary of the Treasury in July, 1945, made little difference, nor the fact that Vinson was later supplanted by John Snyder. The differences were deeper than personalities; they lay in two fundamental philosophies of the role of money and credit.

In July, 1945, Eccles had proposed that the preferential discount rate of 1/2 per cent on loans secured by Treasury bills and certificates, which had been established at all Federal Reserve banks in October, 1942, be discontinued. The Treasury indicated its opposition and the rate was retained. In April, 1946, the Board of Governors acceded to the recommendation of the twelve Reserve banks and approved the discontinuance of the preferential rate despite Treasury opposition; early in 1947 it was successful in persuading the Treasury to accept a free market rate on Treasury bills, and the 3/8 per cent buying rate was terminated. The rate on Treasury certificates was allowed to rise from 7/8 per cent to 1 1/4 per cent. These were modest achievements.

As banking assets continued to rise, however, further measures were advanced, but with less success. As early as 1945, the Board had proposed that the banks be required to hold a special reserve of obligations of the United States or cash as the Open Market Committee might determine in the light of credit conditions. The effect of the special reserve would be the immobilization of government securities held by banks; that is, it would prevent them being sold to the Reserve banks in order to increase the member banks' reserves and hence banking power; at the same time the special reserve would not deprive the banks of the earning power which would be lost if the regular reserve requirements were raised (since the banks do not receive interest on reserves maintained with the Reserve banks). The proposal met strong banking opposition, as expected, but Eccles hoped to carry the plan by reason of the fact that President Truman, growing concerned over the mounting inflation, had called Congress into special session to enact a ten-point inflation control program, of which the restraint of consumer credit and the special bank reserve plan were supposedly principal items. However, political considerations prevailed and the President's message omitted any reference to these measures.

Despite this rebuff, the Federal Reserve Board returned to its proposal in its Report for 1947. It pointed out that the commercial banks then held nearly $70 billion of Government securities and that there were another $70 billion floating supply in the market, not to mention $60 billion of non-marketable securities that were practically redeemable on demand.

All these bonds were quasi-money or what might be called multiple money, since any member bank that was short of lending power could always sell them or discount them at its Reserve bank and thereby obtain additional reserves. The Board therefore renewed its recommendation that banks be required to hold special reserves of cash assets or government bonds that could not then be used as banking reserves for the purpose of multiplying the banks' deposit power.

The most that the Federal Reserve was able to obtain was a Joint Resolution of August 8, 1947, which continued the authority to control consumer credit under Executive Order 8843 until not later than November 1. This authority soon lapsed but again in 1948 (August 16) a Joint Resolution restored the authority over consumer credit to June 30, 1949.

A Joint Resolution of the same date also amended Section 19 of the Federal Reserve Act to give the Board additional authority to increase reserves for a period ending June 30, 1949, within limits of 30 per cent for central reserve city banks, 24 per cent for reserve city banks, 18 per cent for other banks, and 7 1/2 per cent for time deposits. This authority was not renewed when it expired.

At this juncture, Eccles' wings were unexpectedly, and somewhat mysteriously, clipped by Truman's failure to redesignate him as Chairman of the Board at the end of his term on February 1, 1948. Truman did not notify Eccles of his decision until nine days before his term expired and the reason for this sudden act, so embarrassing to Eccles, has never been explained.*

Truman professed no lack of confidence in Eccles and promised to nominate him for Vice Chairman, but this appointment was never made. At the same time there was delay in naming a new Chairman of the Board and Eccles continued to act as interim Chairman until the appointment of Thomas A. McCabe April 15, 1948.

Eccles' reduction in rank combined with the outbreak of war in Korea in July, 1950, to bring the issue between Treasury and Federal Reserve to a pyrotechnic climax.

During the fall Treasury financing of that year the Reserve allowed the rate on one-year Treasury notes to rise to 1 1/2 per cent despite a Treasury announcement of its intention to refund $13,570 million issue

---

*Eccles attributes it to the influence of the Giannini interests of California whose hostility Eccles incurred by his opposition to the expansion of the branch banking system of the Giannini-controlled Bank of America National Trust and Savings Association, the largest banking chain in the U. S. and today the largest banking institution in terms of total assets. (*Op. cit.* Part 7, ch. 3, pp. 434-FF.)

at a cost of 1 1/4 per cent. By this act the Federal Reserve proclaimed its independence of the Treasury so far as short term yields were concerned; but the central bank's open market operations on the long end of the market remained inhibited by the asserted need for maintaining a 2 1/2 per cent yield ceiling on the Treasury's longest-term bonds.[2]

Apparently with the object of tightening the rein on the Federal Reserve, on January 18, 1951, Secretary of the Treasury John Snyder issued a statement without consulting the Board, to the effect that the rate on long-term bonds would be held at 2 1/2 per cent. The announcement declared that the determination had been made at a joint conference with the President and Chairman McCabe.

The announcement created consternation not only in the Federal Reserve but in the banking community, and the *New York Times* commented:

> In the opinion of this writer [Edward H. Collins] last Thursday constituted the first occasion in history on which the head of the Exchequer of a great nation had either the effrontery or the ineptitude, or both, to deliver a public address in which he so far usurped the function of the central bank as to tell the country what kind of monetary policy it was going to be subjected to. For the moment, at least, the fact that the policy enunciated by Mr. Snyder was, as usual, thoroughly unsound and inflationary, was overshadowed by the historic dimensions of his impertinence.[3]

On January 25, Senator Taft questioned Eccles in a hearing of the Joint Committee on the Economic Report.* Eccles restated the Federal Reserve view.

"To prevent inflation," he declared,

> we must stop the overall growth in credit and the money supply whether for financing government or private deficit spending. The supply of money must be controlled at the source of its creation, which is the banking system.
>
> Under our present powers, the only way to do this is by denying banks access to Federal Reserve funds which provide the basis for a six-fold expansion in our money supply. The only way to stop access to Federal Reserve funds is by withdrawing Federal Reserve support from the government securities market and penalizing borrowing by the member banks from the Federal Reserve System.

He went on to say:

---

*According to Eccles, Chairman McCabe begged off from testifying, finding himself in the dilemma of either defending the Treasury's position or opposing it and resigning.

As long as the Federal Reserve System is required to buy government securities at the will of the market for the purpose of defending a fixed pattern of interest rates established by the Treasury, it must stand ready to create new bank reserves in unlimited amount.

This policy makes the entire banking system, through the action of the Federal Reserve System, an engine of inflation.[4]

On the thirty-first, the Board's Open Market Committee was summoned to the White House for a lecture from Truman on the need to support the government credit and immediately following the meeting the White House announced that the Federal Reserve Board had given its pledge "to maintain the stability of government securities as long as the emergency lasted." Within an hour a Treasury spokesman announced that this meant that the Federal Reserve was committed to stabilize the market for government securities at existing levels.[5] At the same time Secretary Snyder issued a challenge to critics of a cheap money policy, warning that an increase in average interest rates would add to mounting inflationary pressures on the economy unless passed on to the public in the form of taxes—which the Administration did not propose to do.

"It should be thoroughly understood," he said in an interview, "that an increase of as much as one half of 1 per cent in the average rate on long-term government securities would mean an increase of $1 1/2 billion in annual carrying charges on the public debt."[6]

To box the Federal Reserve in, the President wrote a letter to McCabe and released the letter to the public, stating:

> Your assurance that you would fully support the Treasury defense financing program, both as to refunding and new issues, is of vital importance to me. As I understand it, I have your assurance that the market on government securities will be stabilized and maintained at present levels in order to assure the successful financing requirements and to establish in the minds of the people confidence concerning government credit.[7]

Eccles now determined to cast politics and his political future to the winds, and played his final stroke. It was on a Friday afternoon that the White House released the President's letter. Chairman McCabe had gone for the weekend. A memorandum of the critical meeting of the Open Market Committee with the President had been drawn, at the Committee's request, by Committee member R. M. Evans; the only copy, however, was in the custody of the Secretary of the Board of Governors, Sam Carpenter. Eccles now routed him from his home, and got him to deliver the memorandum to him. Eccles had it copied, and next day, after sleeping on his decision, gave it to the *New York Times,* the *Washington Post,* and the *Washington Star,* where it was front page news in the Sunday editions of February 4.[8]

At the same time Eccles gave an interview to the *Times'* Felix Belair, Jr., in which he declared, "I am astonished. The only answer I can make is to give you a copy of the record of what took place at the White House meeting.[9]

The Federal Reserve–Treasury differences were now a national issue, no longer to be ignored. Eccles was no longer in control of the Federal Reserve, but just a month later, on March 4, the Treasury and the Federal Reserve issued a joint announcement that read:

> The Treasury and the Federal Reserve System have reached a full accord with respect to debt management and monetary policies to be pursued in furthering their common purpose to assure the successful financing of the government's requirements and, at the same time, to minimize the monetization of the public debt.[10]

As a result, the Treasury undertook to exchange for outstanding long term bonds new long term bonds not directly marketable, an operation that paved the way for the discontinuance of Federal Reserve support of government bond prices by purchases in the market. The new bond issue bore 2 3/4 per cent (as against the 2 1/2 per cent rate at which the Federal Reserve had held the market), with a maturity of twenty-nine years, but were redeemable by the holder by conversion into five-year marketable Treasury notes. Following the agreement also, the Federal Reserve withdrew its support of the general structure of federal credit and allowed the market to seek its own level.

Shortly afterward, McCabe found it convenient to resign as Board chairman and member[11] and in June Eccles retired to private life.

The new Chairman, William McChesney Martin, had distinguished himself as a compromiser, and this quality of disposition, despite a conservative tendency, kept him in office and in favor through both Republican and Democratic administrations for the following fourteen years, and permitted him to lead the Federal Reserve System to its jubilee year intact but shaken as to its independence.*

---

*Martin had been made president of the New York Stock Exchange in 1938, when he was only thirty-one years old, as a compromise candidate between two contending factions. After the war he had been made president of the Export-Import Bank and later, as Assistant Secretary of the Treasury, had helped negotiate the "accord" that compromised the differences between Eccles and the Treasury. Republican Eisenhower found his views on credit restriction and currency discipline congenial, but when Kennedy was elected Martin went

The bold action of Marriner S. Eccles seemed to have restored to the Federal Reserve System its statutory independence, and indeed this may have continued to be the case, but for a new set of circumstances, arising out of post-war foreign policy, that gradually drew the Federal Reserve System into a new entanglement and subserviency—now not to Treasury as much as to State Department.

This was the embarkation of a new foreign policy of world-wide military alliances and a cultivation of world opinion and support through a massive expenditure under a program of assistance to other countries.

---

along with the new Administration's desire for easy credit and a monetary policy of stimulation. In 1965, however, through some slip, he made a speech pointing out the parallels between the conditions preceding the Great Depression and the prosperity which President Johnson's Great Society was enjoying—a speech that catalyzed a stock market break and that threw the Administration into consternation.

30.

The Role of Atlas

T HE FIFTH DECADE of the Federal Reserve System was a period of
placidity, like the uneventful years of senility, as the System drifted
in the overhung backwaters of Treasury influence—and later State Department policy. The significant development of the period was the rise
of State Department influence, and the subservience of Federal Reserve
activities to the changing objectives of diplomacy rather than to the needs
of domestic business. Illustrative is the dichotomy that arose regarding
interest rates—the effort to maintain a high rate to attract deposits from
abroad and deter the export of gold, at the same time a low rate to
encourage capital investment and business expansion. But of that later.

The post-war years had witnessed a remarkable shift in American public sentiment, from isolation and non-involvement in world affairs to assumption of world wide responsibilities and commitments for which the
political experience and the economic power of the people were of doubtful adequacy. The first manifestation was U. S. sponsorship of a series
of international agencies to interlace the political and economic fabric of
the world. The most imposing of these was the United Nations Organization, which came into existence June 25, 1945, following a conference of
delegates of fifty nations at San Francisco. More influential, however, in
effecting practical solutions to the world's problems were two international
economic institutions, gestated a year earlier by the Bretton Woods (N.H.)
Conference of July 1–22, 1944. These were the International Monetary
Fund and the International Bank for Reconstruction and Development.*

---

*These institutions did not begin actual operations until 1946.

The International Monetary Fund was set up to provide a reserve pool of the currencies of the members and to make them available on application to meet currency needs of indigent members, and thereby prevent exchange fluctuations, and international currency crises. The significant thing about the International Monetary Fund was that it restored to sanctity the gold exchange system, first hallowed by the Geneva Conference of 1922, but so thoroughly discredited thereafter by the worldwide collapse of 1932.

The heart of the new gold exchange standard was the U. S. dollar, which was equated with gold in the Fund's Articles of Agreement.

Let us say Country A (one of those nations now called "less developed" or "developing") had a deficit in its international transactions—that is, it was unable to sell abroad as much as it wished to buy abroad—and needed money to pay its foreign creditors. Its own currency was unacceptable to its creditors. It could, under the rules, apply to the Fund and obtain dollars to tide it over, hopefully, until it could set its house in order. In exchange for the dollars the Fund would receive currency of the borrowing country in an amount equivalent—that is, theoretically equivalent—to the dollars obtained. Obviously, the currency of Country A would not be of equivalent value of the dollars received or the foreign creditors themselves would accept Country A's currency in settlement of debts owing, and Country A would not be under necessity of applying to the Fund for aid.

The subordinate currencies were not equivalent mainly because their central banks were unable, or unwilling, to deliver gold for their currencies on demand, and importantly because many of them had no nominal gold equivalents—that is, in the language of the Fund, no par values had been established. One of the first tasks of the Fund was to get the member countries to establish par values, or gold convertibility, for their currencies. This required more internal fiscal discipline than most countries were willing or able to exercise.

The Fund started business with a pool of $7.47 billion nominal value of currencies subscribed by the participating members, of which $2.75 billion was subscribed by the United States. The United States, however, was the only member country that maintained gold convertibility of the dollar,* that is, that freely delivered gold at the statutory parity of $35 an ounce to foreign governments and central banks in exchange for

---

*International convertibility, that is. Since 1933 U. S. citizens have been unable to obtain gold for their paper currency.

dollar deposits or dollar currency. It followed that for the following decade the Fund was really a device for making sound dollars available to various countries in exchange for their less valuable currencies, and after a time the Fund's quotas were increased, with the devious object of making more dollars available to indigent countries. By 1963, the total subscribed capital of the Fund was $15 1/2 billion, of which the U.S. share was $4.125 billion.

The theory behind this procedure was that there existed a "world shortage of liquidity," also called a "dollar shortage," and as part of its contribution to post-war reconstruction the U.S. would by various means put its stock of money at the service of the world community. At the end of the first ten years, that is, on April 30, 1956, of $1,242,-600,000 put at the disposal of members of the Fund, all but $207 1/2 million consisted of U.S. dollars, the balance being largely British sterling.[1] Shortly thereafter, as we shall note further on, a remarkable reversal in relative liquidities occurred, and the U.S. became an applicant for the Fund's assistance.

The International Bank for Reconstruction and Development was created to provide funds, by way of loans, under long-term repayment conditions, to member governments and their agencies, for strictly economic development purposes. Member governments were required to subscribe to the capital of the Bank in varying proportions, and the total authorized capital was $10 billion. Again, as the sellers of goods and services needed for the projects wanted payment in good money, it fell out, not unexpectedly, that most of the loans were made in dollars. To provide a sufficient supply of dollars, the Bank could borrow dollars in the ordinary capital markets, against the credit of the United States, but eventually an increase of the subscribed capital became necessary. By the end of 1963 this capital subscription had been increased to $21.1 billion, of which the U. S. subscription was $6.35 billion.

At the end of 1963 the Bank had outstanding loans in the amount of $5 billion, and to provide this sum it had gone into the market and borrowed $1.9 billion in U. S. dollars, and $620 million in other currencies; the balance it had provided from its own capital reserves, mainly U. S. dollars.*

---

*An interesting question is why the Bank, with $21.1 billion capital subscriptions, and loan investments of only $5 billion should be obliged to go into the market for funds to lend. The explanation is an illustration of the sophistries in which international financial diplomacy operates. In the first place, most of the Bank's assets were in currencies that no one wanted to borrow, and its holdings of U. S. dollars (from the U. S. subscription) were

That the financial power of the U. S. should undergird the world's economy during the period of reconstruction was a proposition increasingly understood and accepted by the American electorate. This electorate had been suffering a form of guilt complex ever since the close of World War I for what was called abroad its grasping self-interest in regard to repayment of the war loans it had made to its allies.

Abroad the popular caricature of the United States had become Uncle Shylock, and American travellers in Europe were slyly taunted on our ingratitude to the mother cultures. The argument was made that European economic stagnation was due to the transfer problem which the U. S. had created by requiring war debt payments and at the same time making obstacles through its high tariff policy which impeded the entry of merchandise by which to discharge the debt.

This theory overlooked the fact that U. S. imports from Europe rose from $765 million in 1921 to $1,334 million in 1929, whereas U. S. exports to Europe actually declined slightly, from $2,364 million in 1921 to $2,344 million in 1929, and that Europeans were at the same time earning large sums from shipping and other services to the U. S. economy and from the spending of U. S. tourists. It also neglected the fact that Europeans could also have reduced their buying of U. S. goods, not all of which went—contrary to popular belief—to feed hungry mouths or to rebuild bomb damage.

Nevertheless, U. S. popular opinion was greatly influenced by the arguments and this was reflected in various official steps to repair that fault. The burden of the war debts was eased by a stretch-out of the payments and later by a moratorium granted by President Hoover, which is still in effect. Under President Roosevelt a general reduction of tariffs was undertaken under what is known as the reciprocal trade policy, whereby it became settled that the U. S. tariff rates should be steadily lowered.

Following World War II the cry again arose from Europe for assistance to avert economic and political collapse. It played upon the sense of discomfort suffered by many Americans over their seemingly undeserved material blessings* which combined with a natural philanthropy on the

---

insufficient to meet the demand for loans. In the second place, the capital subscriptions of the Bank are illusory since subscriptions had to be paid up only to the extent of 10 per cent. Thus, of total subscriptions of $21.1 billion, only $798 million had been paid in U. S. dollars.

*Prof. Helmut Schoeck of Emory University has given most thought to this phenomenon. *See* "The Evil Eye: Forms and Dynamics of a Universal Superstition," *Emory University Quarterly,* October, 1955, pp. 153–61, and "The Envy Barrier," ch. 5 in *Foreign Aid Re-Examined* (Washington: Public Affairs Press, 1958). The general presuppositions in John

part of many more, and a growing suspicion of Soviet Russia by everyone, to lead this country eventually to assume the burden of Atlas supporting the globe.

Since the fiscal sinews of this undertaking were nourished from the vascular streams pumped by the Federal Reserve System like an inexhaustible heart, a sketch of the process by which U. S. world responsibilities multiplied and became an Old Man of the Sea upon the back of the American electorate is in order.

During the war the U. S. had joined an inter-allied relief organization to provide assistance in liberated areas; this became the United Nations Relief and Rehabilitation Administration to which the U. S. eventually contributed, until it ceased operations in 1947, some $2.67 billion of its total resources of $3.66 billion.

The first overt assumption of political responsibility in post-war Europe, however, occurred in Greece and Turkey. The Soviet drive to dominate the Middle East, through pressure on Turkish and Greek sovereignty, had led the U. S. to agree with Great Britain in 1946 to provide economic aid to these two countries while Great Britain provided military aid. In February, 1947, Great Britain notified the U. S. that its own financial difficulties were forcing it to stop further assistance. This put the business squarely on American shoulders. President Truman went before Congress on March 12, 1947, for approval of an appropriation of $400 million for military and economic aid to the two countries.

U. S. public sentiment was still opposed to overseas entanglements, but the temporary nature of the commitment was emphasized, and witnesses testified in the hearings that this was a crisis situation that would not extend beyond fifteen months ending June, 1948. The Administration declared that this was not to be regarded as a precedent, and that it had no intention of making this particular kind of response to every instance in which free peoples were threatened.[2]

The appropriation was voted, and the ink was hardly dry on the bill when the press was filled with portents of European collapse unless U. S. aid were extended there also. The data were impressive. In 1947, it was pointed out, over-all production of goods and services in Western Europe was still 7 per cent below pre-war. This output had to be shared

Kenneth Galbraith's *The Affluent Society* are manifestations. *See also* Edward G. Banfield, *American Foreign Aid Doctrines.* Monograph. (Washington: American Enterprise Institute, 1963)

among a population that had increased by some 8 per cent. Recovery lagged in the key sectors of coal and steel. This had produced shortages of tools and articles manufactured from steel and slowed down production, due to lack of fuel. This in turn hampered the export of goods needed to buy necessary supplies and equipment from abroad. The deficit, it was urged, could only be met by supplies provided by loan or grant. During 1947, particularly, Europe had suffered a series of crises. A cold winter had aggravated the fuel shortage and a drought the following summer had curtailed the harvest. In 1947, also, the British effort to restore the convertibility of the pound had collapsed after six weeks, and this had spread a fog of gloom and despair throughout the markets of Europe.

The American people were not surprised therefore on June 5, 1947, when General George C. Marshall, then Secretary of State, in an historic address at Harvard University, accepted on behalf of the United States a moral and financial commitment for the support of Europe. Marshall declared:

"Europe's requirements for the next three or four years of foreign food and other essential products—principally from America—are so much greater than her present ability to pay, that she must have substantial help or face economic, social, and political deterioration of a very grave character."

Congress assembled in January, 1948, to be confronted with an imposing array of reports on European necessities prepared by three Presidential committees. In addition, representatives of sixteen countries of Western Europe had met in Paris during the summer and had prepared their own report of the needs and resources for economic reconstruction. Their report estimated that they would need some $22.4 billion from the United States in the next four years. The three Presidential committees all concluded that the United States could well afford the cost and if it were not forthcoming, "free institutions everywhere, including those in the United States, would be in jeopardy." On March 13, 1948, after extensive hearings, the Senate voted 69 to 17 to support the European Recovery Program as outlined, and on March 31 the House by a vote of 329 to 74 accepted the financial commitment. The total amount of the commitment was never explicit but it was commonly understood that the program would extend over a four-year period and would be in the neighborhood of $14 billion, of which $5.3 billion would be provided in the first year.

The Greek-Turkish aid program did not, of course, terminate in 1948, nor did the Marshall Plan end in 1952. In 1948 the Greek-Turkish program was merged with the European Recovery Program. This in turn was soon to be expanded into a worldwide program of foreign aid. President Truman, in his inaugural address on January 20, 1949, announced "a bold new program for the making the benefits of our scientific advances and industrial progress available for the improvement and growth of underdeveloped areas." This became known as the Point 4 program, for its being the fourth item in his Administration's program. It evoked world wide enthusiasm, and the Congress went along.

Meantime, although the Marshall Plan had been designed for European necessities, it had soon been expanded to include economic stabilization and development in non-European areas. The China Aid Act of 1948 (Title IV of the Economic Cooperation Act) authorized technical and other (military) aid to China. On January 1, 1949, Truman gave the Economic Cooperation Administration (ECA) responsibility for administering economic aid in Korea, and thus shifted the emphasis from relief to economic development. Indonesia first received aid as a Dutch dependency. Aid programs began in Burma, Indo-China and Thailand when the ECA suggested to Congress that funds left over from the mainland China program be expended in the "general area of China." The earlier post-war relief and reconstruction operations in the Philippines were expanded to include economic development.

Truman's Point 4 program of technical assistance to underdeveloped areas now opened the door to long-term, though presumably inexpensive, advisory operations throughout Asia, Africa and Latin America. This was followed up in July, 1949, after the ratification of the North Atlantic Treaty Alliance, by a Presidential request for authority to give "military aid to free nations to enable them to protect themselves against the threat of aggression"—a *carte blanche* that included practically every country in the world that could maintain a reasonably persuasive diplomatic representative in Washington. This became the Mutual Defense Assistance Act of 1949 which in turn became the first of a long series of enactments, each broader and more vague in the limits it set to the outpouring of U. S. dollars.

This is not the place to explore the philosophy or the results of this concept in foreign policy; our interest here is with its effects upon the Federal Reserve System with which we are primarily concerned in this work. We need note that by the end of fiscal year 1963 the total post-war foreign aid expenditures had exceeded $103 billion; that the Greek-

Turkish Aid Program, originally budgeted at $400 million with a termination date of 15 months, still was in existence and total outlays had cost $7.7 billion; and that Western Europe, excluding Greece and Turkey, had received more than $45 billion (a figure which includes some $16 billion of military supplies) and despite economic recovery and boom time prosperity was the recipient of $900 million in fiscal year 1963.

By 1963 the cost of the foreign aid program had grown to in excess of $7 billion annually. The figure does not include the payments made abroad in support of U. S. garrisons, particularly in Germany and Korea, and of a long list of military, air, and naval bases around the world. These overseas military costs (that is, only the costs that must be paid in foreign currencies) were of the order of $3 1/2 billion annually. Nor does the figure include the large sums made available indirectly, through loans by the various international lending agencies and assistance institutions that sprang up following World War II. We have already mentioned two, the International Bank for Reconstruction and Development and the International Monetary Fund: these have proliferated into the International Finance Corporation; the International Development Association; the Inter-American Development Bank; the Social Progress Trust Fund; and a number of agencies of the United Nations Organization to which the U. S. contributed, chief among them being the United Nations Special Fund and the Expanded Technical Assistance Program.

The total cost to the U. S. taxpayer of all these various assistance operations was actually around $10 billion annually—a magnitude not generally realized by the American public, largely because of the multiplicity of the programs in which the cost had been concealed in the various appropriation bills.

31.

The Not So Golden Years

LENIN is reputed to have dismissed the utility of gold to its value as paving for latrines. Two centuries before, of course, John Law had persuaded the Regent of France that it was possible to abolish gold or any other standard for money in favor of the fiat of the sovereign. In 1905 the German economist George Friedrich Knapp had decried the value of metals as money in his *Staatliche Theorie des Geldes,* and in the 1920s Irving Fisher of Yale had created a following for his proposals of a "commodity dollar" the value of which would rest upon a weighted price index of a list of common articles of trade.[1] Modern economists, disciples of Keynes, incline to sneer at the gold stored at Fort Knox, and say that the world would hardly know the difference if it should suddenly disappear in an earthquake. Nevertheless, few of them are willing to argue the complete disutility of gold in transactions. The prevailing school would reduce its services to the settlement of international balances. Those who retain their convictions that money must be intrinsic, that is, consist of, or be representative of, gold (or silver) have so compromised their positions with their fractional reserve theories as to have lost all authority in the field.

We need not marshall and assess the arguments pro and con: for our present purpose it is sufficient to point out that, although now a euphemism, the value of the dollar is defined by law in terms of gold, and that until the collapse of the gold (convertible) dollar on August 15, 1971, the International Monetary Fund required that the par value of the currency of each member be expressed in gold—and what is more significant to our purpose—"or in terms of the United States dollar of the weight and

235

fineness in effect on July 1, 1944."[2] It also required that all charges imposed on its members be paid in gold.[3]

With this background we may now examine the effects of the policy of foreign aid and military alliances upon the ability of the Federal Reserve System to maintain the gold value of the dollar and its own integrity as a monetary institution. In 1949, which may be taken as the year in which foreign aid became a continuing foreign policy, the gold stock available to support the monetary and credit structure was in excess of $24 1/2 billion, or some 70 percent of the free world visible gold supply. The position of the dollar was unimpeachable.

Beginning in 1949, however, the United States experienced a deficit in its international transactions.* The manifestation of this deficit was an outflow of gold and an increase in foreign holdings of dollar exchange (bank deposits in U. S. banks, Treasury bills, and other credits.) It was, however, not until 1958, when a hemorrhage of $2.3 billion occurred, that the gold outflow began to cause alarm. By the end of 1963 the gold reserve of the country had been reduced to $15 1/2 billion and the soundness of the dollar was everywhere in question.

Meantime a complacent Federal Reserve System had accepted the political philosophy of the Truman Fair Deal, the Eisenhower Crusade, and the Kennedy New Frontier, that tolerated fiscal deficits and demanded easy money. The return of peace, therefore, had not meant balanced budgets and a reduction in the public debt. Between the end of 1945 and the end of 1963 the federal debt held by the banks and public† rose from $227.4 billion to $261.5 billion. At the same time the commercial banks were reducing their holdings of governments to provide funds for expanding commercial demand. To supply the credit for all these needs the Federal Reserve banks added to their holdings of governments. Thus, as we have noted, between 1947 and the end of 1963 Federal Reserve banks increased their portfolios by a good third, that is, from $22.6 billion to $30.6 billion.

In addition, the Federal Reserve Board authorized a series of reductions of the reserve requirements of member banks, bringing down the

---

*The balance of international payments is generally defined as the difference between the payments to foreigners for goods and services and the receipts from foreigners for goods and services, which may be settled by shipments of gold or the increase or decrease of liabilities. The analysis of the balance of payments is complicated by the fact that investments made abroad create a form of balance sheet liability which must be offset by actual shipments or services, or by per contra liabilities.

†Excludes government obligations held by government agencies and trust funds, including the Federal Reserve banks. Gross public debt rose from $257 billion to $309.5 billion.

rates for central reserve cities from 26 per cent in 1948 to 16 1/2 per cent, for reserve city banks from 22 per cent to 16 1/2 per cent, for country banks from 16 per cent to 12 per cent (with a temporary reduction to 11 per cent from 1958 to 1960), and for time deposits from 7 1/2 per cent to 4 per cent.

The effect upon total bank credit is seen in the increase in money supply, or what is now known as M_1, that is, bank deposits and currency in circulation, from $180 billion at the end of 1945 to $300 billion at the end of 1963. By this time the gold available to meet these obligations was only 4.7 per cent of total liabilities, compared with 7.4 per cent during the period just preceding the Great Crash in 1929.

Since 1934, however, no bank depositor or note holder has been able to demand gold for his note or deposit slip. Thus, the threat to gold did not arise from domestic demand, but from abroad. By its undertakings with the International Monetary Fund, the Treasury was committed to deliver gold to foreign central banks of government members of the Fund, at the rate of $35 per ounce. Under this assurance, foreign central banks and international institutions had accumulated some $12 billion of dollar deposits or short term Treasury bills, which they treated as the same as gold in their statements of reserve.

In addition other foreign holders had accumulated dollar quick assets (bank deposits or Treasury bills) to an additional amount of $14 billion all of which could, through sale to their respective central banks, be converted into claims for U. S. gold.

Here was the dilemma faced by the Federal Reserve System in the final days of its fifth decade, its jubilee year. As during the 1920's, foreign central banks had erected a tottering structure of bank money upon a feeble foundation of gold and dollar exchange. Again, they found themselves caught in an inflationary spiral of rising note volume for which increasing quantities of coin or metal were required if the parity of the paper with its stated metal equivalent were to be maintained.* World gold production was not enough to provide these reserves. Except for South African production, gold production had been static or declining,

---

*An over-all statistic for the expansion of money supply is not available, but figures for a few representative countries are illustrative. Using 1953 as a base of 100, the International Monetary Fund reported that between 1948 and 1961 (at which date the index base changed) money supply rose as follows: France, from 47 to 238; Germany, from 49 to 232; Italy, from 53 to 231; United Kingdom, from 92 to 110; Netherlands, from 85 to 147. For the U. S. the index of money supply rose from 85 to 113.

because of the rising costs of mining. Moreover, despite widespread restrictions on the possession of, or trade in gold, increasing amounts were going into private hands. Of estimated free world* gold production in 1963 of 39.2 million ounces ($1.37 billion) some 28 1/2 million ounces ($1 billion) went into private hands. Only the circumstances of short crops and other misfortunes in Soviet Russia, that forced it to sell an estimated 600 tons of gold in the world's markets, together with the corresponding balance of payments difficulties of the U. S. that required a transfer of some $465 million to foreigners, enabled the central banks of Europe to increase their gold reserves as they did. Even so they were compelled increasingly to rely upon dollar exchange to provide reserves for their expanding monetary liabilities.

The increment of dollar exchange which they needed had been provided largely from the U. S. foreign aid program, by creating a net debit in the U. S. balance of payments. But these increments increased the strain upon the dollar, and created apprehension in the U. S. and led to popular agitation for curtailment of the foreign aid program. The practical effect of this would be deflationary. Foreign central banks would find it necessary to curtail the credit they had been extending so freely. The prospect of another depression, triggered by a stoppage of the flow of U. S. credit abroad, generated widespread consternation.

The frailty of the situation was cloaked under the sophistry of the "international liquidity problem." Various schemes were advanced—the Bernstein, the Triffin, the Maudling plans—which space does not warrant our detailing here. All of them evaded the issue of the inadequacy of the gold stock to support such an inflated money supply, and offered palliatives.

Meanwhile, such was the decay of confidence in the dollar that the Treasury, for the first time in its history, was compelled to borrow abroad in monetary units other than the dollar. That is, foreign governments, or their central banks, increasingly doubtful of the ability of the Treasury to redeem its obligations in gold, quietly but insistently pressed for obligations payable in currencies in which they had more confidence. Thus it happened that the government, which during the darkest days of the Civil War never borrowed in any terms but dollars, was compelled in 1961 to go "hat in hand" to the governments of European powers seeking their assistance to maintain the integrity of the U. S. dollar. By the end of 1963, the Treasury had incurred debts totaling the equivalent of $760 million

---

*Free world, i.e., countries not under Communist government.

payable in various foreign currencies (Swiss francs, German marks, Austrian schillings, Belgian francs, Italian lire). No bonds, however, were issued payable in French francs—a circumstance we shall comment on further on. In addition, the Federal Reserve, through a devious device known as "swap arrangements," entered into arrangements with various foreign central banks to obtain foreign currencies in order to strengthen the dollar abroad.

In short, the Federal Reserve System ended its fifth decade with a paradox of the so-called gold exchange standard. Its dollar obligations represented prime reserves of foreign central banks whose currencies, supported by these dollar obligations, were in turn the support for the dollar obligations. If this seems a bit confusing, one can think of the little island where supposedly everyone lived by taking in each other's wash.

32.

〜〜〜〜〜〜〜〜〜〜〜〜〜〜〜〜

The End of a Dream

TOWARD THE END OF 1963 the *New York Times* reported that "a quiet revolution has been taking place in the Federal Reserve System."[1] Within the preceding two and a half years, the *Times* announced, "the nation's money managers have reshaped their tactics and reforged their weapons for carrying out their responsibilities."

The nature of this "revolution," it appeared, went beyond routine questions of the techniques to be employed in easing or tightening credit. It "involved a basic shift in the concept of monetary management."

"The Federal Reserve," the *Times* stated hopefully, "is now following a dynamic course, pursuing an aggressive policy of managing money." This represented an about face from the "passive course followed in the nineteen fifties" when the Federal Reserve "all but abdicated its responsibility for monetary management."

This passive role, it was explained, consisted of "self-imposed restrictions on open-market operations," of reliance upon the discount function, and of disuse of member bank reserve requirements. These had now been abandoned in favor of a willingness to experiment with new techniques in response to changing conditions. "Now, for the first time," said the *Times*, "flexible monetary policy is in operation."

In detailing the specifics of the new dynamism, however, the *Times* account grew understandably vague. It reported that the Reserve had relaxed its "rigid technique for conducting open market operations, and could claim some measure of success for expanding the supply of credit and at the same time holding up short-term interest rates to defend the dollar." It raised the discount rate—"the first time that it had been used to safeguard the international status of the dollar." And it now engaged in extensive foreign currency operations, "another indication of its new look." These seem to be the sum and substance of the "revolution" as reported by the *Times*.

A more accurate reflection of the status to which the Federal Reserve had fallen is found in the violent attacks upon it by Representative Wright Patman. Patman, a Texan from Texarkana (which straddles Arkansas and Texas) who had represented his Eastern Texas district in Congress since 1928, had been an ardent exponent of the Bryan cheap money school and, as his influence rose along with his seniority, became the leader of that persuasion. He favored lower interest rates, a greater abundance of circulating media, abundant and easy credit. As chairman of the House Banking and Currency Committee when the Democrats controlled the House, and senior minority member when the Republicans were in control, Patman was in a position to exert great influence and to some measure control legislation in this field.

It was therefore a matter of note, if not alarm, to defenders of the Federal Reserve System when, early in January, 1964, Patman announced lengthy hearings on a series of bills he had introduced that would alter the structure of the System. He had promptly cut the ground from the opposition in his announcement in which he declared that "any Federal institution that has not been looked into for nearly thirty years should have a check-up . . . we are living in a new country and a new world—we should look at the most powerful banking system on earth, the Federal Reserve, in the light of the United States, 1964."[2]

His bills proposed a drastic diminution of the independence—such as it was—of the Federal Reserve System. They would abolish the System's Open Market Committee and transfer its functions to the Reserve Board; enlarge the Board to twelve members with four-year terms, the twelfth member to be the Secretary of the Treasury and at the same time chairman of the Board; abolish the system whereby the member banks owned the stock of the Reserve banks, and theoretically determined their policies; require audits of the System by the General Accounting Office; and finally require the Federal Reserve to operate under annual Congressional appropriation. In short, the institution would be made *de jure*, as it was *de facto*, an arm of the Federal government. Two other bills would permit commercial banks to pay interest on demand deposits (forbidden since 1933 by the Banking Act of June 16, 1933), and would require the banks to pay interest to the Treasury on government deposits.

Despite the audacity and violence of this assault, the actual threat to Federal Reserve solvency came from another quarter—from old and until recently indigent friends, and from one ancient ally—the French Republic.

Europe had made an astounding recovery from the depression and despair of 1947, which had brought on the Marshall Plan. How much of this recovery was due to the dollars distributed so freely, and how much to innate European vitality, and indeed how much to the restoration of morale which was, even more than the dollars, the chief fruit of American concern and goodwill, all are matters for debate. In Germany, for instance, where following defeat the mark had depreciated to the point where the cigarette had become the preferred medium of exchange, the restoration of a sound currency had had an electric effect. Overnight, shop windows that had been empty were filled, streets that had been deserted now swarmed with traffic; suddenly new buildings were rising on every hand and the air was filled with the sound of the hammer and the steam shovel. Men who had been aimlessly walking the streets seeking work or food were now employed and fed. Overnight the universal look of apathy was turned to joy and expectation.[3]

The German currency reform had occurred in June, 1948, before the impact of U. S. economic aid. The year before, as we have noted, the British attempt to restore the pound sterling had collapsed, with consequences felt throughout Europe. On September 18, 1949, the pound was devalued to a parity of $2.80 with the dollar.* The pound continued to be a feeble currency, however, and in 1961, the United Kingdom was compelled to borrow $900 million from the United States and European countries. When this loan could not be repaid, the government was forced to borrow $1 1/2 billion from the International Monetary Fund and to obtain an additional $1/2 billion stand-by credit.†

In France, monetary instability continued until 1958, with the value of the franc subjected to successive alterations. In 1945, following the liberation from German control, the franc had been revalued at 119.1 to the dollar; in 1948, the rate was reduced to 214.39 to the dollar; in 1949 reduction was made to 329.8; in 1949, to 350, and in 1957 to 420 to the dollar.[4]

---

*Since the dollar had itself been devalued in 1934, the new pound represented $1.654 in terms of the 1914 dollar, compared with the parity at that time of $4.867.

†In November, 1964, a further crisis occurred, compelling a spectacular, overnight rescue, led by the New York Federal Reserve Bank, in which 11 countries provided short-term credits totaling $3 billion.

In June, 1958, conditions in France had reached the state of revolutionary crisis that brought General Charles de Gaulle to power with the authority of a dictator and a mandate to draft a new Constitution. As with Bismarck, with Napoleon, with Constantine the Great, almost his first step in the reform of the state was the restoration of a sound currency. On December 29, under the guidance of the French economist Jacques Rueff, the franc was again revalued, from 420 to the dollar to 493.706 to the dollar, and at this point the franc was abolished in favor of a new franc equivalent to 100 of the former. The restoration of stable currency, the resolution of the Algerian war, and the firmness of the de Gaulle rule now produced a remarkable economic resurgence. Within five years France regained its historic position as the political and economic leader of Europe.

The French revival occurred along with the deterioration of the U. S. international position, which we have already charted, and was accompanied by a foreign policy of independence from, if not veiled hostility toward, the United States. From the days of the French Occupation, when de Gaulle was a young leader of the Free French forces, the proud and lofty Frenchman had never forgotten the cavalier treatment he had received from Churchill and Roosevelt; he continually referred to the "Anglo-Saxons" as an earlier age referred to the Mongols; he spoke frankly of the necessity of resisting "Anglo-Saxon imperialism" in Europe. He was the cause of rejection of the British from the European Common Market—an economic and quasi-political association of France, Germany, Italy, the Netherlands, Belgium and Luxembourg, that had been created in 1957 with American sponsorship and blessing.* He reduced French support for the grand alliance forged by U. S. diplomacy, the North Atlantic Treaty Organization (NATO); and later offended U. S. sensibilities by entering into treaty relations with Red China, which was then abhorrent to American policy makers.

What permitted de Gaulle to indulge his independence and veiled hostility toward the U. S. and enfeeble any diplomatic counter-reaction was, paradoxically, the French power to dictate U. S. monetary policy, the result in turn of the strengthening of the French monetary position at U. S. expense and the corresponding weakness of the U. S. monetary position.

The Federal Reserve System held now less than $2.4 billion in free gold

---

*Actually, an outgrowth of the Organization for European Economic Cooperation set up in 1948 to implement the Marshall Plan.

—that is, gold not required under the Federal Reserve Act to be held as reserve against note and deposit liabilities outstanding. Meantime, French holdings of dollars had risen to nearly $1 1/2 billion. It was uncomfortably apparent to all that the French were in a position to precipitate a dollar crisis merely by converting these dollars into gold and demanding delivery. That the French leadership was not averse to such tightening of the noose was made evident in 1963 by their refusal, which we have noted above, to accept U. S. Treasury obligations stated in French francs.

As the balance of payments deficit deepened and uneasiness spread abroad over the stability of the dollar, the Treasury in 1961 indicated its need for assistance from the International Monetary Fund, but as the Fund's resources were depleted it was necessary to appeal to the principal powers.* Out of this emerged the Committee of Ten† which reluctantly agreed to create "special borrowing arrangements" whereby a pool of $6 billion credit would be created (of which the U. S. share would be $2 billion), upon which the United States would have certain drawing privileges. Significantly, however, the restrictions (which were imposed at French insistence) were so severe, requiring for instance a two-thirds majority consent of the lenders, that the arrangement became a practical nullity, and the device was adopted, to which we have referred, of bilateral swap arrangements between the Federal Reserve and certain foreign central banks.

At the International Monetary Fund's annual meeting in Vienna in 1961, the French finance minister, Wilfred Baumgartner, was caustically critical of U. S. fiscal policies, and foreshadowed a further withdrawal of French cooperation. It was recognized however that a complete break would bring down the house of Dagon upon the French as well, and that some support of the dollar was in order. The mechanism of cooperation became the Committee of Ten in which the French exercised a decisive voice and which appropriately met in Paris.

At the International Monetary Fund's 1963 assembly the U. S. voice was considerably subdued, and Secretary Dillon, who a year before had

---

*The Fund held on December 31, 1961, $2.1 billion in gold and $11.5 billion in member currencies, but these currencies were largely of the "soft" variety. Apart from dollars, the Fund held only $1.6 billion in hard (convertible) currencies. (Testimony of Secretary of the Treasury Douglas Dillion before the Senate Foreign Relations Committee, March 30, 1962. Hearings on H.R. 10162)

†U. S., United Kingdom, Germany, France, Italy, Belgium, Netherlands, Canada, Sweden, and Japan.

disparaged any view that U.S. authorities could not keep their own financial house in order, indirectly conceded the need for aid. As a consequence several committees were created to study means of warding off the approaching crisis.

Meantime, as evidence of the frailty of the Federal Reserve structure, Congressman Abraham J. Multer introduced a bill in Congress in 1961 to remove the 25 per cent gold reserve requirement on Federal Reserve notes and deposits. This would release gold to meet foreign demands for conversion of dollars.

Actually, as many students have recognized, there is nothing sacrosanct about a fixed minimum reserve ratio, the idea having originated in the Bank of England practice, before Peel's Act of 1844, of maintaining a 33 per cent gold reserve against notes and deposits. That basis seems to have been adopted with certain qualifications when the German Reichsbank was instituted by Bismarck in 1875. The theory was subsequently adopted in the Federal Reserve System, and because of its early worldwide influence the practice of a percentage reserve became widespread.[5] Today, however, the requirement is maintained in Europe only by Belgium and Switzerland. The International Monetary Fund had, of course, long before abolished the gold reserve requirement of its members, in favor of a gold exchange (U.S. dollars); and as we shall note further on, with the disappearance of gold convertibility for that currency in 1971, the system of gold as an international currency became only a recollection of things past.

The fact is, of course, that when confidence is threatened no reserve requirement short of 100 per cent will meet the bill. No commercial creditor would lend money to a debtor who undertook to maintain assets to only a fraction of the amount lent, and no banker would make a demand loan to a borrower who could not show quick assets equivalent to, or greater than, the amount lent. Regrettably for the cause of sound money, influential schools of conservative monetary economists* boxed themselves in and became ineffectual advocates by reason of their accepting the delusion of the fractional reserve theory.

Nevertheless, so strong then was the attachment to the fixed ratio reserve—or perhaps the general alarm over the state of the dollar—that Multer was compelled to drop his bill even before hearings by reason of the widespread protests that arose.

---

*Long headed by the Economists' National Committee on Monetary Policy founded by Walter E. Spahr.

Following the British sterling crisis, the French government announced on January 7, 1965, that it would reduce its holdings of dollar exchange by converting an increasing amount into gold beginning with an initial purchase of $150 million. It indicated that within the year it would draw down possibly $1 billion in gold.

The effect was an ill-concealed panic in Washington fiscal circles. Already, the twelve Federal Reserve banks were making daily adjustments among themselves in order to maintain their minimum gold requirements, and on January 28 President Johnson asked Congress to repeal the gold reserve requirement against Federal Reserve deposit liabilities in order to free gold in defense of the dollar abroad.

Representative Patman now abandoned for the time being his crusade against the Federal Reserve, and after hurried one-day hearings, brought out, on February 1, a bill meeting the Administration wishes. Representative Patman had in reality no further need of his campaign. Whatever the appearances, the Federal Reserve System was completely captive to the Treasury, in turn captive to the State Department.

The bill was passed and became law on March 3, 1965. The System was now freed of the major restraint on the excessive creation of debt through Federal Reserve lending power; the other restraint, the gold reserve against note issue, would soon fall.

The consequences of this profound change, that accelerated to a crisis within the following decade, will now occupy our attention.

3 3.

~~~~~~~~~~~~~~~~~~

The Chute

THE HISTORIAN OF THE ROMAN EMPIRE, Theodore Mommsen, characterizes inflationary progress in the third century as a "chute." Something like that now began in the U.S.—an accelerating drop in the purchasing power of the irredeemable currency on which the economy had subsisted since 1934.

In October, 1960, a near panic had occurred in the exchanges with the London market price of gold rising to $41 an ounce, a premium of $6 over the official price, before the Treasury was able to throw sufficient metal into the breach. The cost of maintaining the official parity of the dollar at $35 an ounce was the loss of 200 million ounces of gold from the Treasury stock. As usual, the cry arose laying the blame upon unpatriotic citizens, and President Eisenhower, as one of his last acts in office, issued an executive order forbidding U. S. citizens from owning gold anywhere in the world. In 1963, Congress followed up this autocratic act by passing the "interest equalization tax" on foreign securities sold in the U. S., as a measure to discourage American citizens transferring to foreigners dollar claims payable in gold. These official actions, and various so-called voluntary programs of restraint under official suasion, did little to counter the effect of a continually diluted currency. During 1961–65, the balance of payments deficit increased by nearly $13 billion, and another 106 million ounces of gold were paid out. The federal budget remained also in chronic imbalance, with a cumulative deficit for the years 1960–65, inclusive, of $27 billion, of which half was financed by Federal Reserve purchases of Treasury securities.

The gold panic of 1960 had led the U. S. and six major European countries to form a "gold pool" to subdue any speculative tendencies born of distrust in the dollar, by funneling all gold sales to the public through one agency managed by the Bank of England, with the U. S. Treasury providing 59 per cent of the gold.

Extraordinary measures were also taken to shore up European currencies, all of them weak from the double fault of inflationary domestic policies and of reliance upon U. S. dollar claims as good-as-gold equivalents. In 1961, and again in 1965, massive loans were made to Great Britain to support the pound sterling—a currency that was once, but no longer, the standard of the world—while reeds leaned upon reeds in the "swap" arrangements whereby the fragile dollar was propped up by a fund of borrowed European currencies equally fragile, or more so.

An added peril to the monetary system developed from the U. S. military involvement in Southeast Asia—an involvement that began as a "police action" but grew into a full-scale war lasting nearly fifteen years. As the conflict expanded, under the administration of President Lyndon B. Johnson, concern and opposition spread, marked by reversals at the polls at home and by a demand for gold from abroad. Further political settlement occurred in March, 1968, when a "dove," Senator Eugene J. McCarthy, won 40 per cent of the vote in the New Hampshire primary against the "hawk" Johnson. The London gold pool was now losing $100 million a day, with a hemorrhage of nearly $400 million on March 14.

"That night," reported the *New York Times,* "Queen Elizabeth was awakened by her ministers for her to sign a proclamation closing the gold markets."

"The central bankers and finance ministers," the *Times* continued, now "hurried off to another huddle, this time in Washington. On Sunday, March 17, they announced a two-tier system. Speculators would trade among themselves at free market prices and governments would deal with each other at $35 an ounce. In London, thousands of British youths stormed the American Embassy in further protest over Vietnam."

With access to gold increasingly difficult the American public turned to the feeble barricade of paper money as a defense against the threats of another bank closing. The circulation, that had been rising at the rate of some $300 million annually, now began to increase at the rate of $2 billion. Since by law the note issue required a gold backing of 25 per cent, the closing of the London gold market in March was followed almost at once by an act of Congress (March 18, 1968) ending the gold reserve requirement of Federal Reserve notes (as, earlier, the gold reserve against deposit liabilities had been removed). Removed now, and for the foreseeable future, was any impediment (except public dismay) to the unlimited issue by the Federal Reserve of irredeemable paper notes passing as money, and a corresponding open sesame to unrestricted spending by the government without regard to budgetary balance. By this time the U. S. gold stock was down to 300 million ounces from a peak of 700 million ounces in 1949.

Significant of the generally unrecognized revolution that was taking place in monetary theory and practice, the legend that had appeared on all Federal Reserve notes that they were "redeemable in lawful money" now quietly disappeared—by whose authority diligent enquiry by this author was unsuccessful in discovering.

Paradoxically, although no gold coin was in circulation and although the note issues and the subsidiary coinage no longer bore any legal relation to gold, the dollar was still defined by statute as consisting of so many grains of fine gold (1/35 of an ounce).

Of passing interest in the account of international efforts to maintain a facade of stability to an increasingly unstable structure of managed currencies was the experiment of "special drawing rights" in the International Monetary Fund. A simple explanation of this phenomenon is that each member of the Fund was allocated a quota of SDRs, an SDR being in the nature of a basket of member currencies together having a theoretical gold value according to their several official gold parities. However, since none of the component currencies was actually convertible into gold, the effect was a statistical fiction, a bookkeeping entry; even so, indigent countries preferred the currency of the stronger, however intrinsically weak, and the tendency was to exchange their SDR's for dollars to the extent possible. The Act of June 19, 1968, that authorized U. S. participation in the special drawing rights, also authorized their use as a reserve asset against Federal Reserve notes, and very soon thereafter some $1.3 billion nominal amount of this "paper gold"—as it came to be called—was monetized into legal tender currency through the mechanism of the Federal Reserve System.

The special drawing rights having proved to be another reed to lean on, the demand for gold from the U. S. Treasury resumed, and on August 15, 1971, President Nixon abruptly closed the "gold window" by ending further conversion of foreign held dollar claims. So ended the Bretton

Woods system of gold parities supported by the U. S. dollar, and for the trade of the entire world there now existed only various paper currencies of fluctuating and uncertain value.

Under the Articles of the International Monetary Fund, however, the U. S. was committed to deliver gold to foreign central banks at $35 an ounce, and in December, at a meeting of the ten principal central bank powers, Nixon obtained agreement—an agreement which he described as "the most significant monetary agreement in the history of the world" —to a devaluation of the dollar to 1/38 ounce of gold (the so-called Smithsonian Agreement). This was given legal force by the Par Value Modification Act of 1972 (P.L. 92-2b8, March 31, 1972).

The following year a further devaluation was made (September 21, 1973), reducing the gold value of the dollar to 1/42.22 ounce of gold.[1]

The principal effect of these changes was to increase the dollar liabilities of the U. S. to the International Monetary Fund by the difference in the new value of gold. So far as the market was concerned, the actions were meaningless, for by the end of 1974 gold was trading in the European markets at $195 an ounce.

There remained the prohibitions of law and edict against U. S. citizens holding or trading in gold. Congress now recognized the inconsistency, and in 1974 removed these restrictions.

In 1976, the U. S. Treasury declared U. S. policy to be the demonetization of gold, not only domestically but internationally—in effect, the abandonment of use of a metal that had throughout history provided a universally accepted medium of payments. Characteristic of administration timidity and uncertainty about the effects was the fact that the announcement was entrusted to a deputy assistant secretary of the Treasury and made before an obscure meeting of miners in Spokane, Washington. The language of the announcement was also timorous. It read:

> The judgment that gold does not and cannot serve as a sound or stable basis for a monetary system is almost universally accepted by governments throughout the world. The force of events . . . have [sic] led to the point where [gold] no longer serves an important monetary role in virtually any nation. . . . Under the amended IMF Articles of Agreement gold will no longer have an official price. It will no longer be the legal basis in the Articles for expressing the value of currencies.[2]

Confusion and dislocations only increased in a world trade compelled to transact business and settle accounts in currencies that were forever fluctuating in value against each other and against basic forms of wealth, their course dictated by bureaucracies dominated by an equally confusing mixture of personal, political and economic interests. An important commodity of that trade was petroleum, the principal sources of which were in the Middle East and Africa under control of peoples newly released from European colonial rule, and somewhat testy about their prerogatives. Seizing control of the producing properties they now began to dictate world prices for petroleum, functioning through the Organization of Petroleum Exporting Countries—OPEC—which they dominated. The renewal of war between Israel and its neighbors in October, 1973, together with the gradual weakening of the dollar in the exchanges, gave them further opportunity; prices were multiplied four times, and the trade balance in their favor mounted into the billions. How to settle these balances in continually depreciating currencies now became a concern to the world's monetary authorities. Fortunately, hugely ambitious development programs provided objects in which to spend some of these billions, and other billions were allowed to accumulate in paper currency accounts abroad.

But not for long. As the universal settler of balances, gold now came again into play. The "barbarous relic" acquired new interest. Gold that sold at the end of 1974 at $195 an ounce by 1979 sold at more than $350 an ounce, with the end not yet in sight.

Like Canute bidding the waves recede, however, authorities persisted in the fiction. In 1976 the International Monetary Fund, largely at the instigation of the U. S. announced that some 50 million ounces of its 103 million ounce reserve would be disposed of—one-half to the member countries and one-half offered on the market. A little later, in 1978, the U. S. Treasury announced a program of gold sales on the ground that gold was no longer needed in the monetary system. (The program was discontinued in 1979 after less than 16 million ounces were offered.)

Shrewder money managers, however, were not misled. In 1967 the government of South Africa, suspecting a market for a good gold piece, began coinage of the one-ounce gold Krugerrand, and the issue became so popular that by 1979 some 49 countries were issuing gold coins—though continuing to maintain their shaky paper notes as the legal standard of payments.

34.

~~~~~~~~~~~~~~~~~~~~~~~~~~~

Into the Pit

A PERSPECTIVE UPON THE POLITICAL, social and moral influences
flowing world-wide from the adoption of the monetary theories
enacted in the Federal Reserve System requires a step back into the
nineteenth century—specifically, to the coronation in 1876 of Victoria,
queen of England, as empress of India. That event, occurring just a
century following the U. S. Declaration of Independence and the appearance of Adam Smith's *Wealth of Nations,* produced not only a revolution
in the British political structure but in monetary practice. India, though
long a British dependency, governed indirectly by a British proprietary
company, the East India Company, was now integrated into an imperial
system, and British economic interest in India required a similar integra-
tion of the monetary system.

The problem arose from the fact that England was on the gold standard, with the paper circulation convertible into gold coins, while in India
paper notes were unknown and the circulation consisted of silver rupees
of high quality. (The thirteenth century Mongol overlords of the East had
introduced paper circulation into China, but had never succeeded in
doing so in the Middle East and South Asia.) In India, where banking
institutions were undeveloped, silver coinage provided both a satisfactory medium of exchange and a store of value, particularly for the great
masses of the poor. British colonial practice had been to assure a supply
of rupees through the system of free coinage, by which anyone could take
silver to the mint and, for a small mintage charge, have it coined into legal
tender with purchasing power never lower than that of the market value
of the metal.

As the relative market values of gold and silver fluctuated, the result was a continual uncertainty in the exchange parity of the monetary units. To resolve the problems of unifying two monetary systems, one based on gold and the other on silver, a royal commission was appointed to study and to recommend a method.

During the hearings of the Commission, influential Indian opinion arose in defense of the existing system and cited a statement made earlier (in 1877) by the government. The statement deserves quotation for its clarity and the integrity of its premise:

> A sound system of currency must be automatic and self-regulating. No civilized government can undertake to determine from time to time by how much the legal-tender currency should be increased or decreased, nor would it be justified in leaving the community without a fixed metallic standard of value, even for a short time.[1]

What emerged from the Commission, however, was what is euphemistically known as the gold exchange standard, which we have briefly discussed above,[2] and which John Maynard Keynes described as follows: "The gold exchange standard arises out of the discovery [*sic*] that, so long as gold is available for payments of *international* indebtedness at an approximately constant rate in terms of the national currency, it is a matter of comparative indifference whether it actually *forms* the national currency."[3]

Despite Indian opposition, the government of India now closed the mints to the free coinage of silver and gradually restricted the quantity of metallic circulation to that determined by government policy. To provide circulating media it also introduced paper notes of rupee denomination, the acceptance of which was cultivated by making them convertible into sterling (and hence, into gold).

Keynes, arch apostle of manipulated money, extolled the policy for its blessings, even as he condemned the Indian people for "wasting their resources in the needless accumulation of the precious metals." With the complacency of the times in the effectiveness of authoritarian governments he declared that "the Government ought not to encourage in the slightest degree this ingrained fondness for handling hard gold [and silver]."[4]

The gold exchange system was instituted in 1893. The experiment lasted little more than two decades. With the outbreak of World War I, Great Britain promptly suspended convertibility of its sterling circulation to conserve its gold stocks, with resultant rupee inconvertibility. The consequences in India, of a vast population deprived of a traditional money, compelled to use pieces of paper of uncertain worth, were economic distress and political unrest. In order to provide silver to the masses, and allay discontent, Great Britain appealed to the U. S. for aid; an act of Congress authorized the melting of 350 million silver dollars for shipment to India to restore confidence and retain loyalty to the British raj.

With return of peace, Britain neglected to profit from the lesson and proceeded to compound the error by degrading the rupee coinage to only half silver with the difference in base metal alloy. The effect was further erosion of Indian confidence and further unrest among the masses. During World War II the U. S. again came to the rescue of the British government—as well as to the Dutch and French, which had aped British monetary policy in the administration of their overseas dependencies. In the process, over 410 million ounces of silver were provided to bolster European colonial regimes. (Fortunately for this purpose, as a result of the various silver purchase acts enacted from 1876 through 1934 to absorb the shock to the mining industry from the general demonetization of silver in those years, in 1942 the U. S. Treasury held an enormous stock of silver, some 1,365 million ounces.)

The second attempt to impose a fictitious paper money circulation in the ancient lands of the East was also a failure. By 1949 India was irretrievably lost to the British crown, and in the following years nearly all British colonial dependencies were swept away—a fate followed by those of other European powers.

It is not too much to say that an underlying—and generally unrecognized—cause of discredit of the presiding sovereignties, and rising resistance to their rule, was the loss of integrity of their money, carrying with it disbelief in the integrity of the governments themselves.*

It is now necessary to notice that the Federal Reserve System suffered the same fate as the British Indian—and within about the same time span. Within two decades from the institution of the Federal Reserve the System was forced to suspend gold redemption of its currency.

---

*It is not without interest that Reza Shah of Iran lost his throne within a decade of his demonetization of silver and institution of a paper currency, and that the absence of good metallic circulation among the masses at a time when wealth was pouring into the country from abroad may have been a factor in the revolution that cost his son Mohammed Shah his throne in 1979.

That bankruptcy was inevitable should have been apparent from the steady dilution of the reserves to meet the obligations of the System. By 1933, total note and deposit obligations of the System convertible into gold amounted to $5.9 billion against gold holdings of $3.8 billion. This, of course, is only the tip of the iceberg. Since the Federal Reserve bank deposits were the prime reserve of the banking system generally, the total demand obligations of the banking system, provisionally convertible into gold, amounted to some $15 billion.

Circumstances at home and abroad continued to increase the gold reserve of the System through the Great Depression and World War II to a maximum of some $27 billion by 1949—some 70 per cent of world monetary gold stocks. But the obligations of the System, both direct and indirect, continued to outrace the reserve. After 1949 the gold reserve began a steady decline, while, as we have noted, succeeding enactments of Congress freed the System of any mathematical relationship between its obligations and its gold reserves.

By 1968, when the central banks of the world ceased to deliver gold to the market at monetary parities, the Federal Reserve note circulation had increased to $42.3 billion in addition to which were some $5.3 billion in debased coinage. Demand liabilities of the banking system had risen to $148.5 billion. The gold stock had dropped to $10.9 billion. During the following ten years the "money stock," as the note and coin circulation and demand deposits were now called, rose to $361 billion, and if all banking obligations are included (savings accounts and time deposits), the total ran to upwards of $500 billion—a forbidding sum of dollar liabilities to blanch the advocates of a circulating metallic currency.

The consequences of a depreciating currency—consequences that are immediately economic but spread from there to tincture the social and political fabric of a country, infecting it with the virus of moral decay— have been the subject of many treatises and will only be summarized here. Mommsen's history of the Roman Empire and Andrew White's classic *Fiat Money Inflation in France* describe in vivid terms these effects; those in post-war Germany are of too recent memory to require retelling.

Despite the tragic history of depreciating currencies advocates of monetary expansion continue to be lured by the prospect of cheap money— easier credit, abundant purchasing power for everyone. Paradoxically, the effects are the opposite, and here we find the core of the moral malaise implicit in the process—that avarice, the desire for unearned wealth, is self-defeating.

Thus, we find that as a fiat circulation increases, its purchasing power drops as its cost rises. This may be observed in the price structure. It takes more and more so-called money to buy a given amount of commodities and services, while the cost of acquiring this so-called money continually rises. The influence is frequently concealed, and when visible is attributed by the authorities to other causes.

Prices, of course, are affected by many forces, natural and man-made, from droughts and other natural catastrophes to wars, political upheavals, violence and corruption. It is not possible to separate mathematically their relative influence. Over a period of time, however, the recurrence of normal weather and other natural conditions, the resumption of peace or social tranquility, tend to establish a general line of regression, and any divergence of trend may be associated with the money system and supply.

Thus, during the first 20 years of the Federal Reserve System, except for World War I and its aftermath, prices rose by one-third, measured by the Bureau of Labor Statistics consumer price index of 35 in 1914 and 45 in 1933 (1957–59 = 100). Following suspension of gold convertibility prices rose until the outbreak of World War II by about 50 per cent (to an index high of 50 in 1937). By 1958 prices had doubled, partly under the influence of U.S. military involvement in Korea and thereafter in Southeast Asia, the expenses of which were financed increasingly by Federal Reserve purchases of Treasury obligations; by 1977 prices had again doubled, and the rate by then was accelerating to reach and to exceed 10 per cent annually.

Not only does an unhinged currency lead to steadily rising prices (decline in purchasing power of the circulation), but as the amount of circulation increases, so does its cost; that is, the rental rate of money, interest.

Interest rates, like prices, are affected by many things, principally the stability of a government and the confidence it gives that repayment of a loan will not be jeopardized by war or civil disturbance. During the Civil War, for instance, a period of the greatest threat to its political existence in the history of the United States, the federal government was able to finance its war needs at interest rates that generally did not exceed 7 per cent.[5]

Despite the steady increase in circulation under the Federal Reserve System and the intervention of two world wars, interest rates on U. S. government long-term bonds (those with maturities of 15 years or more) declined to a mean of 2.2 per cent in 1946. Thereafter began a steady upward pressure to above 5 per cent in 1968, accelerating to as high as 9 per cent in 1979 (on bonds of 20-year maturity).

The reciprocal of rising interest rates is a decline in the principal, or capital, value of fixed-rate obligations acquired earlier—mortgages, bonds, preferred shares. If the going rate of interst is 9 per cent, then a long-term bond of 5 per cent coupon acquired at 100 will be marked down to a principal value that will yield the buyer 9 per cent on his investment. The consequence is an unwillingness of lenders to put their funds out at long term. This may be noted in the mounting difficulty of the Treasury in selling its long-term obligations. Thus, in 1941 of the total public debt of $41.6 billion, $8 billion, or 19 per cent, was in short term bills, notes and certificates. By 1968 the percentage had risen to 64 per cent, and a decade later, when the total interest bearing debt had reached $782 billion, of which $493 billion was marketable, only $46 billion, or less than 10 per cent, was in maturities of over 10 years.

The effect of rising prices can be devastating for persons of fixed income from savings and pensions—the older citizens who as a group are generally increasing in numbers, in proportion, and in political influence to the total population, and who, as the elders of society, should be a stabilizing influence. For them, the pinch of outgo against income leads to unrest, disillusionment and resentment rather than support of the political establishment.

Since prices never rise and fall in unison, the inflow of fiat purchasing power into the market from new currency emissions, breeds further price and market dislocations that offer opportunity for the shrewd, for traders and speculators. The same rising prices, however, adversely affect the actual creators of wealth, for whom costs of materials and labor tend to rise faster than selling prices, while planning and programming are frustrated by price uncertainties, both as to the future costs of materials and supplies and the selling prices, the latter even more uncertain by reason of uncertain future demand.

The problem of inflation accounting has recently engaged official and financial market attention, because of the distortion of profit figures caused by price movements. Capital investment depreciated on a cost basis, for instance, must be replaced at a higher rate, the difference being an actual reduction in nominal profits. This phenomenon led the regulator of corporations, the Securities and Exchange Commission, to require corporations to estimate the losses from inflation in their financial reports, but this does not resolve the problem, due to the many imponderables. On a wider frame proposals are advanced for indexing wages, rents, profits, taxes, and other monetary entries, that is, to adjust the nominal amounts by the drop in prices; but no one has yet designed a satisfactory index of prices, and in any case the effect is that of putting the cart before the horse.

More insidious, however, because less visible in statistics, is the political unrest and moral decay that is served if not promoted by depreciating money. Beginning in the 1960's, as many observers have noted, there occurred a widespread dissatisfaction with not only government—which may have been the result of involvement in an unpopular war—but with "establishments" unrelated to politics—from school to church, including conventions of behavior and dress. Young people took to living together without benefit of clerk or clergy; homosexuality emerged from the closet, like vermin from an upturned plank, and became a political influence; the use of narcotics and drug stimulants became open and even fashionable. Accompanying these happenings was an enormous increase in crime—bank robberies, murder, rape and sodomy, masochism, torture, child abuse.

Endemic also was the declining *esprit* and morale of government functionaries: teachers, police, firemen, upon whom the security of society rests, no longer hesitated to raise demands and enforce them by strikes.

Governments, straitened for funds, now regarded gambling more leniently and state after state established official lotteries and encouraged their citizens to gamble. "You Got to Play to Win" was the plea that federal bureaucrats living in nearby Maryland found beaming at them from billboards and posters, a subtle but demoralizing influence on their official rectitude. In the stock market, the big speculation was no longer shares but commodity futures and options to buy shares—forms of speculation that put the little fellow in the game—while the less sophisticated in finance found opportunity at the race track under an official betting system. The price of race horses rose to fantastic figures. "It's getting so a modest owner like myself can't afford to buy a horse by himself anymore," the *New York Times* quoted the head of a large newspaper chain and owner of a dozen race horses. And well he might complain when one filly at a 1979 sale in Lexington, Kentucky, sold for $1.4 million.[6]

Probably no more descriptive of the general state of affairs in the ninth decade of the century, or prophetic of the future, is the comment of a leading track operator, reported in the *Times:* "I have a recurring dream," said John Finney, who managed the Saratoga sales, "that I am auctioning tulip bulbs"—a reference to the seventeenth century tulip mania in Holland.

35.

Out of the Pit

THE QUESTION may now be raised as to what specific reforms are required to restore integrity to the monetary system. It is a question which we have avoided, preferring to leave the answer to monetary technicians, on the principle succinctly stated by the British poet Alexander Pope: "For forms of government let fools contest; / That which is best administered is best."

Essentially, the answer lies in the devotion to moral integrity on the part of the electorate—a conviction, however, that is mightily assisted by the realization that such devotion is not abstract idealism, but of practical consequence in a more harmonious, contented and prosperous society. It is only "if you will keep my commandments," as the Lord reminded the children of Israel, that a people is led into a land of milk and honey. High among these commandments is that of "just balances, just weights, a just ephah and a just hin."

Certain heresies persist, however—false gods of doctrine which economists and money managers have long sanctified—demons that must be exorcised before a sound and honest monetary system can be re-established.

First among these is the conception held by many conservative economists that an expanding economy needs a continually expanding money supply, and that as the quantity of precious metals is limited and new production inadequate, the metallic circulation may—and must, if necessary—be supplemented by a fiat-paper circulation. While this proposition is a subject of vast literature, few question the basic premises, and the argument is generally over the rate of expansion and the quality of the circulation.

Simply expressed, the proposition says no more and no less than that if a cloth merchant doubles his yardage sales he must double the number of yardsticks in his establishment. So obvious is the distinction that some theorists include in their equation a factor for "velocity of circulation," but regrettably, the raw material of their data do not permit such fine factoring. Since production of economic wealth is expressed in monetary terms, as the only common denominator, the theory becomes a cat chasing its tail, for the production figure will rise as prices rise, themselves a function of the monetary supply, and as no satisfactory price index has ever been devised that will satisfy all interests, so no deflator has been devised to exclude the effect of the money supply in the equation. For that matter, neither has "velocity of circulation" been adequately defined.

A second misconception is that prices must be stable or rising—and the attempt to maintain stable prices through monetary manipulation became a swamp which the Federal Reserve entered in 1923 and in which it has been hopelessly mired ever since.[1]

Actually, if advancing technology means anything, it is that goods should gradually decrease in price as the forces of nature are harnessed for their greater production. The only reason prices must be stable, or rising, is that of supporting a burden of interest payments on a burden of debt that steadily rises as a function and effect of the monetary system.

A third misconception is that debt, or debt instruments, can be or serve as money. To accept this view is to cast aside the traditional definition of money as a medium of exchange, a standard of deferred payments, and a store of wealth. Since a particular debt must be repaid—at least such is commonly believed—the extinguishment of a debt instrument that has been monetized, that is, has been made the basis of legal tender currency, would cause a contraction of the "money supply" and, supposedly, economic catastrophe. Therefore new debt must be incurred and monetized to maintain the former equilibrium. To encourage such debt attractive terms must be given; that is, the monetary authority must advance legal-tender currency in exchange for the debt at lower terms than the prevailing market. This is known as the discount rate. That the Federal Reserve is continually in the market buying debt instruments—either private or public (Treasury)—is a persistent stimulus to the creation of debt. The amount of this debt today defies calculation.

A fourth misconception is as to the power of the Federal Reserve to influence the economy—a misconception written into law in the Full Employment Act of 1946 and the later Full Employment and Balanced Growth Act of October 27, 1978. "Fine tuning" became a phrase to describe its efforts to achieve these political ends by adjusting the so-called money supply. It did so—at least in theory—by buying or selling its own debt instruments, which thereafter became money equivalents in the banks to which they were sold, and permitted the banks to extend their own debt commitments through deposit liabilities.

Apart from the debased subsidiary coinage, money supply was defined as the legal tender currency in circulation plus demand deposits in the banks and designated M_1. Neither represented substance; rather they were debt instruments. The awareness soon dawned that M_1 was not an adequate measure of the demand debt outstanding, since savings banks customarily paid out time deposits on demand. The money-supply concept was now broadened to include such deposits and termed M_2. Eventually there was an M_3, an M_4 and an M_5 to designate various levels of debt. By the time M_5 was reached the monetary authority was struggling to control or modify a mass of debt in the market totalling some $1.6 trillion in various forms and extensions.

Vast and powerful as its resources were, here was a behemoth of debt to which no bit could be fitted, upon which no bridle nor saddle could be laid. But the end was not yet. Struggling to determine the extent of its responsibility, the Federal Reserve has of late been trying to determine how much money-equivalents are in circulation in the form of credit card credits, and when that is done they may proceed down the scale until it encompasses such items as the IOU's that circulate around the poker tables and game boards of the land.

In sum, the theory that money supply can be controlled, when it exists in the form of debt, is little short of ridiculous.

An allied misconception is that of the power conferred on government to manage the economy supposedly found in the Constitutional authority of Congress to coin money and regulate the value thereof. During the debates in the Constitutional convention the proposal to give Congress the authority to "emit bills of credit"—forbidden to the States—was voted down; the power to regulate the value of coinage had nothing to do with the economy, but related to the fact that coins of two different metals, gold and silver, were legal tender. The maintenance of an official parity between the two when the market value of the metals diverged had created a continuing dilemma for governments of the time. The problem of bimetallism was not solved for Great Britain until 1814, when gold became the standard, and for the U. S. in 1900, when the standard became the gold dollar.[2]

The misconception that debt can be a form of money arises from a further misconception of the nature of money, that its essence is purchasing power. Purchasing power is an attribute of money, but not its essence, as fragrance is an attribute of the rose, but not its substance—nor will the fragrance of new baked bread satisfy hunger. Whatever is in the market has purchasing power, from a woman's smile to a tenor's song or a lawyer's opinion, but none of them is substance, far less the substance of money. A money system can be erected on nothing less than a transferable substance of market value, and any system lacking that cannot be called a monetary system.

A prevalent misconception is that the banking system is sound and solvent and that in any case depositors are protected by the bulwarks of the Federal Reserve lending power and the guarantees of the Federal Deposit Insurance Corporation. These are false hopes, and the guarantee instruments are self-defeating and counterproductive. The Federal Reserve was at the height of its power and influence in 1933, with ample gold reserves, but was powerless to prevent universal bank insolvency. The subsequently created system of bank deposit guarantee serves to allay disquiet on the part of depositors, who should rather be constantly alert and questioning as to the soundness of their depositary institutions, while the presence of these guarantees only leads the managers of bank funds into an equally false sense of security and encourages them to extend loans to the very edge of credibility.

Officials responsible for the guarantee program have recently shown concern for these conditions. Thus, William M. Isaac, director of the Federal Deposit Insurance Corporation, in an address in 1979 pointed out that in 1945 risk assets of the banking system—total assets less cash reserves and U. S. Treasury obligations—were only 22 per cent of total assets, but by 1965 were 68 per cent and in 1978 had risen to 80 per cent.[3]

After pointing out the added effect upon the soundness of assets from the rising inflation rate, he commented:

"One would think that with banks assuming a greater degree of risk, and the economy becoming more volatile, capital ratios would be increasing. In fact, just the opposite occurred. The ratio of equity capital to risk was approximately 30 per cent at the turn of the century. . . . After World

War II the ratio steadily declined to 14 1/2 per cent in 1960, 11.3 per cent in 1970, and approximately 8 per cent last year."

Chairman Irving H. Sprague of the Corporation also expressed his concern, noting that in 1969 there were under supervision as "problem banks" no bank with deposits in excess of $1 billion and only two with over $100 million deposits, but in 1979 five banks with deposits in excess of $1 billion were in trouble and 30 with deposits of $100 million to $1 billion.

Still another monetary misconception is that the supply of precious metals is inadequate to serve as money. It was upon the cry of metal famine, in fact, that the euphemism arose of the need to "economize gold" by creating fiat paper. Yet relative to production no metal is in greater supply. It is reliably estimated—and the figures are commonly used in the reports of the Director of the Mint—that some 40 per cent of all the gold mined since the discovery of America is still visible—with probably much more in private hoards and jewelry. For most commodities a visible supply of over a year's production is enough to depress the market.

The fact is that the precious metal supply will always be adequate to the demand for use in transactions, for the amount of the metal required to make an exchange will adjust itself to the value of the exchange. If this seems a bit esoteric we may note that at $350 an ounce, the market price of gold in 1979, an ounce of gold would pay the cost of travel by air from New York to London and return—a purchasing power of gold unprecedented. At $400 an ounce, a price toward which the market was climbing as this was written, the gold held by the Treasury (acquired, incidentally, at $20.67 an ounce) would be sufficient to put a reserve of 100 per cent behind the total circulation, and thereby permit a return to a gold or gold-certificate currency.

A final and major misconception to be mentioned is that sovereign majesty is sufficient to gull a public into complacency over its hypocrisies, sophistries, and outright fraud. The scriptural admonition "Be sure your sins will find you out" applies to institutions as well as individuals. Eventually a defrauded people will turn against their government as they did in France in 1789 and in Iran in 1979.

Let us list some of these official immoralities:

(1) The enactment of a monetary system that permitted the issuance of paper currency redeemable in gold to an extent of two and a half times the amount of gold held to redeem the paper. A comparable case would

be that of a man laying aside for emergency 100 Krugerrands, only to discover when he needed them that 60 were nothing but lead covered with gold leaf. Since the Federal Reserve is the "reserve of last resort" for the entire U.S. banking and economic system, the dilution of its reserve, as permitted by law, was a total and unwarranted fraud. However much it was practiced in the open, by law, the great masses of the public were led to believe that their currency was the equivalent of gold.

(2) The expropriation in 1933 of gold held by private citizens. However rationalized as legal by a compliant Supreme Court, the action was contrary to accepted and traditional morality, and indeed contrary to the plain reading of the Constitution which declares, "nor shall private property be taken for public use, without just compensation" (Amendment V).

(3) The repudiation in 1933 of domestic gold delivery contracts, both public and private. While such action was not explicitly prohibited to the federal government by the Constitution, the principle was enunciated in regard to the states, which were forbidden to pass any law "impairing the obligation of contract" (Article I).

(4) The repudiation in 1971 of the international obligation taken in 1945 (in the Articles of the International Monetary Fund) to maintain gold convertibility of the dollar.

(5) The persistence in defining the dollar in terms of gold when gold has not been delivered at that rate since 1933, or at *any* rate.

True reform of the monetary system must begin with a return to a freely circulating metallic currency (or inviolable certificates of deposit of such money), the amount of which is self-regulating. The security of such a system would no doubt need a Constitutional amendment opening the mints to the free coinage of gold by the public (except for mintage cost); the establishment of a gold-coin dollar of a given weight and fineness as the standard of value, with gold as the only legal tender for public payments; prohibition against the issue by Congress of legal-tender bills of credit (as forbidden to the states) or any form of paper currency except certificates of deposit of gold in a federal depositary; and a prohibition against any official seizure or sequestration of such deposited metal.

Since gold coinage by reason of its content and uniformity and its legal tender quality commands a premium over the market price of the metal, a revaluation of the Treasury's gold stock at slightly above present prices, would permit redemption of the total note issue. Such action would provide the market with a gold-coin or gold-certificate circulation, and put the Federal Reserve in possession of a gold reserve that it could use by making it available to the market for currency exigencies.

The Federal Reserve System would thus be returned to near its original design—as a sort of safety valve against credit explosions—in which short-term needs would be served by the issuance of Federal Reserve bank credit only against short-term, self-liquidating commercial paper, with the credit retired as the exigency passed. Such credit would not be legal tender, but like cashier's checks, would serve as quasi-credit superior to that of the discounted commercial instruments. As we have noted earlier, such a system (in the form of clearing-house certificates) served well to curtail the 1907 panic.

Implicit in such a reform would be a prohibition against the issue of Federal Reserve credit against U. S. Treasury obligations, either purchased or discounted, and the abolition of the Open Market Committee as well as any authority of the Federal Reserve to acquire, on its volition, any debt instruments, its credit to be issued only against such short-term commercial obligations as were qualified and presented for discount.

Whether Americans are prepared for such basic reform of a monetary system so touted and copied throughout the world as has been the Federal Reserve System, is questionable. Indeed, it may be questioned whether a work like this is designed to achieve reform so much as to witness to a truth.

Efforts to reform institutions or societies by public appeal too often fail from diffusion. The seed must be drilled rather than broadcast. For the popular palate the strong vinegar of verity must be diluted to flatness; the message must be softened to a coax. Jeremiah, proclaiming to Judah its impending destruction, was cautioned by the Lord that the prophet's warning would go unheeded. When Elijah complained that the people had forsaken the Covenant, thrown down the altars, slain the prophets, and that only he was left, the Lord rebuked him with the reminder that there were yet "left seven thousand in Israel, all the knees which have not bowed to Baal." This is the word of hope. There remain always a Remnant who are bearers of the word and doers of the deed. If the message is sent to them in simplicity and sincerity, it will not return empty.

Notes

Preface.

1. *McCulloch v. Maryland,* 4 Wharton 413. *See* A. Barton Hepburn, *A History of Currency in the United States* (New York: The Macmillan Company, 1915), chapter 7.

Chapter 1.

1. See R. N. Burnett, "Stuyvesant Fish," *Cosmopolitan,* Vol. 35, p. 647.
2. Quoted by Robert A. Lovett, *Forty Years After: An Appreciation of the Genius of Edward Henry Harriman (1848–1909),* pamphlet (New York, Newcomen Society in North America, 1949), pp. 17 ff.
3. *See* Edwin Wildman, "The 'Jekyll–Hyde' Harriman," *Overland Monthly,* March, 1908.

Chapter 2.

1. George E. Kennan, *E. H. Harriman, A Biography* (Boston and New York: Houghton, Mifflin Company, 1922), Vol. I, chapter 12.
2. *Ibid.,* Vol. II, chapter 25.

Chapter 3.

1. *New York Times,* January 3, 1907.
2. *The Economist* (London), March 16, 1907. Quoted in Kennan, *op cit.,* p. 304.
3. *New York Times,* February 27, 1907.
4. Kennan, *op. cit.,* p. 306.
5. *Ibid.*
6. *New York Times,* March 22, 1907.
7. *See* Kennan, *op. cit.;* Otto H. Kahn, *Edward Henry Harriman,* an address (New York: C. G. Burgoyne, 1911); *also* Lovett, *op. cit.*

Chapter 4.

1. *New York Times,* October 4, 1907.
2. *See* Stewart H. Holbrook, *The Age of the Moguls* (New York: Doubleday & Company, 1953), pp. 156 ff.
3. *See* Frederick Lewis Allen, *The Great Pierpont Morgan* (New York: Harper and Brothers, 1949), chap. xxii.
4. *New York Times,* October 20, *et. seq. See also* Walter Lord's racy account of the Panic in *The Good Years* (New York: Harper and Brothers, 1960).
5. John K. Winkler, *Morgan the Magnificent* (New York: The Vanguard Press, 1930), p. 260.
6. *New York Times,* October 23, 1907.
7. *See* U. S. National Monetary Commission, Vol. XXI, *Statistics for the United States,* Part III (Washington: G.P.O., 1911)
8. October 24, 1907.
9. *New York Times,* October 27, 1907.
10. *Op. cit.,* p. 270. *See also* Walter Lord, *op. cit.,* upon whose account we have relied for certain details of the events.

Chapter 5.

1. January 1, 1908, editorial.
2. *Ibid.*
3. N.W. Stephenson, *Nelson W. Aldrich: A Leader in American Politics* (New York: Charles Scribner's Sons, 1930), pp. 332 ff.
4. January 16, 1908.
5. *New York Times,* February 17, 1908.
6. *New York Times,* March 3, 4, 1908.
7. May 4, 5, 1908.
8. *Ibid.*
9. May 9, 1908.
10. *New York Tribune,* May 16, 1908.
11. May 25, 1908.
12. *New York Times, New York Tribune,* May 31, 1908.

Chapter 6.

1. Secretary of the Treasury, *Annual Report,* 1914.

Chapter 7.

1. August 20, 1908.
2. Paul M. Warburg, "Defects and Needs of Our Banking System," *New York Times: Annual Financial Review,* January 6, 1907.

Chapter 8.

1. Vol. XXII, *Seasonal Variations in Demands for Currency and Capital.*
2. November 10, 1911.
3. *12 Statutes at Large 709. See also* Hearings on S. 3702 and S. 3714 before Senate Committee on Banking and Currency. June 24, 1960 (Committee Print), for an excellent concise summary, "Coins and Currency of the United States," a memorandum prepared by the Office of the Technical Staff, Office of the Secretary of the Treasury.
4. Act of December 24, 1919 *(41 Statutes at Large 378).*
5. Sec. 26 of Draft Bill.

Chapter 9.

1. September 17, 1909.
2. *New York Times,* December 18, 1912.
3. December 19, 1912.

Chapter 10.

1. July 3, 1913.
2. June 29, 1913.
3. *New York Times,* October 9, 1913.
4. October 9, 1913.
5. October 27, 1913.
6. November 16, 1913.
7. October 16, 1913.
8. An event of January 28, 1871.
9. November 14, 1913.
10. *New York Times,* December 25, 1913.

Chapter 11.

1. *New York Times,* January 6, 1914.
2. *Ibid.,* April 1, 1914.
3. *Ibid.,* December 31, 1913.
4. *Ibid.,* January 3, 1914.
5. *Ibid.,* January 6, 1914.
6. *Ibid.,* February 4, 1914.
7. *Ibid.,* April 1, 1914.
8. *Ibid.,* April 5, 1914.
9. *Ibid.,* April 7, 1914, May 1, 1914.
10. *Ibid.,* April 22, 1914.
11. July 25, 1914.
12. *New York Times,* August 1, 1914.
13. Secretary of the Treasury, *Annual Report,* 1914, p. 479.

Chapter 12.

1. *New York Times,* August 1, 1914.
2. Secretary of the Treasury, *Annual Reports,* 1914, 1915.
3. *Ibid.*
4. Secretary of the Treasury, *Annual Report,* 1914, p. 483.
5. November 24, 1914.

Chapter 13.

1. Sec. 13.
2. February 14, 1914.
3. February, 1914 (Vol. xviii, no. 2, p. 101).
4. *See* Charles O. Hardy, *Credit Policies of the Federal Reserve System* (Washington: The Brookings Institution, 1932).
5. New York: The Macmillan Company, 1930.
6. *Op. cit.,* p. 91.
7. *Ibid.*

Chapter 14.

1. *Op. cit.,* p. 150.
2. Board of Governors of the Federal Reserve System, "The History of Reserve Requirements for Banks in the United States" (*Federal Reserve Bulletin,* November, 1938).
3. Board of Governors of the Federal Reserve System, *Annual Report,* 1916. pp. 23–6, 139–45.
4. *Ibid.*
5. Board of Governors of the Federal Reserve System, *Banking and Monetary Statistics,* 1943.
6. Board of Governors of the Federal Reserve System, *The Federal Reserve System,* 1954, p. 38.
7. p. 8.

Chapter 15.

1. *Congressional Record,* December 13, 1913.
2. *Ibid.*
3. *New York Times,* April 4, 1920.
4. U. S. Bureau of Labor Statistics.
5. Thomas S. Berry, *Western Prices Before 1861* (Cambridge: Harvard University Press, 1943), records a drop in prices in Cincinnati from an index of 140 in 1820 to 86 in 1821 (based on 1824–46=100). *Historical Statistics of the U. S.* Series E 90–95 (Washington: G.P.O., 1960).
6. Board of Governors of the Federal Reserve System, *Banking and Monetary Statistics,* 1943 and *Federal Reserve Bulletins.*
7. December 15, 1920.

Chapter 16.

1. *The Federal Reserve System—A Retrospect of Eight Years.* XXXVII, 1922.
2. Vol. XI. No. 2. (June, 1921).
3. *Ibid.*
4. p. 8.
5. *See* Willis H. Parker, *The Federal Reserve System* (New York: The Ronald Press Company, 1923), chapter 44.
6. p. 31.

Chapter 17.

1. A. E. Feavearyear, *The Pound Sterling* (Oxford: The Clarendon Press, 1931).
2. Warbug, *op. cit.,* p. 385.
3. *See* John Maynard Keynes, *Indian Currency and Finance* (London: Macmillan and Company Ltd., 1913, 1924), chapter 2.
4. Adapted from Madden, John T. and Nadler, Marcus, *Foreign Securities* (New York: The Ronald Press Company, 1929).

Chapter 18.

1. Source for the indexes cited is *Historical Statistics of the United States* (Washington: G.P.O., 1960).
2. *Annual Report,* 1929.
3. *Ibid.*

Chapter 19.

1. *Federal Reserve Act.* (Boston News Bureau Co., 1914).
2. Board of Governors of the Federal Reserve System, *Report of the Committee on Member Bank Reserves of the Federal Reserve System* (Washington, 1931).
3. Section 14, Federal Reserve Act.
4. Board of Governors of the Federal Reserve System, *Banking and Monetary Statistics* (Washington, 1943), pp. 35, 36. The foregoing and subsequent discussion (chapter 20) is largely the same as that presented in the author's *Money and Man* (Norman: University of Oklahoma Press, 4th ed., 1976).

Chapter 20.

1. President's Research Committee on Social Trends, *Recent Social Trends in the United States* (New York: Whittlesey House, McGraw-Hill Book Company, 1934) I, 256.
2. *New York American*, November 9–15, 1931.
3. Letter from Moody's Investors' Service. The figures are found in *Moody's Manual of Investments, Government and Municipal* (New York) for the years in question.
4. Franklin W. Ryan, "Family Finance in the United States," *Journal of Business of the University of Chicago*, III, 4 (October, 1930).

Chapter 21.

1. *New York Times*, August 21, 1927.
2. September 19, 1927.
3. *New York Times*, September 6, 1927.

Chapter 22.

1. Lucien Lévy-Bruhl. *Primitives and the Supernatural,* translated by Lilian A. Clare (New York: E. P. Dutton & Co., Inc., 1935).
2. *Genesis*, xxxiv.
3. *Jeremiah*, xxxi, 29, 30; also in variant form in *Ezekiel*, xviii, 2–4. "What mean ye, that ye use this proverb concerning the land of Israel, saying, The fathers have eaten sour grapes, and the children's teeth are set on edge? As I live, saith the Lord God, ye shall not have occasion any more to use this proverb in Israel. Behold, all souls are mine; as the soul of the father, so also the soul of the son is mine; the soul that sinneth, it shall die."
4. *Luke* xii, 6, 7, also *Matthew*, x, 29–31.
5. "Wherefore thou art no more a servant, but a son; and if a son, then an heir of God through Christ" (*Galatians*, iv, 7).
6. *John*, x, 10.
7. *Romans*, viii, 21.
8. November 23, 1929.
9. *I Samuel*, viii, 5.

Chapter 23.

1. *Op. cit.* p. 30.
2. *The General Theory of Employment, Interest and Money* (New York: Harcourt, Brace and Company, 1936), p. 383.
3. *The Economic Consequences of Mr. Churchill* (London: L. & V. Woolf, 1925).
4. *General Theory of Employment* etc., p. 76.
5. *Ibid.* p. 137.
6. *Ibid.* p. 175.

7. *Ibid.* p. 113.
8. *Ibid.* p. 75.
9. *Usury & Usury Laws* (Boston and New York: Houghton, Mifflin Company, 1924).
10. *Op. cit.* p. 61.
11. *Ibid.* p. 40.
12. *Ibid.* p. 41.

Chapter 24.

1. William E. Leuchtenberg, *Franklin D. Roosevelt and The New Deal* (New York: Harper and Row, 1963), p. 38.
2. In the author's *Money and Man* (Norman: University of Oklahoma Press, 4th ed., 1976), Bk. II.
3. Emergency Banking Act of March 9, 1933 (48 Stat. 1, Ch. 1).
4. The conference is reported by Ernest K. Lindley in *The Roosevelt Revolution* (New York: The Viking Press, 1933), p. 119, and by James P. Warburg in *The Money Muddle* (New York: Alfred A. Knopf, 1934), p. 99. *See also* Raymond Moley, *After Seven Years* (New York: Harper and Brothers, 1939), pp. 160–1.
5. Of the extensive literature on the New Deal we mention four works: Broadus Mitchell, *Depression Decade* (New York: Holt, Rinehart and Winston, 1947); William E. Leuchtenberg, *op. cit.;* Arthur Whipple Crawford, *Monetary Management under the New Deal* (Washington: American Council on Public Affairs, 1940); and Joseph Dorfman, *The Economic Mind in American Civilization,* 5 vols. (New York: The Viking Press, 1946–1959).

Chapter 25.

1. Board of Governors of the Federal Reserve System, *Annual Report,* 1932.
2. His major works, with Frank A. Pearson, are: *Prices* (New York: J. Wiley & Sons, Inc., 1933) and *Gold and Prices* (New York: J. Wiley & Sons, Ltd., 1935).
3. The foregoing chronology is drawn from the *Annual Report* of the Secretary of the Treasury, 1934 (Exhibit 25).
4. John Morton Blum, *From the Morgenthau Diaries* (Boston: Houghton, Mifflin Company, 1939), pp. 65–70.
5. Secretary of the Treasury, *Annual Report,* 1934, p. 327.
6. *Ibid.*
7. *Historical Statistics of the United States* (Washington: G.P.O., 1960).

Chapter 26.

1. *Beckoning Frontiers* (New York: Alfred A. Knopf, 1951), pp. 131–2. These and other quotations are reprinted with permission of author and publisher.
2. *Ibid.* p. 83.
3. *Ibid.* p. 130.
4. *Ibid.*
5. *Ibid.* p. 131.
6. *Ibid.* p. 132.
7. *Ibid.* p. 173.
8. *Ibid.* p. 185.
9. *Ibid.*
10. *Ibid.* p. 174.
11. *Ibid.* p. 208.
12. *Ibid.* p. 210.
13. *The Federal Reserve Act,* as amended to October 1, 1935 (Washington: G.P.O., 1935).

Chapter 27.

1. *Op. cit.* p. 252.
2. *Ibid.* p. 253.
3. *Ibid.* p. 290.
4. *Ibid.*
5. *Senate Report No. 180, 76th Congress, on S. 1855.*
6. *H.R. 8585 and H.R. 9800, 75th Congress.*
7. *H.R. 4931, 76th Congress.*
8. *S. 31, 76th Congress and S. 2606, 76th Congress. See* Arthur Whipple Crawford, *Monetary Management under the New Deal* (Washington: American Council on Public Affairs, 1940).

Chapter 28.

1. Eccles, *op. cit.,* p. 332.
2. Board of Governors of the Federal Reserve System, *Annual Report,* 1940, p. 67.
3. *Ibid.*
4. Eccles, *op. cit.,* p. 355.
5. *Ibid.,* p. 357.
6. p. 3.
7. Board of Governors of the Federal Reserve System, *Annual Report,* 1941, p. 24; 1942, p. 17.
8. *Ibid., Annual Report,* 1945, p. 2.
9. *Annual Report,* 1945, pp. 4,5.
10. *Op. cit.,* p. 382.

Chapter 29.

1. *Historical Statistics of the United States* (Washington: G.P.O., 1960).
2. *New York Times,* January 2, 1951.
3. *Ibid.,* January 22, 1951.
4. *Ibid.,* February 1, 1951.
5. *Ibid.,* February 2, 1951.
6. *Ibid.*
7. *Ibid.,* February 3, 1951.
8. Eccles, *op. cit.,* pp. 486 ff.
9. *New York Times,* February 4, 1951. Also Eccles, *op. cit.,* p. 496.
10. Board of Governors of the Federal Reserve System, *Annual Report,* 1951, p. 3.
11. March 31, 1951.

Chapter 30.

1. International Monetary Fund, *First Ten Years of the I.M.F.* (Washington: 1956).
2. House Committee on Foreign Affairs and Senate Committee on Foreign Relations, *Assistance to Greece and Turkey.* Hearings on H.R. 2616 and S. 938. 80th Congress, 1st Session. See also *U.S. Foreign Aid,* Legislative Reference Service, Library of Congress (Washington: G.P.O., 1959).

Chapter 31.

1. *See* the author's *Money and Man;* also Charles Rist, *History of Monetary and Credit Theory,* translated by Jane Degras (London: G. Allen & Unwin, Ltd., 1940).
2. Art. IV. Sec 1 (a).
3. Art. V. Sec. 8 (f).

Chapter 32.

1. September 2, 1963.
2. *New York Times,* January 20, 1964.
3. Ludwig Erhard, *Prosperity Through Competition—The Economics of the German Miracle,* tr. and ed. by Edith Temple Roberts and John B. Wood (New York: Praeger, 1958).
4. *See* the author's *Decay of Money,* monograph (Washington: Institute for Monetary Research, Inc., 1962).
5. *See The International Gold Problem.* Collected Papers. A Record of the Discussions of a Study Group of Members of the Royal Institute of International Affairs, 1929–31 (London: Oxford University Press, 1931).

Chapter 33

1. Par Value Modification Act of 1973 (P.L. 93–110, September 21, 1973).
2. *Annual Report, 1977, of the Secretary of the Treasury,* Exhibit 44 (p. 413).

Chapter 34

1. *Report of the Indian Currency Commission* (London, 1893), p. 786.
2. *Supra.,* pp. 132 ff.
3. *Op. cit.,* p. 30.
4. *Ibid.,* p. 99.
5. Sidney Homer, *A History of Interest Rates* (New Brunswick, N.J.: Rutgers University Press, 1963), chapter 16.
6. *New York Times,* August 26, 1979.

Chapter 35

1. *Supra.,* pp. 124 ff.
2. *Documentary History of the Constitution* (Washington: Dept. of State, 1894).
3. Before the Florida Bankers Association, March 16, 1979.

Selected Bibliography

Albert, John C. *Roosevelt and the Money Power*. New York: Sudwarth, 1908.
Allen, Frederick Lewis. *The Great Pierpont Morgan*. New York: Harper and Brothers, 1949.
Andrew, A. Piatt. *The United States and the Money Market*. Boston (?). 1907 (?).
Blum, John Morton. *From the Morgenthau Diaries*. Boston: Houghton, Mifflin Company, 1959.
Board of Governors of the Federal Reserve System. *Banking and Monetary Statistics*. Washington, 1943.
    Federal Reserve System. Washington, 1954.
    Banking Studies. By members of the staff. Washington, 1941.
    Annual Reports, Federal Reserve Bulletins. Washington.
Chandler, Lester V. *Benjamin Strong, Central Banker*. Washington: The Brookings Institution, 1959.
Chapman, Charles C. *The Development of American Business and Banking Thought, 1913–1936*. London, New York: Longmans, Green & Co., 1936.
Corey, Lewis. *The House of Morgan*. New York: G. H. Watt, 1930.
Crawford, Arthur Whipple. *Monetary Management under the New Deal*. Washington: American Council on Public Affairs, 1940.
Dewey, Davis Rich. *Financial History of the United States*. 12th ed. New York, London: Longmans, Green & Co., 1936 (1st ed. 1903).
Dorfman, Joseph. *The Economic Mind in American Civilization*, 5 vols. New York: The Viking Press, 1946–1959.
Eccles, Marriner S. *Beckoning Frontiers*. New York: Alfred A. Knopf, 1951.
Eckenrode, Hamilton James, and Edmunds, Pocahontas Wight. *E. H. Harriman, The Little Giant of Wall Street*. New York: Greenberg, 1933.
Erhard, Ludwig. *Prosperity through Competition—The Economics of the German Miracle*. Translated and edited by Edith Temple Roberts and John B. Wood. New York: Praeger, 1958.
Feavearyear, A. E. *The Pound Sterling*. Oxford: The Clarendon Press, 1931.
Glass, Carter. *An Adventure in Constructive Finance*. Garden City (N. Y.): Doubleday, Page & Company, 1927.
Goldenweiser, E. A. *Federal Reserve System in Operation*. New York: McGraw-Hill Book Company, Inc., 1925.
Groseclose, Elgin. *Money and Man*. Norman: University of Oklahoma Press, 4th ed., 1976.
    ———. *Decay of Money, A Survey of Western Currencies, 1912–1962*. Monograph. Washington: Institute for Monetary Research, Inc., 1962.

Harding, William P. G. *The Formative Period of the Federal Reserve System.* Boston and New York: Houghton, Mifflin Company, 1925.

Hardy, Charles O. *Credit Policies of the Federal Reserve System.* Washington: The Brookings Institution, 1932.

Hazlitt, Henry. *The Inflation Crisis, and How to Resolve It.* Westport (Ct.): Arlington House, 1978.

Hepburn, A. Barton. A History of Currency in the United States. New York: The Macmillan Company, 1915.

Holbrook, Stewart H. *The Age of the Moguls.* New York: Doubleday & Company, 1953.

Homer, Sidney. *A History of Interest Rates.* New Brunswick (N.J.): Rutgers University Press, 1963.

Howland, Harold J. *Theodore Roosevelt and His Times.* New Haven: Yale University Press, 1921 (*Chronicles of America.* Vol. 47).

The International Gold Problem. Collected Papers. A Record of the Discussions of a Study Group of Members of the Royal Institute of International Affairs, 1929–31. London: Oxford University Press, 1931.

Josephson, Matthew. *The Robber Barons.* New York: Harcourt, Brace and Company, 1934.

Kahn, Otto H. *Edward Henry Harriman.* An address delivered before the Finance Forum in New York, New York: C. G. Burgoyne, 1911.

Kennan, George. *E. H. Harriman, A Biography.* 2 vols. Boston and New York: Houghton, Mifflin Company, 1922.

Keso, Edward Elmer. *The Senatorial Career of Robert Latham Owen.* Abstract of thesis. Nashville (Tenn.): George Peabody College for Teachers, 1937.

Keynes, John Maynard. *A Treatise on Money,* 2 vols. New York: Harcourt, Brace and Company, 1930.

———. *Indian Currency and Finance.* London: Macmillan and Company, Ltd., 1913, 1924.

———. *The General Theory of Employment, Interest, and Money.* New York: Harcourt, Brace and Company, 1936.

———. *The Economic Consequences of Mr. Churchill.* London: L. & V. Woolf. 1925.

Laughlin, James L. *The Federal Reserve Act: Its Origins and Problems.* New York: The Macmillan Company, 1933.

Leuchtenberg, William E. *Franklin D. Roosevelt and the New Deal.* New York: Harper & Row, 1963.

Lévy-Bruhl, Lucien. *Primitives and the Supernatural.* Tr. by Lilian A. Clare. New York: E. P. Dutton & Co., Inc., 1935.

Library of Congress, Legislative Reference Service. *U. S. Foreign Aid.* Washington: G.P.O., 1959.

Lindley, Ernest K. *The Roosevelt Revolution.* New York: The Viking Press, 1933.

Lord, Walter. *The Good Years.* New York: Harper and Brothers, 1960.

Loucks, Henry L. *The Great Conspiracy of the House of Morgan.* Watertown (S.D.): Author, 1916.

Lovett, Robert A. *Forty Years After: An Appreciation of the Genius of Edward Henry Harriman (1848–1909).* Pamphlet. New York: Newcomen Society in North America, 1949.

Mitchell, Broadus. *Depression Decade.* New York: Holt, Rinehart and Winston, 1947.

Moley, Raymond. *After Seven Years.* New York: Harper & Brothers, 1939.

Moody, John. *The Masters of Capital.* New Haven: Yale University Press, 1921 (*Chronicles of America.* Vol. 41).

The New York Times.

Owen, Robert Latham. *The Federal Reserve Act.* New York: The Century Co., 1919.

Palmer, Jr., James E. *Carter Glass, Unreconstructed Rebel.* Roanoke (Virginia): The Institute of American Biography, 1938.

Pringle, Henry F. *Theodore Roosevelt, A Biography.* New York: Harcourt, Brace and Company, 1931.

Prochnow, Herbert V. *Federal Reserve System.* New York: Harper and Brothers, 1960.

Rist, Charles. *History of Monetary and Credit Policy.* Translated by Jane Degras. London: G. Allen & Unwin, Ltd., 1940.

Ryan, Franklin W. *Usury and Usury Laws.* Boston and New York: Houghton, Mifflin Company, 1924.

Satterlee, Herbert L. *J. Pierpont Morgan—An Intimate Portrait.* New York: The Macmillan Company, 1939.

Smith, Rixey and Beasley, Norman. *Carter Glass, A Biography.* New York: Longmans, Green & Co., 1939.

Sprague, O. M. W. *A Central Bank of Issue.* New York: The Bankers Publishing Co., 1910.

Stephenson, Nathaniel Wright. *Nelson W. Aldrich: A Leader in American Politics.* New York: Charles Scribner's Sons, 1930.

U. S. Department of Commerce. *Historical Statistics of the U. S.* Washington: G.P.O. (periodically issued).

  Statistical Abstract of the U. S. (Annual) Washington: G.P.O.

U. S. National Monetary Commission. *Reports.* Washington: G.P.O., 1911.

U. S. Treasury Department. *Annual Reports.* Washington: G.P.O.

Warburg, James P. *The Money Muddle.* New York: Alfred A. Knopf, 1934.

Warburg, Paul M. *The Federal Reserve System.* New York: The Macmillan Company, 1930.

_____. *The Discount System in Europe.* Washington: G.P.O. 1910.

_____. *American and European Banking Methods.* New York: The Columbia University Press, 1908.

Warren, George F. and Pearson, Frank A. *Prices.* New York: J. Wiley & Sons, Inc., 1933.

_____. *Gold and Prices.* New York: J. Wiley & Sons, Inc., 1935.

Wiggins, James W. and Schoeck, Helmut, editors. *Foreign Aid Re-Examined: A Critical Appraisal.* Washington: Public Affairs Press, 1958.

Willis, H. Parker. *The Federal Reserve System.* New York: The Ronald Press Company, 1923.

Winkler, John K. *Morgan the Magnificent.* New York: The Vanguard Press, 1930.

About the Author

ELGIN GROSECLOSE founded (1960) and currently serves as executive director of the Institute for Monetary Reasearch, Inc., and since 1944 has been head of Groseclose, Williams, and Broderick, financial and investment consultants. With degrees from the University of Oklahoma (AB) and American University (MA, PhD), he is one of America's leading monetary economists.

Dr. Groseclose was the first financial editor of *Fortune*, has taught money and banking at the City College of New York, and has served the federal government in a number of professional and consultative capacities. During World War II he served as treasurer-general of Iran by appointment of the Iranian parliament, charged with the principal task of curbing wartime inflation. He successfully carried out this mandate by returning gold to the marketplace—a measure subsequently adopted with great success throughout the Middle East War Theatre.

Dr. Groseclose's books include *Money and Man* (1976), the fourth revised and enlarged edition of *Money: The Human Conflict* (1934); *Introduction to Iran* (1947); *Fifty Years of Managed Money* (1966), of which this work is a revised and updated edition; and seven novels, among which are *Ararat* (1939; third edition, 1977), winner of a National Book Award and a Foundation for Literature Award; *The Kiowa* (1978), a Gold Medallion winner and Christian Herald Book Shelf selection; and *Olympia,* a story of fourth century Byzantium (1980).

Index